DETERMI[N]
DEMOCRATIZATION
IN AFRICA

A Comparative Study of Benin and Togo

Mathurin C. Houngnikpo

University Press of America,® Inc.
Lanham · New York · Oxford

Library of Congress Cataloging-in-Publication Data

Houngnikpo, Mathurin C.
Determinants of democratization in Africa : a comparative study
of Benin and Togo / Mathurin C. Houngnikpo.
p.   cm
Includes bibliographical references (p.) and index.
1. Democratization—Benin. 2. Democratization—Togo.
3. Political culture—Benin. 4. Political culture—Togo.
5. Benin—Politics and government—1990- 6. Togo—Politics
and government—1960- I. Title.
DT541.845 .H68 2001   320.9668—dc21   2001027894 CIP

ISBN 0-7618-2063-9 (cloth : alk. paper)
ISBN 0-7618-2064-7 (pbk. : alk. paper)

CONTENTS

PREFACE

INTRODUCTION   1

Chapter

1. STATEMENT OF PROBLEM AND RESEARCH
   OBJECTIVES   7

   Statement of Problem   7
   Research Design and Methodology   13
   Research Objectives   15

2. THEORETICAL PERSPECTIVES ON
   DEMOCRATIZATION, CIVIL SOCIETY, THE MILITARY
   AND POLITICAL CULTURE IN AFRICA   21

   Democratization in Africa   21
   Civil Society and Democratization in Africa   37
   The Military and African Politics   49
   Political Culture, Democratization, and African Politics   58

3. BENIN AND TOGO THROUGH HISTORY   65

   Political Development of Benin   65
   Political Development of Togo   72
   Economic Development of Benin   77
   Economic Development of Togo   80

4. NATIONAL CONFERENCE AND POLITICAL
   TRANSITION IN AFRICA   85

   National Conference as a Political Phenomenon   86
   National Conference in Benin   90
   National Conference in Togo   96
   National Conferences in Other African Countries   100

5. THE MILITARY AND DEMOCRATIZATION IN
   AFRICA   117

   The Military and Politics in Benin   119
   The Military and The National Conference in Benin   127
   The Military and Politics in Togo   131
   The Military and The National Conference in Togo   136

6. FRANCE AND DEMOCRATIZATION IN AFRICA   139

   France's Historical Ties to Africa   140
   La *Baule* Conference on Democratization   147
   Democratic Reforms as a "Requirement" in Benin   153
   Political Reforms as a "Recommendation" in Togo   157

7. INTERPRETATION OF FINDINGS   165

   The Culture of Politics in Benin and Togo   166
   Different Stakes and Strategies   171
   France's Policy of Double Standards   176
   The "Military" Society's Difference in Benin   180

CONCLUSION   185

BIBLIOGRAPHY   193

Index   243

About the Author

PREFACE

This study emerges out of concern about the popular belief that democracy's return to Africa is the sole work of civil society. In a now very large body of literature on democratization in Africa and elsewhere, the credit to a return of constitutional regimes seems to go squarely to vibrant social organizations bent on challenging powerful states. Although a variety of causes could be, and are indeed, cited for the explanation of Africa's democratic transition, the critical role of the military cannot be overstated.

My interest in the intellectual pursuit of this issue arose during the national conference of Benin. My witnessing that gathering, and my aversion towards the military institution first led me to follow the conventional wisdom in explaining democratization in Africa: to give credit to civil society for its resilience. However, very soon, my observation of events leading to Benin's national conference, in comparison to the political turmoil in neighboring Togo and elsewhere on the continent revealed a painful truth that the mere will of civil society to change a political system is not enough.

This book, which is a revised and expanded version of a dissertation submitted to the Graduate School of International Studies at the University of Denver, represents the culmination of extensive fieldwork and secondary source research mostly in Africa and Europe. While the cases directly concerned are Benin and Togo, the very nature of the subject requires investigation in other African countries.

Through a series of loosely structured interviews within the armed forces and among civilian politicians in Benin, Togo, Ghana, Nigeria, Niger, and Côte d'Ivoire, a great deal of information allowed a better understanding of state-society and civil-military relations in those countries. I also managed, though painfully, to peruse the national archives of Benin and Togo, the archives in French embassies in both countries, and finally, the French Foreign Office, the *Quai d'Orsay*, where primary source documents delineated the path of my inquiry.

Due to the problems inherent to doing research in Africa in general, and on such a sensitive topic, I was asked by my informants not to disclose their real identity. However, I am very grateful to them and to several individuals and institutions in Africa and in Europe for having made my research feasible. Besides my family, friends and colleagues, I would like to thank Professors Jack Donnelly and David Goldfischer, of the Graduate School of International Studies at the University of Denver, Colorado; Angelique Haugerud at Rutgers University, New Brunswick, New Jersey; and Jendayi E. Frazer at Harvard University, Cambridge, Massachusetts.

Like most authors of academic books, I have relied on the help of a number of people to correct errors in the manuscript, to make suggestions for its improvement, to provide me with data from their area of expertise, and most important, to give me the courage to persevere. Although they all provided insightful comments that I am immensely grateful for, I am solely responsible for the content of this book, which accomplishment will best be judged by the reader.

MCH   Oxford, Ohio (USA) 2001

LIST OF ACRONYMS

ACP	African-Caribbean-Pacific (Countries)
ADEMA	Alliance pour la Démocratie au Mali
ANR	Assemblée Nationale Révolutionnaire
AOF	Afrique Occidentale Française (French West Africa)
ATT	Amadou Toumani Touré
CEAO	Communauté Économique des États de l'Afrique de l'Ouest
CFA	Communauté Financière Africaine
CMLN	Comité Militaire pour la Libération Nationale
CMR	Comité Militaire Révolutionnaire
CMV	Comité Militaire de Vigilance
CNDH	Commission Nationale des Droits de l'Homme
CNID	Comité National d'Initiative Démocratique
CNTT	Confédération Nationale des Travailleurs du Togo
CRN	Comité de Réconciliation Nationale
CTMB	Compagnie Togolaise des Mines du Bénin
CTSP	Comité de Transition pour le Salut du Peuple
CUT	Comité de l'Unité Togolaise
FAC	Fonds d'Aide et de Coopération
FAR	Front des Associations pour le Renouveau
GDP	Gross Domestic Product
GNP	Gross National Product
HCR	Haut Conseil de la République
IMF	International Monetary Fund
LTDH	Ligue Togolaise des Droits de l'Homme
MNSD	Mouvement National pour une Société de Développement
OCAM	Organisation Commune Africaine et Malgache/Mauricienne
OTP	Office Togolais des Phosphates
PCD	Parti Communiste du Dahomey
PCT	Parti Congolais du Travail
PDG	Parti Démocratique Gabonais
PDGG	Participatory Development and Good Government
PRPB	Parti de la Révolution Populaire du Bénin
PTP	Parti Togolais du Progrès
RDP	Rassemblement pour la Démocratie et le Progrès

RPT	Rassemblement du Peuple Togolais
SAP	Structural Adjustment Program
SNES	Syndicat National de l'Enseignement Supérieur
SONADER	Société Nationale pour le Développement Rural
UAC	United Africa Company
UDPM	Union Démocratique du Peuple Malien
UDPT	Union Démocratique des Peuples Togolais
UDSR	Union Démocratique et Socialiste de la Résistance
UFC	Union des Forces du Changement
UGDT	Union Générale des Travailleurs du Dahomey
UN	United Nations
UNTM	Union Nationale des Travailleurs du Mali
USTN	Union des Syndicats des Travailleurs du Niger
UT	Unité Togolaise

Democracy is not achieved simply by the hidden process of socioeconomic development bringing a country to a point where it has the necessary "prerequisites" for it. It is not delivered by the grace of some *deus ex machina*. And neither is it simply the result of the divisions, strategies, tactics, negotiations and settlements of contending elites. Political scientists who conceived of democratic transitions simply in this way miss an important element. That element is struggle, personal risk-taking, mobilization and sustained imaginative organization on the part of a large number of citizens.

Larry Diamond 1992, 5.

INTRODUCTION

> The collapse of single-party regimes throughout Eastern
> Europe and the former Soviet Union set powerful
> precedents for African pro-democracy activists who
> already had begun organizing against human rights
> abuses and political repression. Severe economic
> stagnation and decline in most African economies
> served as the internal spark for political discontent.
>
> Schraeder 2000, 268.

The thaw of the Cold War, equated with the end of the chess
game between the two superpowers, seems to have allowed democracy
back on both academic and political agendas. With the end of the
geopolitical division created at the close of World War II, a new
perception has been established in international affairs, heralding the
possibility of a new fluidity in political thought. According to Held,
"these circumstances [of the post-cold war] present significant
opportunities for the establishment of an international order based upon
the principles of constitutionality and democracy" (1995, ix). Despite
the elusive nature of the concept, democracy, or rather cosmopolitan
democracy (Archibugi and Held 1995; Held 1999) has been presented
as the panacea of Third World ills, generating excitement among both
donor countries and recipient ones.

The Third Wave of democratization (Huntington 1991) has sent ripples to the shores of the Third World in general, and of Africa in particular. Contrary to conventional wisdom, democratic institutions emerged among poor, illiterate, diseased, and war-ravaged populations, even though outside forces helped in providing the impetus, rationale and material support (Anderson 1999, 9). After several decades of autocratic rule, mal-development, disappointment and despair, hope resurfaced on the continent. Reconstituting a new political order in Africa became crucial. There was a sense of a new beginning and Hyden's statement captures the situation on the continent:

> The demand for reconstituting the political order in accordance with the principles of freedom and justice has since spread to other parts of the world where conditions of authoritarian rule have persisted. In many African countries, similar scenarios were enacted. Activists who have been detained in the past for their opposition to government gained more freedom to speak out. As political groups began to articulate their displeasure with dictatorial methods of rule, they quickly received popular support. African governments capitulated to these popular demands for constitutional reform or did so in response to conditionalities placed upon them by powerful foreign donor governments. (1999, 179)

Whether the renewed interest in democracy is due to the strong belief that democracies do not fight each other (Kant 1795; Doyle 1983, 1986; Chan 1984; Weede 1984; Rummel 1985, 1995) or to the positive correlation often drawn between democracy and development (Lipset 1959, Almond and Verba 1963, Huntington 1991), it is clear that democracy or democratization—the process that leads to democracy—has gained a new momentum in International Politics (Hyden 1997, 233). Scholars' understanding of democratization became more sophisticated, emphasizing the dynamic aspects of the process. Democratization is no longer regarded as a mechanical journey toward a predestined outcome. According to Gros,

> Democratization is a transitional phenomenon involving a gradual, mainly élite-driven transformation of the formal rules that govern a political system. Thus democratization is not an end game; rather, it is a means to an end, which is democracy...Because democratization is a process, it is neither unilinear nor static: it can move forward, stagnate, or be reversed. (1998, 2)

In the hope of altering domestic politics in developing nations, both bilateral and multilateral relationships between donor countries and recipient ones are now managed according to the "gospel" of democracy (Hadenius and Uggla 1996, 1635-36). There is a strong belief that only democratic institutions can "enable the mass of citizens to exert control over those governing in their name" (Luckham and White 1996, 3). Consequently, current Western orthodoxy requires that Third World countries democratize if they are to develop, and, aid has therefore become increasingly conditional on political reforms (Conteh-Morgan 1997, 5). Belatedly, international donors re-appraised their objectives for Africa. Their earlier goal of containing communism having vanished, the promotion of multiparty democracy quickly emerged as a central aim (Tangri 1998, 108). On each side of the ideological divide, African "client" states now stripped of their patrons' guaranteed economic and military support, became more vulnerable (Press 1999, 35). Reminiscent of the wave of de-colonization of the late 1950s and early 1960s, Africans seized the new wave of democratization to make the most of what seems to be a new dawn of political and economic freedom.

By the late 1980s, most authoritarian rulers in Africa faced severe crises of legitimacy. In Lewis's assessment, most states in Sub-Saharan Africa failed to meet the challenges posed by global price shocks because of excessive spending, ill-chosen policies, and widespread corruption. The resulting economic crises prompted a rebirth of associational life.

> By the end of the decade [the 1990s], most of Sub-Saharan Africa was in the grips of a sustained economic downturn, reflecting the combined effects of global price shocks, profligate state spending, inappropriate macroeconomic policies and ubiquitous corruption. Economic crises eroded both the extractive and distributive capabilities of many states, fostering a defensive regeneration of associational life. (1998, 148)

Having realized the incapacity of their leaders to solve their basic socio-economic and political development problems, African citizens took matters into their own hands (Bratton and van de Walle 1998, 99). Obviously, these leaders had damaged their own claim to rule by engaging in nepotism and corruption, which led to popular perceptions that only those with access to political office were living "high on the hog" while ordinary people suffered (Bratton and van de Walle 1998,

99). There was clearly a crisis of the state institution, and Chazan and her colleagues are right when they state that:

> By the late 1970s and early 1980s, most, if not all, African states were undergoing an organizational crisis. The first and most widely noted characteristic of the crisis was the fraying character of state-society relations. Many governments, particularly in those countries that had experienced numerous regime changes since independence, had not been able to gain the trust of large portions of their populations. (1999, 65)

With a loss of faith in their leaders and a lack of forum to peacefully air their grievances, Africans, desperate to redress this imbalance, grabbed the only choice they were left with—to remove inept and corrupt leaders from office by force—and, thanks to outside assistance, ousted some authoritarian leaders.

Regardless of conjecture about an ideal sequence, many African countries face a situation of concurrent political and economic reform. If political liberalization enables a departure from the practices and institutions associated with neopatrimonial rule, then democratization in African states can begin to shift the terms of economic governance. There is also a possibility, however, that traditional politics may persist, although perhaps in a different guise. The nature of leadership, the composition of social coalitions, and the capacities of public institutions influence reform.

Left with very little choice, given the bad shape of the economies of their countries, many African leaders had to embark on a democratization path. As Crowder rightly puts it:

> By 1985, a quarter of a century after the *annus mirabilis* of African independence, the dreams had been shattered and replaced by a profound disillusion whereby Africa had become the world's basket case, a permanent *mezzogiorno* for which there was little if any hope...The universal wisdom has become that African independence has been an abysmal failure. (1987, 9-10)

Having sensed a change in the cadence of the music, African leaders tried to coordinate their dance steps. Thanks to pressure, both endogenous and exogenous, a political liberalization occurred on the African continent (Bratton and van de Walle 1998, 36). Since some forms of political openness became unavoidable, leaders from all ideological spectra introduced political reforms geared at bringing about a multiparty political system.

Although the early euphoria has died down due to recent disappointments with the state of democratization on the continent, it is undeniable that a new era has begun in Africa (Wiseman 1996, 35). In his attempt to capture the new fight for political freedom in Africa, Press summarized eloquently the current fervor on the continent:

> A long-simmering discontent and anger with politics as usual boiled over in Africa at the end of the Cold War in 1989. Pervasive poverty and international and domestic pressures for democracy set the stage for change to some degree, but mostly it was the power of an idea, the idea of freedom, that changed the shape of African politics more than at any time since independence. Africans caught a fever of freedom which spread rapidly across the continent, prompting confrontations and other challenges to longtime authoritarian rulers. Ordinary people, not just political opposition leaders, stood up for democracy, often against great odds, sometimes against brutal force. (1999, 3)

However, the roots of such a change remain unclear. While several scholars attribute the political reforms to a more vibrant civil society, the very fact that democratization only occurred in countries where the military has either embraced or at least condoned it suggests alternative source of political change in Africa (Onwumechili 1998, 73). In fact, Welch's view on the wave of democratization on the continent seems to connect the decline of military rule with democracy.

> The rule of the "man on the horseback" is declining, as a consequence of the global political and ideological changes…Civil-military relations are changing dramatically with the spread of the call for democracy around the world. Although armed forces remain primary political actors in most states, their direct political roles have been reduced in recent years. The result, to overstate the case, is fundamental transformation and nowhere is it more marked than in developing countries. The Third World is now witnessing the slow, difficult, but significant consolidation of civilian governments after, in many cases, several decades of military rule. (1993, 71)

Given the military's endemic involvement in African politics (Decalo 1976, 1985, 1989; Luckham 1994), it is difficult to give any scholarly praise to that institution for its contribution to the new dawn on the continent. It is however important that a different assessment of the military be done in the light of its recent behavior *vis-à-vis* democratization in certain countries (Onwumechili 1998, 75-89). Because of the complex civil-military *problématique* in Africa, both civilian leaders and military officers need to reevaluate their relations for a brighter prospect for democracy on the continent.

The major problem of civil-military relations is the "praetorian problem...the need to curb the political power of the military establishment and to make the armed forces into a professional body committed to providing for the external security of the country" (Huntington 1991, 231). While liberal democracies and emerging democracies must guard against the ancient and persistent problem, they more usually need to concentrate on how to manage civil-military relations after the power of the military has been curbed (Bland 1999, 13).

This book explores the determinants of democratization in Africa. While several analysts attribute the new economic and political dawn on the continent to civil society's endurance, a closer evaluation demonstrates otherwise. Without downplaying civil society's credit, it is equally important to note other important factors that contribute to the rebirth of democratic rule in Africa. Among these variables, the determinant role of the military, the political will of incumbent leaders and outside pressure or complacence seem to matter. Through a comparative analysis of two neighboring West African countries, the Republic of Benin and the Republic of Togo, the fate of African democratic transition will be evaluated.

After the first chapter sets the stage for this analysis, by stating the issue at stake, the second chapter will cover the theoretical perspectives on democratization, civil society, the military, and political culture in Africa. The third chapter will give an overview of the historical backgrounds of Benin and Togo, in an attempt to shed some light on the circumstances that demanded democratization. In the fourth chapter, the phenomenon of "national conference" as a new conduit of peaceful transfer of political power in Africa will be explored. Chapter five will deal with the military and democratization in Africa, probing specifically the behavior of the military *vis-à-vis* democratization in both Benin and Togo. The unclear, if not contradicting, stance of France in the democratization process in both countries will then be scrutinized in chapter six. The last chapter will deal with my interpretation of the findings.

CHAPTER ONE

STATEMENT OF PROBLEM AND RESEARCH OBJECTIVES

> It is paradoxical that the third wave of global democratization affected Benin, of all African states, [which became] the pioneer of the "national conference" approach to the rollback of authoritarian rule, and *ipso facto* the first of Africa's new democracies. This is even more perplexing when contrasted to the different evolution in neighboring Togo...where General Éyadéma brutalized the pro-democracy movement into submission and entrenched his military rule with a semblance of electoral sanction.

> Decalo 1997, 43.

Statement of Problem

Can democracy, a system of government that allows *demos* (the people) to decide its own fate through free, fair and periodic multiparty elections, be achieved in Africa without the support of the military? Or does the military, as a practical matter, need to endorse democracy for its birth and survival? In other words, is civil society, the private sphere that challenges state behavior (Bayart 1986; Chabal 1986; Chazan 1991; Robinson 1994; Fatton, Jr. 1995; Keller 1995), strong and vibrant enough to bring about democracy in Africa regardless of the attitude of the military?

Such a question would have been viewed as futile in the early days of what was considered by many as the "second independence" or "second liberation" of Africa (Riley 1991; Allen 1992; Wiseman 1996; Diamond 1998). The euphoria and the rediscovered sentiment of freedom that came with democratization prevented an adequate analysis of how things came to being (Chenu 1991, 7). Given the track records of both the military and civil society in African politics (Austin 1963; Gutteridge 1969; Lee 1969; First 1972; Decalo 1976), it is indeed malapropos to even think of the military as a force that might, be it for its own interests, subscribe to democratization. As Luckham contends, "the military and repressive apparatuses of the state may not seem the best vantage point from which to study democratization" (1996, 119). In fact, the military, whether colonial or post-colonial, has always been heavily involved in politics on the continent, most of the time, at the expenses of the populations (Decalo 1968; Bebler 1973; Bienen 1979).

The legal use of force at the disposal of the African military became its main weapon of oppression. Despite their resentment, African populations had to endure arbitrary, injustice and imposition (Cartwright 1983; Chabal 1986). However, the impotence of African masses was not total. In front of huge obstacles and despite serious risks, several clandestine groups were formed in order to challenge the military's grip on power (Sylla 1982, 26-27).

Even in countries where the military was not directly in charge, different organizations sought to monitor state behavior (Ekeh 1992; Beckman 1993; Hutchful 1995, 1996). That struggle, although very unfair to civil society because of the state's monopoly of violence, started to bear some result when the economic degradation, coupled with new attitudes in donor countries' policies, compelled many (mostly military) African leaders, to open up their countries' political systems (Bayart 1993; Heilbrunn 1993).

Describing the new political overture on the continent, Gyimah-Boadi elaborates as follow:

> Clearly, Africa's civil societies are among the chief engines driving the continent's political development. With their increased sophisticated and mounting capabilities, they are helping to drive the shift from unalloyed state hegemony to nascent pluralism. Their growing self-awareness and determination to defend their autonomy against all efforts at suppression or co-optation (especially those originating from the state) are signs that they are here to stay. The first springtime of African civil society followed hard on the heels of de-

colonization, but soon faded before authoritarianism's onslaughts in country after country. The second springtime, which began in the Cold War's wake, shows promise of enduring far longer than its ill-fated predecessor endures. (1998, 24-25)

While it is easy, from what has been said so far, to jump into a hasty conclusion by giving the entire credit for the change in Africa to civil society for its bravado, the reality on the ground cautions otherwise (Onwumechili 1998, 59-72). Because of persistent pockets of antidemocratic forces on the continent, Chazan is right in stating that "democratic pressures persist while authoritarian rules prevail." In the same vein, Adebayo Adedeji believes that the seeds of "authentic" democracy are yet to germinate in the "psyche" of Africa's political class (quoted in Udogu 1996, 9). The very fact that democratization occurred, or, is in progress, only in countries where the military consented to it, and especially the recent comeback of the military through toppling democratic regimes in Niger and the Congo, demands a critical re-evaluation of the roots of recent political change in Africa (Kpundeh 1992; Conteh-Morgan 1997). In Fatton's views, civil society's *débordement* of the state does not necessarily guarantee democratization (1992, 105-6).

Whether democracy can flourish and endure in Africa seems to depend to a great extent on the attitudes of the military (Conteh-Morgan 1997, 119-142). Unfortunately, the role of the military in African societies, in terms of its support for, and consolidation of, democracy, has yet to receive adequate attention. Although a great deal has been written on the military and democratization in Latin America and Southern Europe (O'Donnell, Schmitter and Whitehead 1986; Stepan 1988; Aguero 1990; Karl 1990; Welch, Jr. 1990), Africa remains to be covered in a systematic way.

While the early mainstream scholarship as seen in the works of Lipset (1959), Almond and Verba (1963), Moore, Jr., (1966), Dahl (1971), O'Donnell (1979), and scores of other distinguished scholars, focused on the search for the necessary conditions and prerequisites for the emergence of a stable democracy, recent writings have been concerned primarily with the dynamics of democratic transition and consolidation (Dabezies 1992; Conac 1993; Pateman 1996; Conteh-Morgan 1997; Bratton and van de Walle 1998).

Democracy has made such a strong comeback in the last two decades that, for the first time in history, almost every region of the world has witnessed some form of democratization. The power of the tide of democratization led Samuel Huntington to view democracy as "the only legitimate and viable alternative to an authoritarian regime of any kind" (1992). Other scholars like Fukuyama (1992) and Rustow (1994) highly praised the new political change in the Third World. As demands for democracy have swept across Africa, dramatic change has affected states on the continent (Riley 1992; Iheduru 1999, 24-26). Frustrated by declining economies and the failures of incumbent governments, Africans from different social strata took to the street to demand an end to authoritarian and totalitarian rule. They were greatly helped by events in Eastern Europe (Bratton and van de Walle 1992; Heilbrunn 1993), and donor countries' pressures (Dowden 1993; Huntington 1991). In response, several African governments were forced to adopt significant reforms allowing greater pluralism and competition within the polity. According to Hyden:

> The discourse on democratization continues to dominate the minds of those who are interested in how Africa's development can be accelerated. The international community and Africa itself have moved a long way from the jargons of the 1980s, which implied that the continent's salvation lay in economic reform. As we approach the end of the century, it is not a matter of "getting prices right" as much as it is of "getting politics right." The latter has become a virtual imperative since the end of the Cold War. The rest of the world is being swept along, whether it likes it or not. Although there are many African leaders who have found it hard to adjust to the new situation, they have had little choice but to acknowledge that "democracy is now the only game in town." (1997, 233)

Throughout Africa, the struggle of civil society for more open, accountable, just and democratic systems of governance has always been present in spite of the ruthlessness with which power holders have responded to these demands (Makumbe 1998, 307). Although the intensity and durability of such struggles have varied from one country to another, the truth is that across the continent, trade unions and academics, peasants, students, civil servants and professionals, interest-based and religious organizations have permanently challenged, although with less success until recently, the ruling authorities, through strikes, mass protests and rallies (Wiseman 1996, 35). But whereas before African governments have always turned a deaf ear to civil society's demands, this time, they could no longer afford to ignore the people's request for political freedom and reform of the structure of governance (Abrahamsen 1997; Bratton and van de Walle 1998).

Indeed, the sharp deterioration in living conditions, the worsening economic crisis and the blatant corruption of politicians have combined with political repression and disrespect for human rights to cause social explosion in many countries on the continent (Sklar 1983; Mbembe 1990; Heilbrunn 1993; Bayart 1993). As Legum puts it:

> Signs of mounting discontent across the entire African continent are reminiscent of the anti-colonial storm that gathered after World War II and bear some resemblance to the current movement of dissent in Eastern Europe. Whereas the anti-colonial movement spearheaded a revolt against alien rule, the present targets are the post-independence African ruling classes and, especially, the political systems they built and now defend. (1990, 129)

In the hope of nipping these movements in the bud, several governments took hasty measures to reform their political systems. However, they realized very early on that political change for change's sake was not what Africans meant (Ergas 1987; Mbembe 1988; Koné 1990). They expect genuine political reforms and economic liberalization and are willing to accept no compromise. Their obstinacy and resilience paid off, and new methods of governance were introduced. Obviously, the impetus for the political change, according to many observers and based on the military's record in African politics, was credited to internal struggles, which had been incubating for several decades (Anyong'Nyongo 1987). Consequently, recent scholarship has tended to focus on the role of political leaders and strategic élites (Diamond, Linz, and Lipset 1988).

In his praise for civil society in the Third Wave of global democratization, Diamond, having acknowledged that the overthrow of authoritarian regimes through popularly based and massively mobilized democratic opposition has not been the norm, states nevertheless that:

> Even in...negotiated and controlled transitions, the stimulus for democratization, and particularly the pressure to complete the process, have typically come from the "resurrection of civil society," the restructuring of public space, and the mobilization of all manner of independent groups and grassroots movements. (1994, 4)

In all fairness, the African masses deserve a great deal of credit for their impact on the democratic transition in Africa. While popular unrest had long been an intermittent feature of African politics, the intensity of recent popular demands was unprecedented (Wiseman

1996, 35-69). However, one needs to be careful in praising civil society without over-emphasizing its role. If the masses were the only trigger of democracy in Africa, there should be no military leaders left in power, given the amount of political protest leveled against them (Mbaku and Ihonvbere 1998). Several facts seem to weaken the theory of civil society as the real source of democratization in Africa, and Press's views remind us of the complexity of African democratization:

> Some of the old-guard incumbents got wise to the new democratic movement. Having seen electoral defeats of incumbents in other parts of Africa, they learned quickly how to adapt, how to make just enough political concessions to take the heat off for a while, how to tamper with the electoral machinery just enough to win again. Some heads of state used outright force or had the potential to do so, which is why there were few pro-democratic victories against military regimes. Most civilian authoritarian regimes were more subtle, calling elections quickly, before opponents could get organized, or not allowing potentially broad-based parties to run for various reasons, or passing laws designed to prevent particular strong potential candidates from running. (1999, 47)

The fact that generals Lansana Conté of Guinea and Gnassingbé Éyadéma of Togo are still in power, in defiance of civil society; recent military re-intervention in democratic experiments in Niger and the Congo Republic (Gros 1998, 7); the military intermission in Sierra Leone, and the fact that the late President Mobutu of former Zaire (now Democratic Republic of Congo) could only yield to military force, demonstrate that the explanation of democratic transition in Africa is undetermined at best, or, does not simply lie in how active or forceful civil society is (Conteh-Morgan 1997; Mbaku and Ihonvbere 1998).

The truth of the matter is that smooth democratic transitions, although short-lived in most cases, occurred only in countries where the military leadership has initially supported democracy (Onwumechili 1998). In the early days of political demands, national conferences with the military on board had allowed the Congo Republic, Madagascar, Mali, Niger, Benin, etc., to enjoy a peaceful transition. At the same time, countries such as Guinea and Togo where the military refused to cooperate for a peaceful political change continue to experience a situation full of uncertainty, despite controversial elections (Heilbrunn 1997; Decalo 1997).

Regardless of one's feelings towards the military on the continent, a survey of contemporary African politics does clearly reveal one fact: the role of the military in bringing about, and eventually consolidating, democracy in Africa is crucial. To explain democratization on the continent, we will have to take into account among others, the military factor (Gros 1998, 10; Tordoff 1997, 207; Onwumechili 1998, 75).

Research Design and Methodology

Through a comparative study of Benin and Togo, this study explores mainly the military variable in African democratization. The choice of these two neighboring countries is simply explained by the contrasting results achieved by their respective democratization processes, despite their similarities.

After the arbitrary carving of Africa by the Europeans at the Berlin conference of 1884-1885, the territory under the control of the kingdom of Danhomê first became a French colony. In 1958, it gained the status of a self-governing republic within the French Community, before becoming independent in 1960 (Decalo 1997, 44). It was then known as the Republic of Dahomey, before changing its name to the People's Republic of Benin as an experimental socialist state, and now the Republic of Benin *tout court* (Glèlè 1969, 1974; Cornevin 1981; Decalo 1995).

As far as the Republic of Togo is concerned, the story is less straightforward. Togoland, of which the Togolese Republic was formerly a part, was annexed by Germany in 1894, occupied by Anglo-French forces during World War I, and proclaimed a League of Nations mandate in 1919 (Decalo 1996). France became responsible for the larger eastern section of Togoland, while the United Kingdom administered the western part. In October 1956, French Togoland became an autonomous republic, also within the French Community, before gaining independence in 1960 (Cornevin 1988).

The two countries under study, Benin and Togo, are therefore former French colonies, clearly still under heavy French influence and dependency. Besides sharing a similar geographic terrain, the fabric of their societies is very alike. Their people share culture, ethnicity and kinship. Both countries had their very first military coup d'état in 1963 (Decalo 1973a, 1973b; Cornevin 1968), only three years after their nominal independence, and had been under military domination until the new challenge for political change. Before their national conferences, generals led both countries: Gnassingbé Éyadéma in Togo and Mathieu Kérékou in Benin. Both men are from the northern part of their respective countries, and had a solid hand over the army (Decalo 1995, 1996). Although it is almost impossible to have perfect similarity between countries, Togo and Benin are alike enough to lead one to expect similar outcomes from a similar social or political phenomenon (Clark 1998, 97). Yet while in Benin, Kérékou and the military leadership agreed to take part in what was dubbed as a "civilian coup d'état," that is the National Conference that engaged the democratization process, in Togo, Éyadéma and the military denounced and refused to attend the Togolese national conference (Heilbrunn 1994, 1997). Consequently, political events unfolded differently in both countries.

Whereas in Benin democratization is seen as a necessary step towards reconciliation and political renewal, Togo seems to still be searching for a more adequate forum for a better political dialogue (Heilbrunn 1997, 241-242). If nothing else, the contrasting result of the national conferences, explained largely by the attitude of the military, provides a clear opportunity to investigate the importance of the military in the democratization in Africa (Onwumechili 1998).

This inquiry is undertaken through Mill's (1863) method of difference, spending less time on the parameters, in order to allow a deeper analysis of the operative conditions. Variables such as the colonial heritage (French heritage), peaceful transition to independence, ethnically structured and highly politicized army, are touched upon (Decalo 1995, 1996; Andereggen 1994; Cornevin 1968, 1981, 1988), but not thoroughly investigated. Rather, the bulk of this study focuses on the variables in the hypothesis according to which the democratization process in Africa depends largely on the military, whose consent is based on three key factors: **the political culture of the country, cost-benefit analysis of the military leadership, and the impact of external power.** Through Alexander George's structured focused comparison that deals only with relevant variables, the research problem is scrutinized.

This study, explanatory in nature, concentrates on hypothesis building rather than theory testing. The data is gathered through government documents, archival records, and interviews. The use of multiple sources of evidence allowed the study to address a broader range of historical, attitudinal, and observational issues, and also helped cope with the validity concern. Official documents were reviewed at the French Ministry of Foreign Affairs and Cooperation, and French embassies in both countries. National assemblies, national armies, national archives and libraries of Benin and Togo, also help clarify the issue at stake. While government documents enlightened on official policies, in-depth and unstructured interviews were very helpful in uncovering the unofficial stances.

Through answers to questions related to civil-military relations, democracy in Africa and France's relations with both Togo and Benin, the rationale of why, according to France, totalitarian (Marxist) regime of Kérékou must go, while the authoritarian government of Éyadéma could stay, became obvious. Although this study's primary focus is Togo and Benin, interviews in countries such as Nigeria, Ghana, Côte d'Ivoire, Sierra Leone, Liberia, Mali and Niger, where civil-military relations remain very complex, helped put the political and economic situations of Benin and Togo in full perspective.

Research Objectives

The comparative literature on regime change offers three basic explanations for the democratic ferment in Africa (Joseph 1991; Bratton and van de Walle 1992). Explaining why democracy is appealing to the world, Stepanek contends that "democratic governments honor universal human rights as values based in law. Democracy is also fundamental to progress because it welcomes initiative, creates ownership, and builds consensus. Democracy is the foundation of development because it defines a process of consensus building and, in turn, ensures that benefits are shared. Centralized control of power, incentives, and distribution is unsustainable" (1999, 159).

The three important aspects of conceptual concern that emerge from recent theories of democratization are: first, structural and contingent factors that create cracks in the edifice of both authoritarian and totalitarian rule (Moore 1967; O'Donnell et al. 1986); second, the relative importance of élite behavior versus mass mobilization strategies of reform (O'Donnell and Schmitter 1986; Karl 1986, 1990; Rueschemeyer et al. 1992); and, third, diffusionist explanations of change (Huntington 1991).

Although contemporary scholars appear to be almost unanimous in the view that democracy and civil society have a dependent relationship, I believe that democracy can be the result of military endorsement. According to Yoshikazu Sakamoto (1991, 121), the struggle for and process of democracy underway in almost every society in the world could also take two different forms. One is "democratization from above" in which the initiatives, at least at the onset, are taken by the élite. The other is "democratization from below" caused by the popular struggle for democracy. Whether it is from above or below, democratization seems, in Sakamoto's view, to be triggered by civil society.

Embracing to varying degrees these conceptualizations, the literature on democratization in Africa can be traced back to *Popular Struggles for Democracy in Africa*, edited by Peter Anyang' Nyong'o (1987). In the book, several essays by respected African scholars detail the emergence of democratic movements, but attribute the phenomenon to the revolt of the popular masses. In his introduction, Anyang' Nyong'o (1987, 15) argued that "broad-based movements of a popular alliance type ...can restore democracy to a country run down by dictatorship."

A year later, Larry Diamond, Juan Linz and Seymour Martin Lipset published *Democracy in Developing Countries: Africa* (1988). In their book, the editors employed a framework of comparative historical analysis. In an effort to link the prospect for durable democracy to the sources of democratization, contributors were asked to make "an exhaustive examination of all the historical, cultural, social, economic, political, and international factors" that "fostered and obstructed the emergence, instauration, and consolidation of democratic government around the world" (Diamond et al. 1988, xiii). In each of the twenty-six countries explored, particular attention was paid to the cultural traditions, colonial heritage, and post-independence history "in order to explain the overall path of a country's political development" (Diamond et al. 1988, xiv).

All along, the emphasis seems to have been on civil society. As a matter of fact, Diamond (1988, 26) believes that a rich and vibrant associational life has developed in many African countries independent of the state, and such pluralism in civil society "has become the cutting edge of the effort to build a viable democratic order." He went on to say later on that "the only absolute requirement for [political] transition (short of foreign conquest and imposition) is a commitment to democracy on the part of the strategic élite" (1993).

In his quite elaborate description of the cause of the new wind of change in Africa, Wiseman focuses squarely on civil society, hardly mentioning the military:

The pro-democratic movements of most African states in the late 1980s and early 1990s represented a remarkable coalescence of political participation by all levels of society from élite to mass élite. At the élite level, pressure came from educated groups that has managed to retain, or were able to assert, some degree of autonomy from state control. Church leaders were especially prominent in a good number of cases. Enjoying a high level of popular respect in highly religious African societies, church congregations often represented one of the few legal ways of bringing people together in large numbers: the "political sermon" became common in this period. Professional associations, especially those organized by lawyers, medical staff and academics, played an important role in the pressure for political reform. Members of these associations, along with students and journalists, were often prominent in the large numbers of groups established to promote the linked causes of democracy and human rights. (1995b, 5)

After several attempts at understanding and explaining the fall of democratic regimes in Latin America and Southern Europe, O'Donnell, Schmitter, and Whitehead (1986), through their four-part series, *Transition from Authoritarian Rule,* gave a major new impetus to the field of transition studies. Following the modernization theory's vanguardist role given to the supposed innovators of change in the development process, this book champions the strategic élite explanation of democratization. Intra-élite division, loss of legitimacy by incumbent authoritarian regimes and a readiness on the part of dissatisfied élites to "overthrow" the regime are seen as necessary and sufficient conditions for democratization.

Although the book also discussed the role of the military in democratic transition because the impetus for democratization in Portugal in the late 1960s emerged from within the armed forces, the emphasis is clearly placed on civil society. An entire chapter is devoted to resurrecting civil society. As a matter of fact, the book's praise for the "critical" role played by groups and individuals in civil society during democratic openings is frequently cited by analysts of popular protest and political reform in Africa (Bratton and van de Walle 1992).

The appeal of civil society as an organizing concept is not puzzling. Indeed, there is widespread agreement across a range of theoretical perspectives that political accountability is an essential condition for democracy, and that the degree of accountability depends on the capacity of a robust, autonomous civil society to curb the hegemony of the state (Lonsdale 1986). Having lost interest in civil society in the 1970s because of the rise of the party-state and personal rule, most Africanists began in the 1980s to once again associate civil society with the prospects for limiting state power (Woods 1992).

Besides Anyang' Nyong'o and his co-authors who believe that "popular struggles" will smash "the neocolonial state," Robert Fatton, Jr., (1992) characterized civil society as a potentially subversive space in which dissidents grounded in private routes to power and wealth may, under certain conditions, force an autocratic regime to accept a democratic pact (Ndue 1994, 51).

Civil society as the most popular of all the perspectives in democratic transition, flows from three main sources. The first is the experience of the Western societies in which civil society, conceived of as the non-statist organizations that occupy the political and social space between the individual and the state, has historically functioned to limit the power of the state and uphold pluralism. The second is the liberalization that has been implemented side-by-side with democratization in many countries. The third is the role civil society is expected and encouraged to play in the process of democratic consolidation (Osaghae 1992, 192).

It is believed that civil society has the capacity to keep the transition process from backsliding and that if ingredients of democracy—accountability and respect for constitutional rules—are well ingrained, it can play crucial roles in the building and sustenance of democratic cultures (Bratton and van de Walle 1998, 147). The civil society perspective provides a very important framework for evaluating the impact of ordinary peoples—their demands, actions and orientations—on the transition process.

Clearly, the significance of a lively civil society in achieving democracy, cannot, and should not, be ignored. There are instances in which the democratic struggle by civil society has, by itself, succeeded in bringing authoritarianism and military rule to an end in Africa (Decalo 1968, 16-17; Oyugi 1988). However, the current literature on democratization tends to over-emphasize the importance of civil society in African polity. Contrary to widely held views, democratization does not simply depend on civil society's behavior. This research discovered that, to even burgeon, democracy in Africa requires the cooperation of the military (Onwumechili 1998, 1), and the fact that several emerging democracies reversed to military dictatorships testifies to that observation.

Recent military coups d'état in the Gambia, the Congo, Niger, Sierra Leone, the January 2001 failed military coup in Côte d'Ivoire, and the military's inclination to cling to power on the continent (Martin 1997, 96), highlight the importance of this study's effort to comprehend the military's role in democratic transition in Africa (Hutchful 1997, 44). No democratic state can endure for long time without the bedrock of support provided by a democratic society and the habits it nurtures (Ndue 1994, 51). Consequently, until the military is under civilian control at a later stage of democratic consolidation, efforts at democratization must accurately understand and address the attitude and capacity of the military.

CHAPTER TWO

THEORETICAL PERSPECTIVES ON DEMOCRATIZATION, CIVIL SOCIETY, THE MILITARY AND POLITICAL CULTURE IN AFRICA

Given the theoretical spectrum of this study, some concepts and theories are reviewed to clarify the numerous concepts found in the current literature on regime change, and to, therefore, allow a better understanding of this investigation.

Democratization in Africa

Despite renewed interest in democracy adherents have failed to address questions such as whether democracy must be conceived as liberal democracy, whether democracy can only be applied to 'governmental affairs' (and not to the economic, social and cultural realms as well), and whether the most appropriate locus for democracy is the nation (Held 1995, v). Although democracy seems to have scored an historic victory over alternative forms of government (Held 1995, 3), it remains an essentially contested concept (Gallie 1956). The difficulty in giving a defensible definition to democracy can de seen in the sheer number and diversity of its meanings. In Beetham's "small selection" of potential definitions, democracy is, depending on one's ideological stance, equated with

> Rule of law, rule of the people's representatives, rule of the people's party, majority rule, dictatorship of the proletariat, maximum political participation, elite competition for the popular vote, multi-partyism, political and social pluralism, equal citizenship rights, civil and political liberties, a free society, a civil society, a free market economy...the 'end of history,' all things bright and beautiful. (1999, 1)

Although some of these meanings overlap, many are inconsistent with one another, creating a set of mutually incompatible conceptions of democracy. There are therefore several antitheses including:

> Democracy as a descriptive or as a prescriptive concept; democracy as institutional procedure or as a normative ideal; direct vs. representative democracy; elite vs. participatory democracy; liberal vs. non-liberal (populist, Marxist, radical) democracy; deliberative vs. mass democracy; political vs. social democracy; majoritarian vs. consensual democracy; democracy as individual rights or the collective good; democracy as the realization of equality or the negotiation of difference. (Beetham 1999, 1)

The lack of agreement not only affects the definition of democracy, but also its emergence. In a survey of the literature on democratic transition, Huntington (1991, 38) identifies six general propositions on democracy and its causes:

1. No single factor is sufficient to explain the development in all countries or in a single country.
2. No single factor is necessary to the development of democracy in all countries.
3. Democratization in each country is the result of a combination of causes.
4. The combination of causes producing democracy varies from country to country.
5. The combination of causes generally responsible for one wave of democratization differs from that responsible for other waves.

6. The causes responsible for the initial regime changes in a democratization wave are likely to differ from those responsible for later regime changes in that wave.

According to early propositions of democratic theory, a viable democracy depended on higher levels of modernization, illustrated by wealth, a bourgeois class structure, tolerant class values, and economic independence from external actors (Lipset 1959; Almond and Verba 1963; Moore, Jr. 1966; Rustow 1970; Dahl 1971; O'Donnell 1979). But, since the third wave of democratization, the scholarship of necessary and preconditions of democracy made way for the dynamics of democratic transition (Bermeo 1990; Buijtenhuijs and Rijnierse 1993; Buijtenhuijs and Thiriot 1995). Once democratization began to take root in infertile ground, research shifted away from structuralism. Academics were no longer interested in clarifying the role of structures in democratization and indeed, tended to dismiss the idea that it was even possible to identify them (Schmitz and Sell 1999, 30). In Karl's view,

> Rather than engaging in a futile search for new preconditions, it is important to clarify how *the mode of regime transition (itself conditioned by the breakdown of authoritarian rule) sets the contest within which strategic interactions can take place because these interactions, in turn, help to determine whether political democracy will emerge and survive* (emphasis in original). (1990, 19)

However, scholars molded in the modernization paradigm continued to seek confirmation of their assumption through their initial responses to the "Third Wave." According to Remmer, they offered four possible explanations:

> First, offering modernization theory as an old answer to new questions; second, rejecting theory altogether and linking political outcomes, at best, to 'choices of particular political elites' and, at worst, to '*virtù* and *fortuna*;' third, advocating 'barefoot empiricism' in order to generate a new agenda; or fourth, dismissing the developments as significant or a mere 'wave in the cyclical alternation of democratic and authoritarian regimes.' (1991, 481)

In its structural explanations, modernization theory's causal link between socio-economic development and democracy, and its sweeping claims of its early days failed to stand up to in-depth scrutiny. Modernization theory also remains incapable to explain why authoritarian regimes decide to liberalize their political system. The role of economic growth in that process remains a mystery, as much as liberalization in places where modernization theory was completely unable to predict any such development (Schmitz and Sell 1999, 29).

Because democracy has emerged in an infertile terrain, several scholars have tried to understand how, without fulfilling all the prerequisites, some countries in the Third World were able to democratize or at least open up their political systems (Charlton 1983; Berton 1992; Conac 1993; Callaghy 1994; Chabal 1998). Like democracy itself, democratization, evidently, means different things to different people. Many writers, including Schumpeter, Dahl, Przeworski, Lipset, Huntington, have spent their scholarly lifetimes teasing out the subtleties and nuances associated with conception of democracy. Yet, the concept remains elusive, and highly contested in analytical and ideological discourse (Wiseman 1996, 8).

Etymologically, democracy derives from a Greek word meaning the "rule by the people," the classical notion of "government of, by and for the people." However, because by "people," Greeks referred to a particular social class, it is more appropriate to translate democracy as the rule of the "many."[1] Although any political system can claim to further people's interest, only a democracy allows the majority to rule, and not just benefit (Monga 1996, 19-20). According to Schumpeter,

> democracy does not mean and cannot mean that people actually rule in any obvious sense of the terms "the people" and "rule." Rather, it comprises institution and procedures that ensure plural centres of power and competition for office between contending political élites. It is more a technique of government than an ideal to be pursued over the long term; more about government for than of the people. (1943, 284)

Besides the complexity of the concept of democracy, raised by Schumpeter, it is also important to mention that any system that incorporates political participation is not necessary a democracy (Daloz and Quantin 1997). Democracy is more than a set of procedural mechanisms and some have argued that it stands for values such as equality and individual liberty. In Catt's views:

> In most theoretical writings, democracy is not valued in itself but because it provides other desirable ends. Central to the arguments for democracy and its gradual acceptance are the basic ideas of equality and individual liberty and what these concepts entail. However, both

of these central ideas can be interpreted in a variety of ways and the exact nuances that are stressed affect the type of democracy that is seen as justifiable. Another problem is that individual liberty can be restricted by the implementation of equality and can also hinder equality. The ways in which tensions between the key ideas of equality and liberty are dealt with are at the centre of arguments for different types of democratic procedures. (1999, 7)

The concept of democracy has two variants: a maximalist definition and a minimalist or procedural version. In its maximalist form, democracy is supposed to be the vector to solve all the problems a society is facing (Muller 1988; McFerson 1992; Good 1997). This concept equates democracy with economic development. The original statistical research in the 1960s on the correlates of democracy was partly inspired by, and also contributed to, a prerequisite on socio-economic development, labeled "modernization theory," which expected societal "goodies" to go together: increased incomes, more modern and positive social values, enterprise, socio-economic diversity, income equality and democracy (Moore 1996, 60). In its maximalist expression, democracy is associated with "welfarist" public policies and relatively good performance on the components of human development indices. Several scholars who argue for the dualism of economic stability and democratic sustainment maintain that "Africa has no chance of attaining meaningful economic growth and development unless it first moves squarely into modalities of governance that include political accountability, participatory politics and free market economy (quoted in Udogu 1996, 9). Ake concurs with this view when he asserts that "the problem of persistence of underdevelopment is related to lack of democracy in Africa…democracy is not just a consummatory value but also an instrumentalist one (1990, 2).

A simpler form counters this approach, contesting socioeconomic advances as defining criteria intrinsic to democracy. According to minimalist proponents, (Schumpeter 1942; Dahl 1971; Di Palma 1990; Huntington 1991; Przeworski 1991), democracy is simply a method that allows the majority to have a say in the political decision-making process. According to Schumpeter's "another theory of democracy," "the democratic method is that institutional arrangement for arriving at political decisions in which individuals acquire the power to decide by means of a competitive struggle for the people's vote" (1942, 269). Schumpeter's analysis came out of his conviction that average citizens were incapable of rational reflection or realistic consideration about public affairs, but would, rather, yield to extra-rational or irrational prejudice or impulse (Beetham 1999, 2). To equate, however, democracy with mere electoral competition for public office, is to "elevate a means into an end," and "to confuse an instrument with its purpose (Beetham 1999, 3). According to its critics (Held 1987; Dahl 1989), constitutional democracy does not in itself guarantee development, nor does it meet the demands of democracy itself. It excludes many interests, and it puts unacceptable and unnecessary limits on the possibilities of politics itself. Democratic government does even have to be necessarily "good," since "governments produced by elections may be inefficient, corrupt, shortsighted, irresponsible, dominated by special interests, and incapable of adopting policies demanded by the public good. These qualities may make such governments undesirable but they do not make them undemocratic" (Huntington 1991, 10). Through institutional arrangements for arriving at political decisions, individuals acquire the power to decide by means of a competitive struggle for the majority's vote. In a way, minimalist democracy simply gives the citizenry the opportunity to "kick the rascals out" (Wiseman 1996, 8). However, disagreement over the meaning of democracy spills over into the literature on the process by which it is attained.

The current literature on democratization is dealing with how to reach a political system that grants that kind of freedom to citizens. Scholars generally agree that the route to democracy is normally a gradual, staged process rather than an abrupt and dramatic one (Keller 1995, 224). However, there is no commonly-agreed number of stages to the process. Schmitter and O'Donnell (1986, 7) suggest two broad phases leading to democratic outcomes: liberalization and democratization.

While liberalization encompasses the more modest goal of merely loosening restrictions and expanding individual and group rights within an authoritarian or totalitarian regime, democratization includes expanded civil and political rights (Shin 1994, 142). Without a distinction between liberalization and democratization, any move towards a less closed political system might be confused with a democratization process. Liberalization is a necessary but not a sufficient condition for democracy. As a first step towards a government by the majority, democratization requires that political leaders be elected through regularly held free elections (Maclean 1994; Stromberg 1996, 3-15).

Democratization is a complex historical process with four analytically distinct but overlapping stages: (1) decay of authoritarian or totalitarian rule, (2) transition, (3) consolidation, and (4) the maturing of democratic order (Shin 1994, 143). This book, which espouses the procedural or minimalist view of democracy, will focus on the second, that is, the transition to democracy. Because many African countries are still struggling to attain the most rudimentary forms of political liberalization, focusing on the second stage, transition, will yield key policy guidance for those countries. Transition comprises the time from the breakdown of the old regime to the formal establishment of a new government, and during which new rules of the political game are set (O'Donnell and Schmitter 1986, 6).

After the turning of the page of dictatorship in Africa (Iheduru 1999, 21-23), the continent needs a genuine democratic transition to begin a new era. In an effort to capture the different transition paths in Africa, Joseph (1991) identifies seven models: (1) the National Conference, (2) government via democratic elections, (3) co-opted transitions, (4) guided democratization, (5) recalcitrant and piecemeal reforms, (6) armed insurrections culminating in elections, and (7) conditional transitions. None of these routes guarantee a successful democratic transition since success seems to result from the willingness of incumbent regimes to transfer and also from the strategies adopted by challengers.

The story of democracy in Africa is a long and sad one. Although there still is a debate about the extent to which pre-colonial Africa was democratic, given the elements of caste, slavery, and gender discrimination found in pre-colonial societies, ancient African communities had several ingredients of democracy (Kunz 1991, 227; Mair 1977). Without claiming that all traditional African societies were democratic, because several of them were ruled by despotic and vicious monarchs, it has been evidenced that some of them were relatively democratic in their practices (Onwumechili 1998, 1-14). Corroborating democratic practices in Ashanti societies in Ghana, Busia contends that:

> The Ashantis of Ghana have one of the large kingdoms in Africa, and yet there were various elements of democracy in their government. The powers of the *Asantehene* were not absolute, because he had to abide by the custom and advice of a representative council. If an *Asantehene* decided to ignore these checks on his power, he could be deposed [destooled]. Though the throne of *Asantehene* was hereditary, the electors had a choice of replacement from "other members of the same lineage. (1968, 30)

Concurring with Busia, Kunz found in African political culture a tradition of checks and balances when he states:

[This] tradition [exhibits a] rich body of varied constitutional practices in African societies long pre-dating the colonial period, a set of 'leadership norms' often enshrined in oaths, song and drum texts, maxims/proverbs, prayers on ceremonial occasions. Cumulatively, they gave shape to the rival 'principle of equality' or equal potentiality to authority ('the king in every man') and they constituted what Maxwell Owusu has referred to as "fiduciary obligations of trusteeship," subordinating the wielders of political power to 'constitutional law.' Conversely, they established the "right" and duty of the subjects to disobey and even kill an autocratic or tyrannical ruler. (1991, 226-7)

Unfortunately, European invaders, in order to justify their action, had to "civilize," altering profoundly conquered societies (Ayoade 1986, 25). Concerned about France's policies *vis-à-vis* African democracy, Martial Merlin, French General Governor (1919-1923) observes that the "fierce struggle against chiefs" had been a misguided crusade inspired by the republican ideology of France's newly triumphant bourgeoisie (Conklin 1997, 188). Still troubled by France's adamant desire to subdue Africa's democracy, Merlin contrasts France's policies to the England's in a report:

What have the English done? They have allowed democracy to persist, under the resemblance of a doctrinaire liberalism, all that is oppressive in the feudal regime that was in place when they arrived. This fundamentally aristocratic regime, which did not allow them to recruit even a twentieth of the men we were able to during the war, is now condemned by all important colonial figures [because it risks alienating the mass of African subjects]...Less liberal in its proclamations, but more democratic in terms of its affects, our policy consisted, in contrast, in preserving for ourselves alone all sovereignty. In conciliating the masses, however, we alienated the sympathy of the dispossessed chiefs, who were reduced to simple intermediaries. Is there not room for a mixed policy that simultaneously respects the *amour propre* of the ruling classes and the essential rights of the masses? (quoted in Conklin 1997, 190)

By the time Europeans left the continent, any democratic practices in African societies were diluted or destroyed (Coquery-Vidrovitch 1992b, 6). Rupert Emerson (1960, 113) even predicted that "democracy in Africa, as in Asia, would bleed and die on the altars of national consolidation and social reconstruction." Alluding to the history of democracy in Africa, Pfaff maintains that:

it seems fair to say that when Europeans first came to Africa there
were coherent, functioning societies of varying degrees of
sophistication, some of great political subtlety and artistic
accomplishment, others simple hunting and gathering communities,
some extremely cruel in their practices, but all possessing their own
integrity and integrated into the natural environment of the continent.
This was destroyed by colonialism. (1995, 3-4)

At independence, African leaders were left with somewhat
democratic colonial states (Sylla 1982, 26). Africa inherited liberal
democracy in its British, French, or Belgian version from the accelerated
and panicky processes of rapid de-colonization (Jackson and Rosberg
1985; Clapham 1993, 425). It was only in the last decade of colonialism,
when independence became a certainty that the imperialist powers
gradually began to institute democratic reforms in what had hitherto been
structures of exploitation, despotism and degradation.[2] According to
Udogu (1996, 9), "the colonial administrators socialized the African
leaders in an authoritarian form of governance, but expected those to
whom they handed the baton of leadership to become democrats in due
course." These expectations were simply not fulfilled and democracy
eluded the continent until recently. Almost as if to fulfill Emerson's
prophecy regarding the fate of democracy on the continent, most new
leaders imposed a one-party system in the name of unity and nation
building (Jackson and Rosberg 1985, 293).

One paradox of the latter days of colonial autocracy was the
encouragement of democracy in order to perpetuate exploitative
capitalism and dominance by the former colonial powers. Another
paradox was based on the logic that to withdraw from the colonies would
enable Europeans to regulate the colonial economies at a time when their
focus had shifted to economic security (Conteh-Morgan 1997, 48). The
history of the de-colonization is splattered with many more instances of
colonial power intransigence, repression, and exploitation. These
undemocratic structures would later haunt the post-colonial national élite
and be used by them to consolidate their authoritarian rule (Conteh-
Morgan 1997, 49). In Sklar's words, "Africa's post-colonial states are
successors to profoundly anti-democratic colonial forms of governing"
(quoted in Press 1999, 29).

Although it does not fully justify the behavior of post-independence
African leaders, the political system bequeathed by European powers does
explain the root of authoritarianism on the continent, and Gordon is right

in his assessment of the political scene in Africa on the eve of independence:

> democratic governmental models developed by the French and British for their colonies were essentially alien structures hastily superimposed over the deeply ingrained political legacies of imperial rule. The real political inheritances of African states at independence were the authoritarian structures of the colonial state, an accompanying political culture, and an environment of politically relevant circumstances tied heavily to the nature of colonial rule. Imperial rule from the beginning expropriated political power. Unconcerned with the needs and the wishes of the indigenous population, the colonial powers created governing apparatuses primarily intended to control the territorial population, to implement exploration of natural resources, and to maintain themselves and the European population. For all European colonizers – British, French, Belgian, Portuguese, German, Spanish, and Italian – power was vested in a colonial state that was, in essence, a centralized hierarchical bureaucracy. Specifically, colonial rule was highly authoritarian and backed by police forces and colonial troops. Under this circumstance, power did not rest in the legitimacy of public confidence and acceptance. There was no doubt where power lay; it lay firmly with the political authorities. (1996, 57)

In a way, the idea that government was above self-interested political activity was never conveyed by colonial administrators. As a result, notions that authoritarianism was an appropriate mode of rule became part of the colonial political legacy (quoted in Gordon 1996, 57).

African leaders never fully accepted the precepts of the European political model. Few were enthusiastic about it, and most tolerated it as a means to their own selfish end (Clapham 1993, 428). They argued that a competitive party system was inappropriate for African conditions, because political parties only represent and perpetuate social classes. Another political ground for rejecting liberal democracy is the Marxist argument that it is only a mask for bourgeois domination. Given that mistrust of "bourgeois" democracy, one would expect African leaders to devote their energy to the betterment of the lives of their compatriots. Unfortunately, they simply replaced the colonizers and performed very poorly (Sandbrook 1988, 249). They built support through local constituencies made up with kinship and ethnic groups. Ethnic constituencies became crucial to the survival of new governments. In the meantime, they either ran the opposition underground or defused it by coopting into government members willing to bestow their political support and personal loyalty in return for political compensation (Gordon 1996, 71-72).

Chazan and her colleagues believe that "because state institutions in Africa are fragile and command only limited public acceptance, informal networks of personal relationships emerge in society to link a relatively powerful and well-placed patron with a less powerful client or clients for the purpose of advancing their mutual interests" (1999, 113). In the same vein, Lemarchand contends that "clientelism can lead to a pyramiding of client-patron ties, and, through the recruitment of new brokers, to an expansion of local or regional reciprocities on a more inclusive scale" (1972, 86).

Power evolved around individuals and constitutions were ignored, altered or set aside. There was a near-consensus that Africa was different and should develop its own forms of democracy, more suited to its history and culture.[3] That position was even praised by some scholars. Ruth Schachter (1961), for example, hailed the one-party regime as a necessary and inevitable modernizing agency if different ethnic groups were to be mobilized and constituted into one nation. At the same time, Frantz Fanon already saw in such a system the root of all the problems the continent might face. In his condemnation of the corruption of Jean-Jacques Rousseau's "General Will" which emerged in the early 1960's in the form of the one-party doctrine in Africa, Fanon (1968, 165) said poignantly: "the single party is the modern form of the dictatorship of the bourgeoisie, unmasked, unpainted, unscrupulous, and cynical." Through one-party political systems, new leaders crafted pervasive clientelistic networks that ensured the flow of powers through their hands rather than through formal institutions that might impose unwanted constraints on them.

Later on, the one-party ideology gave birth to "developmental dictatorship" (Sklar 1983). According to A. James Gregor (1987, 87), the principles of developmental dictatorship, first formulated by Italian Marxists, entrusted responsibility for the direction of a country to a "vanguard elite." However such a system suppresses liberty, regiments and exploits labor, curtails freedom of movement and restricts personal choice (Coquery-Vidrovitch 1992b, 7).

For his study of the African vanguard élites' leadership, Richard Sklar (1983) distinguished four types of 'democracy' in early post-independence Africa. The first model is liberal democracy, exemplified by Senegal and Botswana, wherein law limits the powers of government and citizens enjoy freedom of association to compete for office in regularly held free elections (Levallois 1996, 14). Most liberal democracies bequeathed to Africa by the former colonial rulers were rudely swept away by military coups, political usurpation and constitutional changes shortly after independence (Sklar 1983, 12). The second type, guided democracy, accepts the principle of accountability but denies multiparty elections. Jomo Kenyatta's Kenya was a prototype (Sklar 1983, 14). The third model, or social democracy, extends the concept of democracy beyond the mere precept of accountability, to the idea of social justice. Late Julius Nyerere's Tanzania would be a good case (Sklar 1983, 15). Sklar's fourth type of democracy is the one-party participatory democracy of Kenneth Kaunda's Zambia. Although this type of democracy bears some resemblance to Pateman's concept of participatory democracy,[4] it is simply an attempt to induce popular participation through channels controlled by the state party (Sklar 1983, 16).

There is a fifth model of democracy, but with no legal guardian in Africa, although its adoption is often contemplated: consociational democracy (Sklar 1983, 17). That type of democracy, which, in fact, is a version of liberal democracy with special arrangements to protect the vital interests of social groups, is recommended for deeply divided societies. (Lijphart 1977). At the same time, there is a brand new type of democracy, the "no-party" democracy (Tordoff 1997, 22). Ugandan President Yoweri Museveni, who believes that most African states are not ready for multiparty democracy, has experimented with this "no-party" model or "movement democracy" (*West Africa*, January 19-25, 1998, 63).

Until 1989 when the wind of change started blowing on the continent, only a few countries like Botswana, Mauritius and Senegal qualified as democracies in the Western sense. The wave of democratization was probably perceived first as an anomaly, since democratization was not supposed to occur on the continent. According to the main theories about the prerequisites or favorable conditions for democracy (Lipset 1959; Moore, Jr. 1966; Edvardsen 1997), most African countries are far from fertile ground. The continent was too poor, too culturally fragmented, and insufficiently capitalistic to embark on a democratization road. It lacked the requisite civic culture. The middle class, weak and more bureaucratic rather than entrepreneurial, was often co-opted into authoritarian political structures. The working classes were too embryonic to trigger democratization (Muravchik 1993, 646). According to some, excessive division on basic matters, such as race, culture class, or religion could be a severe handicap to democracy (Stromberg 1996, 135).

In the views of Niebuhr and Sigmund (1969) democracy creates too many rifts in the organized communities united by a common language or race, or exacerbates divisions within a community divided by religious loyalties. Reviewing Gann and Duigan's book, *Colonialism in Africa*, Eric Stokes observes that "liberal democracies with the panoply of civil liberties are the exotic product of relatively homogeneous national communities in the West, whilst most African states are plural societies in the ethnic, if not in the economic sense (quoted in Stromberg 1996, 135). Bernot Marrah carried this point even further when he argues that:

> The enemies of democracy in the modern world are primarily the forces that tend to destroy the homogeneity of nations, and introduce principles of division which go beyond differences of opinion, and rend the society asunder by conflicts of doctrine, or of real or alleged interests, in which there is no common ground to form the starting point, and the finishing point, of argument. (1942, 34)

In a similar vein, Lijphart (1977) also warned that in the context of heterogeneous, and divided societies, majoritarian electoral system can actually undermine national stability. Besides instability, it can also generate two other possibilities, neither of which is conducive to democratization. In some African countries emerging from one-party rule, multi-party elections are likely to result in a *de facto* one-party-dominant party-system, which allows opposition parties only a marginal role in the political system. Alternatively, they might generate regional one-party systems, making national government difficult and marginalizing minorities (van Cranenburgh 1999, 101). Although others (Lerner 1958; Dealy 1974) also maintain that democracy does not flourish in a society too organic, several scholars continue to value consensus and community as the best ingredients of democracy.

The divisiveness within African nations coupled with the absence of other preconditions for democratization, led many scholars to consider democracy in Africa to be an impossibility. In 1984 when Huntington wrote that, "with a few exceptions, the limits of democratic development may well have been reached," he certainly did not have in mind African countries as the exceptions. As a matter of fact, he believed that "most African countries are by reason of their poverty or the violence of their politics unlikely to move in a democratic direction." There have been doubts about the possibility of change without "an independent commercial class, elevated literacy rates, and higher levels of per capita income." (Widner 1994, 2).

Similarly, if Dahl (1971) did not expect "any dramatic changes in the number of polyarchies within a generation or two," it is because the chances of African countries becoming democratic must be very remote. Giuseppe di Palma (1990) bluntly characterized the prospects of democracy in "Africa as a whole" as "bleak." By 1989, even committed Africanists like Michael Bratton (1989) began to lose hope for democracy on the continent.

The prospect that African political leaders could be installed and deposed by political will and held accountable while in office seemed too remote before the 1990s (1989). When Crawford Young (1994) described the return of democracy in some African countries by 1991 as "stunning", he spoke for the academic community. At the same time, Young agreed with Rustow (1970) that there are indeed "many roads to democracy."

Despite all the hardships and obstacles that post-independence African regimes impose on the populations, ordinary citizens and some scholars maintain faith in (liberal) democracy. Back in 1971, Gonidec (181) denounced African leaders for declaring that they are committed to democracy while relegating the people to the very fringes of political life. In his view, only free and fair elections, and not plebiscites, could restore the expression of the people's will and thereby show a genuine expression of choice (Kabaya-Katambwa 1986, 27).

In his 1986 edited volume, *Democracy and Pluralism in Africa*, Dov Ronen (194, 202) reviews the role that "sociocultural heterogeneity" or pluralism, self-rule and self-determination or democracy could play in African societies. While David Magang (106) elaborates on Botswana as a good example of African democracy, Lansine Kaba (100) narrates how African form of democracy, with all its shortcomings, contributed to the Songhay Empire of the fifteenth to the sixteenth Centuries. For his part, Colin Legum (179) finds "examples of both authoritarian and democratic systems in pre-modern times."

In his *Power in Africa: An Essay in Political Interpretation*, Patrick Chabal (1992) also deplores the turn of events on the continent. Through a sweeping analysis of politics in contemporary Africa, he exposes the ills of the continent that result from the lack of democracy and accountability. Harry Goulbourne (1991) also depicts multipartyism as the essential ingredient to overcoming the constraints on civil and human rights in Africa.

Although the reasons why Africa's democratic systems fell apart in the recent past might seem obvious because the collapse can easily attributed to Africa's own internal shortcomings (Sandbrook 1987, 25), they are actually a complex mixture of external and internal factors. In Malwal's words:

> When Europeans left power in Africa, most of them were not entrusted in ensuring that an African system of government survived after them; in fact, what was done actually ensured that the political system had little chance to survive after independence. The fight for the spoils went on unabated among the African élites. Three who got to the top, whether by chances or by other means, generally had no concept of human rights – all they cared about was how to remain on top, and they were willing to use any means to stay there. (1986, 89)

In a similar vein, Ayoade echoes:

> Colonialism retarded the growth of traditional political institutions in order to prevent them from competing with the colonial institutions for the allegiance of the people. By undermining these traditional institutions, the philosophical bases of duties and obligations regulating the relationship between the governing and the governed were destroyed. (1986, 25)

Furthermore, the denigration of African traditional religions undermined political duties and obligations by neutralizing religion, which had provided effective civic support for traditional political authority. Colonialism not only destroyed what was in place, but also taught wrong lessons on democracy, in failing to replace traditional structures with adequate forms of political arrangements. In Barry Munslow's words, "the problem was not so much a failure by Africans to learn the lesson of parliamentary government; rather, the lesson of authoritarian colonial rule was taught and learnt too well" (1993, 478).

The colonial legacy confronted Africa with a fundamental contradiction that African leaders failed to resolve, between the imperatives of democracy and the necessity to build bourgeoisies (Bratton 1989, 413-418). Rather, the debris of the parliamentary model gave way to different forms of personal rule that achieved varied degrees of successes with variable degrees of coercion (Finer 1967, 507). While success was precarious, temporary and crippled by its class and ethnic limitations, failure was egregious, massive and tragic (Sandbrook 1987, 20). Where civil liberties remained, they were fragile, vulnerable and under constant threat of sudden death (Chabal 1991). Where despotism prevailed, it was cruel, murderous and incompetent (Jackson and Rosberg 1982).

In the same vein, Jean-François Bayart (1985) and Thomas Callaghy (1994) believe that the emergence of modern authoritarianism in Africa stems from a series of interrelated phenomena rooted in the burdensome and contradictory colonial legacy, the intense and Hobbesian process of class formation, and the severe crisis and dislocation of the structures of production (Bratton 1989, 411). According to most Africanists, the weight of culture and history, the struggle for wealth and privilege, and the vicissitudes of scarcity and poverty have all generated despotic forms of personal rule (Balandier 1955; Bayart 1989; Chabal 1994a).

Until the Europeans' invasion of Africa, traditional rulers understood the importance of having the support of their subjects (Kabaya-Katambwa 1986, 29-30). Without reminiscing about the past, it can be stated that power was more or less in the hands of *demos*. Mostly monarchical in nature, power in pre-colonial Africa took into account the will of the people, and the difficulties Europeans faced while trying to destroy or weaken it testify to the diffusion or acceptance of power among the populations (Mair 1977; LeVine 1980, 658). Traditional political systems demonstrated tolerance, accommodation and peaceful coexistence, as embodied in checks and balances on the power of Chiefs (Ayittey 1992, 37-77). However, colonization eliminated traditional rulers and corrupted what had worked effectively in the past (Coquery-Vidrovitch 1992a, 34). Whether it is the British attempt to "improve what they find" (indirect rule) or the French who prefer to "make all new" (direct rule), their imposition of what Albert Sarraut (1923) called "new and rectilinear architectures" on indigenous authorities did not help the promotion of democracy (Mamdani 1995, 606).

Colonial powers believed that new modern ideas would guide the chiefs in the way of enlightenment, remove abuses from the traditional system, control the infliction of cruel punishments, and monitor the demands that chiefs could make on their subjects. Unfortunately, that vision simply ignored the dynamic nature of social relations in Africa (Hull 1980, 20), by failing to recognize that the traditional relationship of chiefs with their subjects resulted from continuous interaction, in which a balance was struck between the claims of the ruler and the expectations of the ruled (Potholm 1979, 24-25). Except a few cases, like that of the Fulani empires, where conquerors had military power strong enough to enforce the submission of conquered peoples, the subjects more often acquiesced in a rule which they considered worthy and respectable, and the ruler approximated their ideal chief (Potholm 1979, 26; Onwumechili 1998, 2-14).

Without idealizing African traditions, which might not have been democratic in the Western sense of the term, these traditions rested on an equilibrium that made authority acceptable as long as obedience was considered to be worthwhile (Diagne 1986, 68-69). Once that balance was disturbed, obedience could disappear through either a transfer of allegiance by individuals or secession by larger groups (Onwumechili 1998, 15-17). There were cases where the ruler could be removed by popular will as in the case of the Akan-speaking peoples of Ghana, who, among other African communities, had a formal procedure for the removal of chiefs (Mair 1977).

With the annihilation of African traditional power, European colonization destroyed the possibility of an eventual advent of democracy in Africa (Onwumechili 1998, 16). Consequently, nationalist leaders who replaced Europeans at the helm of their countries did not feel obliged to keep intact the pseudo-democracies they were handed (Houngnikpo 1989, 39-40). The African commitment to liberal democracy being shaky and hesitant, it did not take a decade after independence before most countries adopted one-party regimes (Young 1996, 55). In fact, democracy's fate in independent Africa became so doubtful that many scholars lost hope in the return of democracy on the continent. Only a handful of theorists remain optimistic about democracy's resilience. One of such hopeful scholars is Sklar who believes that:

> Democracy dies hard...[it] stirs and wakens from the deepest slumber whenever the principles of accountability is asserted by members of a community or conceded by those who rule. Democracy cannot be destroyed by a coup d'État, it will survive every legal assault upon political liberty. (1983, 11)

Eventually, democracy did survive, owing to a resilient civil society, but also to the will of "military" society.

Civil Society and Democratization in Africa

The role played by civil society in forcing political reforms in Africa explains a strong return of that concept in African studies (Mamdani 1995, 602-603). Although used in a variety of ways, civil society often refers to the emergence of new patterns of political participation outside of formal state structures and one-party systems (Bratton 1989, 407). As one of the necessary conditions for the persistence of modern democracies, civil society has always been determinant in the birth and growth of any democracy since time immemorial (Patterson 1998, 423). According to Baker (1998, 81), "an autonomous civil society is seen as a necessary bulwark against undemocratic state power, whether potential or actual." Alluding to the importance of civil society in democratization, Woods states that;

> The relationship between civil society and democracy is a complicated one. The emergence of a civil society does not guarantee the development of democracy; however, it is highly unlikely that a viable democracy can survive without a civil society. Civil society is a necessary foundation for democracy...It is within civil society that public opinion is formed and it is through independent associations that individuals can have some influence on government decision making. (1992, 94)

Although civil society is closely associated with the state and should be studied with the state (Sachikonye 1995, 7), scholars only recently became interested in civil society. For a long time, the state has captured the imagination of political theorists (Rowley, 1997, 1) because of its importance in answering crucial questions related to the nature of justice, the ideal institutional arrangements that can lead to good life, the provision of dignity and self-respect of human beings, the realization of political morality, etc. Since the time of Plato, the state has emerged as the main corporate actor in political, cultural, social and economic sectors, and consequently civil society has been put on the back burner (Hutchful 1995-1996, 54).

However, a good understanding of the state requires a proper appreciation of the concept of civil society (Mamdani 1995, 605). Although every state possesses ultimate power and performs a set of definite functions, states differ in their behavior, revealing the existence of a variable that shapes the character of the state: civil society. The behavior of a state depends, to a great extent, on the nature of the relationship between the state and civil society (Chandhoke 1995, 9).

Any state will naturally seek to control and limit the political practices of society if there is no buffer zone between the state and society (Blaney and Pasha 1993, 6-7). Civil society forms that zone where mediations and altercations take place, and the site where state and society negotiate their relationship (Neocleous 1996, 2). Classical political theory views civil society as the locus where individuals come to recognize themselves as social beings, capable of reaching their private ends through working with others (Roniger 1994, 210-211). Several scholars have to define civil society. Hegel wrote:

> Through working with others, the individual's particularity is mediated; he ceases to be a mere unit and eventually becomes so socially conscious, as a result of the educative force of the institutions of civil society, that he wills his ends only in willing universal ends. (1942, 353-354)

To Hegel, civil society is an intermediary stage between the unreflective emotions of the family and the universal logic of the state. To Gramsci, civil society is simply the site where the atomistic impulses of the economy and a state-dominated existence meet. In his famous *Prison Notebooks* (1971, 208-209), he asserts that "between the economic structure and the State with its coercion stands civil society." Civil society, as the sphere where the capitalist state constructs its project of hegemony, becomes, in Gramscian terms, a handmaiden to the state (Mamdani 1995, 605).

Such a conception of civil society as a buffer for the state, contradicts the traditional view defended by liberal theorists such as De Tocqueville, who conceptualized civil society as a buffer from the state. Very often, state and civil society are not only seen as dual and oppositional categories, but they are also viewed through different logics (Chandhoke 1995, 36). While the state operates by coercion, civil society represents the sphere of support structures, solidarity, and self-help associations. However, that dichotomy does not necessarily hold. As a matter of fact, turning Hegelian thought on its head, Marx (1843) showed the state is organically linked to civil society, since it is the political representative of the dominant group in civil society. But despite the debate surrounding the concept of civil society, its importance in bringing about and keeping democracy is without controversy (Neocleous 1996, 12-13).

Because the merits of civil society include political participation, state accountability, and publicity of politics, and also due to its institutions, that are associational and representative forums, a free press and social associations, civil society has the potential to interrogate the state (Chandhoke 1995; Bayart 1983, 99-100). As an ideal site for the production of a critical rational discourse to challenge the state, democratic theory privileges civil society as a vital, though not a sufficient, precondition for the existence of democracy (Mamdani 1995, 611). Whether the state can be made accountable to its citizens depends greatly upon the self-consciousness, the vibrancy, and the political visions of civil society (Neocleous 1996, 22).

While an inactive civil society leads to unresponsive states, a politically self-conscious civil society forces the state to remain within its boundaries. In the words of Habermas (1989, 234), the legitimacy of a state lasts as long as the "political public" accepts the boundaries prescribed by the state. Any transgression or redrawing of these boundaries alters previous arrangements and can lead to a rupture of the political discourse (Roniger 1994, 214-215).

Four components of civil society are essential to democracy: first, autonomy from the state; second, the access of different sectors of society to the agencies of the state and their acceptance of a certain commitment to the political community and the rules of the state; third, the development of a multiplicity of autonomous public arenas within which various associations regulate their own activities and govern their own members; and fourth, accessibility of these arenas to citizens. This last aspect demonstrates the importance of civil society itself to be democratic in order to contribute to the democratization of the state (Chandhoke 1995, 51).

The resurgence of civil society after decades of marginalization as a key concept in political theory, besides reducing the importance of the state as a theoretical object of political inquiry, lies in the desire to rectify the boundaries between civil society and the sphere of statist influence (Cohen and Arato 1992). The idea of civil society is central to any discussion of democracy since it raises fundamental questions about the role of societal forces in defining, controlling and legitimating state power (White 1996, 185). Whether in academia or in the public sphere, references to contemporary 'civil society' are frequent. According to Bryant (1993, 397), the formation and reformation of civil society is now widely considered an integral part of "the great transformation" attempted since 1989. Craig Calhoun (1993) agrees when he says that the Fall of the Berlin Wall in 1989 catapulted this concern from academic circles to the broader public discourse. If the 1970s witnessed an obsessive preoccupation with the state, the 1980s and 1990s saw civil society take the floor.

Many theorists are turning to the concept, the language, and the institutions of civil society to explain the generality of the democratic trend. But, although civil society plays a role in democratization and liberalization, it is a far more comprehensive and deeper concept (Blaney and Pasha 1993, 10-13). Whereas democracy can become a mockery and serve as a tool to legitimate an authoritarian/totalitarian regime, civil society stands for a whole range of assumptions, values and institutions, such as political, social and civil rights, the rule of law, representative associations, a public sphere, and above all a plurality of associations (Spalding 1996, 65).

Scholars have resurrected the concept of civil society as a challenge to the power of the state (Chandhoke 1995, 26). The idea of civil society coincided with political theorists' argument about a social community's capacity to organize itself independently of state power (Sullivan 1999, 40-41). The freedom of civil society formed the backbone of democratic movements in eighteenth-century Europe against absolutist states. The importance of civil society grew to the point where for theorists such as Hobbes and Locke, the state no longer defined community, since its own legitimacy rested on the acquiescence of the people (Demirovic 1991).

Civil society became the appropriate tool to curb the overreach of the state in Eastern Europe or to challenge the extended state in the post-colonial world, (White 1996, 178). The strong desire of the state to control its people has led to the erosion of the space where voluntary associations could lay down the parameters of a public discourse and hold the state responsible. Civil society has therefore lost its capital role in keeping the state in check (Kamal 1996, 68).

Fortunately, events in Eastern Europe triggered a revitalization of civil society. Starting with *Solidarnozc* (Solidarity) in Poland, a resilient civil society began to confront the state. According to Arato (1981, 23), the social movements in Poland were the manifestation of the rise of "civil society against the state." For Pelczynski (1988, 363), these contestations represent the "rebirth of civil society." In Latin America, efforts by the states to weaken and hopefully extinguish civil society diminished, and scholars like Stepan (1985) simply equated the concept with democracy. Scholars also applied this framework to Asia, to describe the upsurge of popular movements against the state (Ghosh 1989; Guha 1989; Kothari 1988; Shah 1988; Rubin 1987).

In Africa, the reincarnation of civil society coincided with the renewal of political demands of the late 1980s and the early 1990s. However, "current understandings of African politics tend to posit a simple dichotomy between state and civil society. They portray a 'soft' and decaying authoritarian state stuck in a deadly struggle against an emerging and democratic civil society. The two realms are conceived of as distinct, unconnected, and antagonistic spheres of institutional and social activities" (Fatton, Jr. 1992, 1). Most scholars saw in Africans' successful struggle against despotic rulers, repressive regimes and governments that violated both their individual and their collective rights, civil society in action (Geremek 1992, 3-12). Outlining the importance of civil society in democratizing Africa, Larry Diamond states that:

> civil society performs many...crucial functions for democratic development and consolidations: limiting the power of the state more generally, and challenging its abuse of authority; monitoring human rights and strengthening the rule of law; monitoring elections and enhancing the overall quality and the credibility of the democratic process; educating citizens about their rights and responsibilities, and building a culture of tolerance and civic engagement; incorporating marginal groups into the political process and enhancing the latter's responsiveness to societal interests and needs; providing alternative means, outside the state, for communities to raise their level of material development; opening and pluralising the flows of information; and building a constituency for economic as well as political reforms. (1997, 24)

This re-emergence of civil society in Africa stemmed from two main processes: first, confronted by a massive shortage of resources and the costly obligations of collective public welfare, the higher circles shrank the realm of state obligations and expanded the private sphere of the market. Second, faced with the authoritarian reach of the state and their incarceration in its regimented network of control, subordinate classes retreated into their own private spaces of survival, where they engage in all sorts of self-help activities (Fatton, Jr. 1992, 74).

The praise of civil society in Africa, besides the fact that the concept remains a bone of contention among African scholars, clearly justifies the view by some that Western social scientists expect African civil society to perform the role of civil societies in western liberal democracies (Makumbe 1998, 306). But, before going into the debate about what African civil society is or is not, what it can or cannot do, the history and tradition of civil society in Africa deserves a brief review.

Although centralized regimes ruled by powerful monarchs dominated pre-colonial Africa, challenges and protests occurred daily. Because traditional rulers were born rather than elected or appointed, Africans could not be actively involved in their selection. But once in power, these leaders did not enjoy unchallenged rule. Local authorities struggled to retain their power and privileges and stoutly resisted centralizing tendencies (Hull 1980, 20). In fact, several regions lived under somewhat democratic, politically segmented systems in which power lay in the hands of local chiefs, hereditary clan elders, and ritual priests. Chiefs remained custodians of the ancestral lands and allocated them to deserving subjects. They were also expected to be the most generous men in their localities, winning loyalty through patronage and engaging the population in civic activities, designed to monitor their performance (Hull 1980, 20).

Pre-colonial Africans generally considered society to be a community in which leadership should serve the common good. Unwritten laws bound kings and chiefs who could be dethroned in the event of misdeeds or infirmity. Moreover, they could not rely on the regulative capability of their office to sustain them for long if they behaved irresponsibly or arbitrarily (Potholm 1979, 25). The constitutional checks and balances, translated in an informal institutionalization of a separation of powers as prerequisites for effective restraints on political leaders, did exist in pre-colonial Africa, even if not in a written form.

Pre-colonial African political systems recognized the role of popular participation in decision-making and governance (Kabaya-Katambwa 1986, 27). Major decisions took place after widespread consultations. Unfortunately, it seems that the effectiveness of Africans' political participation was not apparent to outsiders. Early European explorers observed only two types of African political systems—despotic regimes and others that bordered on anarchy (Potholm 1979, 24). While some despots wielded power over protests by their people, their rule does not negate the system of checks on political power. Africans' failure to prevent every tyrant does not distinguish the continent from the European states that sent those explorers.

The conception of Africa as a continent permeated by despotic rule (Murdock 1959, 37) does not correspond to the reality of pre-colonial African politics. Even if what was in place was not civil society as known to the west, the fact remains that pre-colonial Africans never questioned their duty to challenge and monitor their political leaders' performance, and by so doing, fulfilling the functions of today's civil society. Unfortunately, European colonial powers did not allow any challenge to their power and control, dealing a severe blow to Africans' natural tendency to defy political leadership (Busia 1967; Mair 1977; Médard 1991; Mbachu 1994).

Given their goals—to despoil Africa of its resources, human as well as material—colonial governments viewed African civic groups and organizations with suspicion and did everything in their power to destroy them. Concerned that these groups might generate animosity toward colonial rule, Europeans took necessary steps to prevent such a challenge. Africans were qualified to be subjects, taxpayers, or potential military draftees (*Afrique Utile—Useful Africa*) (Lewis 1965; Martin 1983; Manning 1988), but were unqualified to take an active part in the way their life was being run. The only civic groups allowed to be involved in politics during the colonial era were those whose membership comprised settlers and the colonists themselves (Makumbe 1998, 306).

Ironically, such exclusion drew more Africans into the political process. The spread of urbanization during the colonial period allowed the emergence of a clear social space distinct from the state on one hand, and family and kinship groupings on the other (Woods 1992, 86). The various needs and demands of new city-dwellers required the formation of voluntary associations, the backbone of civil society (Balandier 1955, 274-278). Whether based on ethnic, cultural, class, or intellectual ties, these groups gave birth to an African associational life that received encouragement from African intellectuals' desire to challenge colonialism. In Fatton's words:

> While it is true that imperialism can always mobilize the resources necessary to force into compliance recalcitrant African states and ruling classes, it is frequently confounded by their evasive and defensive strategies. The history of the relationship between imperialism and Africa is as much the history of compromises and pacts as the history of repressive violence and reluctant cooperation. While imperialism has profoundly conditioned the states and civil societies of Africa, it has always been constrained by their trenches and defenses. It simply cannot obliterate them. (1992, 16)

As a matter of fact, civil societies eventually helped liberate African states from the grips of European powers. Taking advantage of these civic groups and associations, nationalist leaders started organizing them as formal channels of protest and resistance (Clapham 1993, 435). Gradually, these "innocent" organizations became the crucial fora for the expression of political demands. In Gramscian terms, African intellectuals helped to articulate an "ethnical political" vision of a society and state free of European domination. Many of the political parties of the 1940s and 1950s grew out of the associational activity (Woods 1992, 87). According to Mamdani:

> The history of civil society in colonial Africa is laced with racism, for civil society was first and foremost the society of the colons. It

was also primarily a creation of the colonial state. The rights of free association and free expression, and eventually of political representation, were rights of citizens under direct rule, not of subjects under indirect rule...This dichotomy explains why the colonial state is a Janus-type affair. Its one side, the state that governed citizens, was bounded by the rule of law and an associated regime of rights. Its other side, the state that ruled over subjects, was a regime of extra-economic coercion and administrative justice. It is thus no wonder that the struggle of subjects was both against the "tribal" authorities in the local state and against civil society. The struggle against the latter was particularly acute in the settler colonies, where it often took the form of an armed revolt whose best-known theoretician was Frantz Fanon. This, then, was the first historical moment in the development of civil society: the colonial state as the protector of the society of the colons. (1999, 192-3)

However, after helping to drive out colonial powers, civil groups or associations lay dormant in independent Africa until recently. Until shortly before their departure, the colonial rulers had never tried to exemplify the practice of democracy; they were perfectly content with ruling in a strictly authoritarian manner (Ayoade 1986, 25). In the name of nation building, Africa's independent leaders ruled out any dissent (Médard 1991, 1994). Crawford Young is right when he echoes that:

Once in power, the first generation of African rulers closed the doors of politics and co-opted the colonial discourse of "development." To discourage opposition and perpetuate their power, they argued that the problems of development demanded complete unity of purpose, justifying on these grounds the criminalization of political dissent and the inexorable march to political monolithism. The political kingdom was won; the era of accelerated economic development was at hand. There was a truly extraordinary confidence in the rationality and capacity of the developmental state to plan, organize, and effect rapid transformation, illusions shared by the new political leadership and the new profession of development economics. (1994b, 232)

Many dissenters were detained, killed, maimed, or forced into long exile. In disregard of civil society's important role during the liberation struggle, new leaders sought to control the civic groups through legislation, registration and various other measures. Chazan and her colleagues describe quite well the attitude of the new leaders:

> With alternate power constellations officially enfeebled, reconstructed opposition parties were on tenuous ground when they sought to mobilize support or criticize government actions. The opportunities to voice discontent were also substantially reduced. The notion of a loyal opposition was alien to the colonial and de-colonization experiences of most African leaders; once in power, they typically assumed that hesitations and reservations threatened their positions. Steps were taken to enforce newly formulated sedition laws. The independent press was curtailed or shut down. Vocal opponents of ruling parties and of their methods of government were either incarcerated or exiled. The enfeeblement of opposition in many cases also involved the actual dismantling of the multiparty system. The trend toward the creation of one-party states is perhaps the best known and the most noted of the political changes introduced at independence. In the quest for consolidation, political competition, it was suggested, had to be controlled and some monopoly of the governing political apparatus assured. African leaders throughout the continent, arguing from different perspectives, thus supported the transition to single-party dominance. (1999, 48-49)

Such control was seen as an imperative weapon of national integration (Wallerstein 1964, 132). Although Africans resented the *volte-face*, they hoped that a wise use of their new political power would accelerate the overdue economic development of their nascent nations (Médard 1991, 96).

But very soon, it became clear that the new leadership, through the creation of one-party systems, was more concerned with self-aggrandizement than with the welfare of the populations (Monga 1995). Civic groups and organizations resumed their activities in order to bring the authoritarian state under some control. Unfortunately, their actions failed to duplicate their previous success under colonialism, not only because of the repression they were subjected to, but also due to the lack of intellectual support. In the post-colonial period, African intellectuals did not play the same extensive role in mobilizing and shaping public opinion as they had under colonial rule. African intellectuals, even those who possessed the courage to oppose authoritarian governments, proved unable to lead civil society in an effective resistance movement (Bayart 1986, 120).

With no viable civil society, the absolute state in Africa remained very powerful. De-politicization and withdrawal simply replaced political participation. Several decades passed before intellectuals led civil society out of its coma. In the late 1980s, students, university professors, lawyers, and the clergy, fed up with an arbitrary and ruthless power, started demanding both social and political changes. In Nordlund's words (1996), civil society had been clearly effective in bringing about political and economic reforms in Africa. Several other scholars also contended that the political changes on the continent could not have occurred without the full participation of an active and dynamic civil society (Anyang' Nyong'o 1992; Diamond 1994; Monga 1995; Fatton, Jr., 1995; Hutchful 1995/96; Bratton and van de Walle 1997; Makumbe 1998). In Lewis' words, "democracy will stand or fall on the creation of new political communities and the quality of participation in liberalizing politics" (1998, 137).

In his synopsis of civil society's journey in Africa, Udogu maintains that:

> The development of a civil society pre-dates the emergence of independence in Africa. Indeed, it was the assembly of "intellectuals" in urban settings, and the later articulation of their interests that culminated in the cessation and departure of the colonial powers. In this process, the intellectuals led the political cavalry by amalgamating the various cleavages and (ethnic) groups in their demand for independence. The post-independence era, however, saw a diminution in the effectiveness of social groups that pressed for independence as they were absorbed in the proliferation of one-party rule in the continent. (1996, 11-12)

However, in his criticism of the simplistic identification of the notion of civil society with a successful democratic polity, Zakaria cautioned that not all intermediate associations are equally conducive to the democratic virtues. In his words, "what we want is not civil society, but civics – what the Romans called *civitas*; that is, public-spiritedness, sacrifice for the community, citizenship, even nobility. But not all of civil society is civic minded" (quoted in Sullivan 1999, 32). In Fatton's views, civil society's logic and substance reside in the defense and promotion of private rights and sectional interests. It does not have a national vocation and is ill-equipped to supplant the state in the necessary provision of public goods (1992, 113).

Civil society presupposes the existence of a state that can establish and enforce the law, and maintain peace, order, and social well-being

(Walzer 1984, 217). However, this premise does not always hold true. Several authoritarian governments have tried, unsuccessfully, for years to co-opt civil society in order to legitimize their rule. A democratic civil society cannot exist if the state is undemocratic, ineffective, corrupt, and capricious, because the first task of an undemocratic state will be to smash civil society. If a democratic state presupposes a democratic civil society, then a democratic civil society also requires a democratic state (Chandhoke 1995, 36-37). Cox also cautions about civil society when he contends that "a weak and stunted civil society allows free rein to exclusionary politics and covert powers" (1999, 14).

In his doubt on the African civil society capabilities, Lemarchand posits that "the nature of African civil society is in consequence highly contradictory and that this makes the institutionalization of democratic governance very problematic because the structures of accountability are segmented, syncretistic and fluid (1990, 190). Despite the debate on African civil society's origin, traditions and capabilities (Woods 1992; Bayart 1986; Lemarchand 1992; Hutchful 1995/1996; Osaghae 1995), and Udogu's contention is that "the concept…is problematic because, in general, there is as yet no clear line of demarcation between the African state and society or polity (1996, 11). Concurring with Udogu, Allen echoes that:

> Concepts like 'civil society,'…while providing a bridge to an enormous and exciting literature, are frustrating to use. In Benin there was an obvious flowering of civil society from the late 1980s, as a host of private associations were created, or ostensibly pub ones (like the unions) reclaimed for civil society. That flowering was intimately linked to the political transformation of the same period, providing much of its initial impetus, institutional base, leadership and ideological drive. Yet establishing a more systematic relationship open to theoretical elaboration remains elusive: 'civil society' presents even more analytical problems than does 'democratization.' (1989, 77-78)

The elusiveness of African civil society is also described by Monga when he states that:

> There is little doubt that African civil society cannot be fully comprehended let alone assessed by the classic instruments of analysis. Most institutions which make up society cannot be compared to those which we see working in Europe, where elected local, regional, and national bodies meet regularly to decide policy

and choose leaders. In the African case the leadership, membership, and functioning of such structures are often shrouded in mystery (1995, 362).

In spite of these fundamental difficulties, the contribution of civil society in undermining authoritarian and totalitarian governments in Africa is undeniable. However, civil society has been overly praised at the expense of "military society." Because incipient civil society turned its back on the state for several decades, whether civil society could really develop into a force capable of altering the state's character and becoming the foundation for a new participatory form of democracy is questionable (Cox 1999, 25).

None of the new democracies on the continent burgeoned against the will of the military (Onwumechili 1998). As a matter of fact, all of them enjoyed either an express support—as in Benin, Mali, and Niger initially—or tacit consent—in Gabon, and Côte d'Ivoire for example—from military leadership. Yet, very little, if anything, is said about African military's contribution to democracy on the continent, certainly because of the military's dismal performance in African politics.

The Military and African Politics

The military's position in contemporary African politics has surprised many scholars, who expected the army to be a non-factor in the political realm of the continent. Coleman and Brice were quite blunt in their naïveté when they state that:

> Armies have been the last of the authoritative structures of government to be created in all but a few of the forty-odd political entities of Sub-Saharan Africa. With few exceptions, national armies are either non-existent, or they are fragile structures still heavily dependent upon external support for their maintenance and development. This embryonic and underdeveloped character of Africa's military establishment, coupled with the precipitate and unexpected termination of European rule, underscores the ominous power vacuum that exists throughout that vast continent. (1962, 359)

Unfortunately, this prognostic of the early days of independence soon proved untenable. Following the failure of the civilian leaders' presumed commitment to the goals of rapid modernization, several military officers embarked on a mission of ending poverty, illiteracy, and disease. In a dramatic transformation, the "weak and fragile" African military became a powerful force that African civilian political leaders had to reckon with.

In their study of the "armed bureaucrats" (Feit 1969) in Africa, historians and political scientists proceed from different perspectives and make widely divergent assumptions about the relationships of the military to society (Onwumechili 1998, 37-38). More often than not, they explain the behavior of African armies through the legacy of the colonial and post-colonial periods, paying very little attention to Africa's past. But as Ogot (1972, 1) and Uzoigwe (1975) suggest, understanding the nature and role of the military in post-independence Africa requires, grasping the characteristics of pre-colonial Africa's armies and examining the role and behavior of the colonial armies in their pacification mission in Africa.

By the 19th century, militarism and warfare had become important in pre-colonial Africa. In the conduct of inter-African affairs, military strength served as a precious tool in diplomatic negotiations, especially in the conquest of new territories (Hull 1980, 24). By nature, an empire strives to aggrandize itself, and a huge army instills an enormous amount of fear and respect in the minds and hearts of the potential conquests (Smith 1976, 43). Although some imperialistic rulers conquered purely for the sake of aggrandizement, most leaders inherited confederacies and empires that could maintain only through a strong military presence (Hull 1980, 25).

In his evaluation of the army's role and position in pre-colonial Africa, Onwumechili contends that:

> In most traditional Africa, the nature of the community's needs determined whether a standing or an *ad hoc* army was used…Traditional communities that were engaged in frequent warfare found it necessary to maintain permanent armies (Kingdoms of Zulu, Borno and Kongo…) However, in less war-prone kingdoms such as Yorubaland and the Ashanti kingdom, the *Omo Ogun* (War Boys) in Yorubaland and the *Akonsani* and *Hiawuo* of Ashanti were small scale armies who mainly guarded the king's palace and formed the core of a larger army, which was raised on an *ad hoc* basis when needed. (1998, 5)

Because the army served war-fighting purposes in traditional Africa it lacked an administrative role was conceived for the military. Consequently, military coups occurred only rarely. Most of the time, the African military was under the control and subordination of the civilian administrative authority.

A few years before European conquest, Africa suffered from internal aggression. In East Africa, Ethiopian King Menelik II's army defeated and occupied the Ogaden (Prunier 1991, 10). In southern Africa, Mzilikazi, the chief of the *Khumalo*, used his powerful army to impose his will on Mashonaland. Shaka's regiments, closely drilled and highly disciplined, frequently harassed the Nguni and the Sotho. In West Africa, offensive wars by the empires and kingdoms of Mali, Songhay, Ashanti, Oyo, Danhomê, Benin, and others, are well-documented (Onwumechili 1998, 6).

Obviously, many parts of the continent escaped the ravages of war, and life continued as peacefully as possible. But without question, warfare and militarism existed in Africa before the advent of colonialism (Hull 1980, 24). Contrary to contemporary Africa where the military pursues coups d'état out of ambition, military intervention in the politics of 19ᵗʰ Century Yorubaland was more a response to a clearly disturbed political situation (Smith 1976, 39).

A review of civil-military relations in colonial and post-colonial Africa reveals at least three distinct phases where the military has been used as the main instrument of control and domination. The first phase covering the initial conquest and imposition of colonial rule lasted from the mid-1880s to the end of World War I. During that period characterized by a *de facto* military rule, European powers met resistance and protest from African kingdoms and chiefdoms with sheer military power. Since the Berlin Conference[5] required European powers to demonstrate "effective control" over their colonies and territories in order for their colonial claims to be recognized, heavy land and naval artillery and other types of weapons became necessary to impose an effective order (Frazer 1994).

As critical instruments of conquest, military outposts were created to not only ward off competing colonizers, but also to suppress any rebellion on the part of Africans. Accordingly, and unfortunately, the nascent colonies grew out of military *diktat*. The first administrative structures of pre-World War I Africa combined military and civil functions, and were often run by military officers. The typical colony or "state" had a military governor, a sparse administrative structure in the hands of expatriate officers, and a colonial army composed of African soldiers with European officers (Lewis 1965; Smith 1976; Chipman 1989).

During that phase of military occupation or pacification, it was impossible to distinguish between the state, as a separate entity, and the military as a coercion instrument. Hardly any independent judiciary and legislative bodies balanced the executive power (Cohen 1991). The unchallenged mandate given to the governor or executive authority and the administrative agents, who were active duty officers, was such that the military, although theoretically under the control of external civilian officials, exercised in the colonies tremendous autonomy in policy formulation and implementation. As a matter of fact, military rulers assumed, for quite a while, responsibility for a wide range of political and military issues (Agyeman-Duah 1990).

Although French politicians realized that a policy of economic development was not compatible with a continuing policy of unbridled conquest pursued by the army, it took drastic measures to impose France's desire on the army, as chronicled by Conklin:

> West Africa was sufficiently "pacified" to wind up military operations and begin tapping the resources of the new territories already under French control. The civilian-military disputes taking place in West Africa between 1891 and 1894, coupled with the army's refusal to obey orders from Paris, had, however, already shown that such a "winding up" could not be coordinated from the metropolis. What was needed instead was a civilian representative of the Third republic on the spot, with sufficient authority to bring the military forces to heel, and to overcome the separatist sentiments of the different governors. (1997, 35)

However, France ultimately replaced civilian governors with active duty or former military officers. Such a system of a strong external civilian control and a powerful internal military rule left Africa with three unfortunate enduring legacies. First, the overlap of political and security duties undermined clearly defined spheres demarcating military and civilian responsibilities and prerogatives. Second, the colonial armies developed a tradition of wide jurisdictional boundary *vis-à-vis* other security forces (Frazer 1994). While they were engaged in territorial defense, they were simultaneously involved in internal security during their conquering and pacifying mission. Consequently, the army obtained a legitimate domestic role and also a high level of politicization. Third, there was a clear and deliberate absence of countervailing institutions, because there were enough outside forces to meet army revolts and mutinies in a particular colony. European powers could use their own imperial armies as well as colonial troops from neighboring territories to quell mutinies (Frazer 1994; Bienen 1979; Goldsworthy 1981).

The second phase, during the inter-war years witnessed the consolidation of the military's role in internal affairs. The bureaucracy was "civilianized," but with no clear demarcation between military and civilian authorities. At the same time, there was a reinforcement of the military's involvement in internal affairs for economic purposes (Baynham 1986).

By then the League of Nations' mandate demanded that colonies be developed. Although, European governments first translated the League's injunction into "bringing civilization to the native population for eventual self-rule," they soon faced pressure from their own constituencies to make colonies and territories economically or financially self-sufficient. The new urgent mission, which required competent administrative officers, simply exacerbated the military's involvement in internal affairs (Chaigneau 1984).

Although there was a rationalization of the bureaucracy and professionalization of the administrative cadre, governors and provincial and district administrators, and active duty officers were mostly replaced with retired military officers. New administrators continue to use colonial armies to promote economic policies not necessarily related to national security (Lewis 1965). Besides aiding district officials in collecting taxes and enforcing labor regulations, colonial armies were more often used to suppress African revolts.

With the traditions of the first phase—overlapping civilian and military responsibilities, wide military jurisdictional boundaries, and a lack of countervailing institutions—carried over the second phase, "civilian" governors who took over the authoritarian regimes did not need to define military and civilian spheres. Their external basis of power and authority rendered civilian supremacy in colonial administration in Africa a futile issue (Crocker 1974).

The final phase that lasted from the end of World War II to the 1960s, saw the disintegration of the colonial system. As a result of social unrest that challenged colonial rule, the political context shifted dramatically. Besides new political institutions demanded by indigenous populations, the governor's powers in security affairs devolved to other officials. Colonial powers appointed defense ministers to the executive councils and the legislative councils gained greater oversight of military expenditure and defense matters (Decalo 1990). By late 1950s and early 1960s when most African countries became independent, the struggle to transfer the government and civilian bureaucracy into African hands intensified.

In part because of Europeans' evident reluctance to pass the baton to Africans, especially in the domain of security, their last minute plans to create an African officer corps did not include clear policies and institutions to exercise political control over the new national armies. Given the colonial army's behavior in Africa, "apolitism" was a foreign concept to African armies (Eleazu 1973). The clear separation of realms between civilian and military authorities found in Europe did not exist in independent Africa.

The legacy of colonial armies got civil-military relations in independent Africa off such a bad start, spawning several coups d'état in the first decade of African independence (Luckham 1994). By the twilight of Europe's scramble for Africa, the military had gained ascendancy over civilian leaders in many indigenous governments. According to Hull (1980, 26), "the great leaders of Africa were no longer men of peace and statesmanship, but of war." At independence, government in Africa was almost equated with the military. Having experienced the use of colonial armies for civil repression, tax collection and conquest functions, new leaders were perplexed about the role the military should play in the overdue development process (Feit 1968).

While African leaders still wondered about the proper avenue for a rapid political and economic transformation of their continent, policy-makers and scholars in the West urged the military to participate in politics in the Third World. As early as 1962, Lucien Pye already favored the military's involvement in governmental affairs when he praised military leaders for being more pro-Western than their civilian counterparts (86). In other words, the West valued a friendly Third World government over a competent or democratic regime. Even Edward Shils (1960), who had praised earlier the intellectuals as the creators of political life in their new countries, later divided them into two categories: the politicized intellectuals (civilians) and technical-executive intellectuals (military). In Shils's view only the latter could allow the emergence of a stable and progressive civil society. Similarly, Gaile argues that because the military often exhibited greater leadership and organizational skills than civilian politicians, it could more effectively pursue the goal of national integration in the developing world (1970, 342).

Following that line of thinking, theories and hypotheses on the role of the military in the development process received extensive scrutiny. Many other scholars shared Shils's and Gaile's views that the military ought to play an extensive role in political life (Finer 1962;

Gutteridge 1962; Janowitz 1964). There was an implicit notion that "with its administration and managerial skills, the military's involvement in the politics of new nations is likely to result in favourable consequences as these skills are transferred from the sole administration of military affairs to those of the general society" (Mowoe 1980, 15). These views rested on the core assumption that the Western type of army organization which the new African states copied had a hierarchic structure that emphasized discipline and unity of command. On this assumption, the military, imbued with the spirit of rigor and hard work, should help African military leaders adapt more easily to the problems of modernization.

For Ergas (1986, 314), the armed forces may be able to play the function "of educator, of guardian of the secular character of the state, and guarantor of political stability and honesty in government." Unfortunately, the first wave of military coups and interventions, although a self-fulfilling prophecy, disappointed the proponents of military rule. Once in office, the military's performance did not differ from the civilian governments, belying the prognostications of the organizational model. Consequently, another generation of studies arose to explain the military's behavior in Africa (Bienen 1968; Welch 1970; Luckham 1971).

While many of these studies produced good profiles of the military establishment in particular countries, and in the process challenged previous assumptions, they failed to agree on the main cause of military's intervention in African politics (Bangura 1994). According to the literature, two main themes explained the military's involvement. These centered on military professionalism and the causes of coups (Kennedy and Louscher 1991). In his 1957 seminal work, *The Soldier and the State*, Samuel Huntington compared the professionalism of the Western military to the non-professionalism of Third world military, and attributed the military's intervention in Third World politics to the lack of professionalism of the military establishment.

Other scholars interpret military professionalism otherwise. According to them (Finer 1962; Kennedy and Louscher 1991), the military intervenes only in countries with institutional frameworks. In societies with relatively well-developed institutions of state coercion, but with poorly-developed institutions for popular participation, the military's involvement in politics is seen as arising from the failure of the political system to effectively handle increased demand for popular participation. Out of this debate, it appeared that military's intervention is a direct function of the level and degree of a country's political development (Huntington 1968; Perlmutter 1981; Kennedy and Louscher 1991).

However, Samuel Decalo (1976, 1985, 1989) stresses rather the idiosyncratic and individualistic causes of coups in Sub-Saharan Africa. Most coups occurred simply because the leaders were conditioned by their "socio-economic backgrounds." Mbaku (1994) disputes however this contention, arguing that far from being "irrational buffoons," military leaders involved in coups are rather rational agents seeking to maximize well-defined goals. Although a military coup has been, until recently, one of the most common methods of regime change in Africa (Mazrui and Tidy 1984; McGowan and Johnson 1984; Mbaku 1988; Mbaku and Paul 1989; Jenkins and Kposowa 1990), its causes have always eluded scholars. The history of military intervention in Africa reveals important shifts in the objectives of soldiers turned politicians and in the types of political changes their actions have generated. While initial uprisings such as the 1963-64 mutinies in Kenya, Tanzania and Uganda, represented sheer corporate demands, they did become a precursor of broader army political action (Chazan et al. 1999, 227).

Whether the military has intervened in African politics because of internal institutional characteristics of the military, such as its size, cohesion, hierarchical command, and corporate interests (Janowitz 1964; Cox 1976; Decalo 1976), or because of societal conditions such as low economic development, social cleavages, and low political culture and institutionalization (Finer 1962; Huntington 1968; Perlmutter 1982; Lefever 1970), it is a fact that the military has ruled most of Africa most of the time. Such a usurpation of African politics and government prevented acknowledgement of the military for doing something commendable: allowing either actively or passively, the democratization process in Africa to succeed.

If the war waged on unpopular African regimes, both civilian and military, in the 1980s by Africans represents anything new, it is perhaps its intensity, not the fact that Africans took to the streets to demand more freedom in choosing their leaders (Busia 1967; Bovy 1968; Kabaya-Katambwa 1986). A few years after independence, Africans started raising their concerns about the direction the continent was taking under the guidance of new African leaders (Houngnikpo 1989, 15; Ihonvbere 1998, 9). However, their resentment of post-independence regimes took a milder form, with the hope that "consensus" that is supposed to prevail in African societies will help open a genuine dialogue. Unfortunately, all their complaints fell on deaf ears (Young 1996, 54). Having inherited power from the colonizers and tasted its sweetness, new leaders found all kinds of excuses to remain the sole decision-makers (Ihonvbere 1998, 10). With no real will to share power, their absolute power corrupted them. Faced with such a situation, civil society started searching for ways to make itself heard. However, its lack of organization and resolve thwarted any chance of changing the course of events (Bayart 1986).

Civil society's failure to alter the political system opened up the door to "military" society. On behalf of their post-independence constitutional duty as the guarantor of the nation, the military moved in. Early coups d'état were widely welcomed (Bates 1994, 19), simply because African were fed up with the deplorable state of affairs on the continent (Collier 1978).

These military interventions gave a new twist to civil-military relations on the continent. The lack of clear demarcation of boundaries between civilian and military roles, inherited from colonialism, became evident. According to Schraeder, "the range of military involvement in African politics and society is best characterized as a continuum of civil-military relations, in which each successive model represents a greater degree of military influence over civilian politicians" (2000, 248). Drawing on Liebenow's work, Schraeder offers five models of civil-military relations in Africa. At one extreme is the "civilian supremacy model," in which the military is firmly under the control of civilian politicians. The second type, known as the "watch dog model," represents a greater degree of military intervention within the domestic political system. In the "balance wheel model," which represents a civil-military coalition, the military plays a stronger role. The military officers who adhere to the "direct rule model" of civil-military relations assume that the overthrown civilian leaders, including the heads of individual bureaucracies, are "creatures of their own pasts" and therefore incapable of providing adequate leadership for the country. The final form of civil-military relations, known as the "social transformation model," resembles direct rule in that military officers take charge of individual bureaucracies and government agencies (2000, 248-252).

Unfortunately, the similarity between corrupt civilian leaders and military dictators soon became apparent. Actually, the military leadership turned out to be worse since the legitimate use and control of weapons gave them a *carte blanche* for any action, regardless of the populations' reactions (Bayart 1983; Decalo 1990; Luckham 1994; Onwumechili 1998, 17). Hit with such a reality, civil society resumed its struggle, but from a different perspective. Since basic freedoms such as free association, free speech, free press, etc., were taken away, and opposition had to be covert, only underground organizations could carry on the struggle against incompetent military dictators (Onwumechili 1998). In countries where corrupt civilian leaders were still in charge with no legitimacy, civil society took a harder stance (Koné 1990; Legum 1990; Joseph 1991, 1994). Although neither open actions nor underground challenges really removed pervert leaders, they did weaken their regimes before the wave of political transition from Eastern Europe helped toll the knell of these leaders' power (Conac 1993).

However, contrary to the literature that tends to glorify civil society for its tenacity, the military played a key role in some countries The illustrative cases of Togo and Benin will later demonstrate (Heilbrunn 1993, 1994, 1997) that without the military's consent—almost to show the centrality of the military in Africa—there can be no democratization, even if a country possesses a vibrant civil society and a dynamic political culture.

Political Culture, Democracy and African Politics

Evolved from centuries of generalizing about power's different faces in different places on earth, the concept of political culture could find its interpretation in Plato's "dispositions," Montesquieu's "spirit of the laws," Jean-Jacques Rousseau's "mores," David Hume's "manners," Alexis de Tocqueville's "habits of the heart," Emile Durkheim's "collective consciousness," and Max Weber's "authority systems" (Gendzel 1997, 226).

Despite the lack of consensus on its usefulness in political analysis, political culture has always been associated with democratization and the fact that its "return" to the study of Comparative Politics coincides with democratization is hardly surprising. In fact, Diamond is right when he states that:

> Within Comparative Politics, few problems would seem to be more ripe for illumination from the political culture perspective than the sources of democratic emergence and persistence. Prominent theory of democracy, both classical and modern, has asserted that democracy requires a distinctive set of political values and orientations from its citizens: moderation, tolerance, civility, efficacy, knowledge, and participation. Beliefs and perceptions about regime legitimacy have long been recognized as a critical factor in regime change bearing particularly on the persistence or

breakdown of democracy. The path-breaking works of Almond and Verba and of Inkeles and Smith showed that countries do differ significantly in their patterns of politically relevant beliefs, values, and attitudes, and that within countries these elements of political culture are clearly shaped by life experiences, education, and social class. (1994, 27)

Long before the term *political culture* was coined, political theorists explored the political mores and norms of societies, seeking to determine which attitudes are essential preconditions for a stable democracy. In the fourth century BC, Aristotle associated democracy with the values and outlook of a middle class (Welch 1993). In the eighteenth century, Montesquieu identified integrity and trustworthiness as the critical values for a democracy. De Tocqueville (1990), in *Democracy in America*, went the furthest when he noted that one precondition for democracy was the ability of free citizens to form associations, working together to advance their own interests while respecting the larger needs of the political system as a whole.

The concept of political culture descended from these historical roots, originated as an analytical tool for political scientists using quantitative-behaviorist methods, but historians have so enriched the concept with theories of cultural interpretation that now "one can see grounds for re-borrowing by political scientists of the concept originally borrowed from them" (Welch 1993, 148). It is not an exaggeration to say that while political scientists have come to admit that historically derived "cultural beliefs," not systemic "variables," affect political outcomes, historians also seem to have established the intersection of politics and culture (Welch 1993, 148).

In fact, through wondering how the unique "psychological coherence" or "modal personality" might affect its politics, American social scientists tried to establish a connection, if any, between politics and culture. When, in the 1930s, Lasswell suggested an "extension of the scope of political investigation to include the fundamental features of the cultural settings," he never knew he had triggered a whole series of "national character" studies that only faded because of their hereditary determinism and crude stereotypes (quoted in Gendzel 1997, 227).

The contemporary concept of political culture resurfaced during the Cold War, as a useful concept to single out the "free world." During the intense battle between the West and the East, or between capitalism and communism, each side searched for ways to justify their "democratic nature." It is in that context that Almond's landmark essay (1956) contrasted the "pragmatism" politics of the Western democracies with the "simplism" of totalitarian states. Later writings by Almond and Verba (1963) and Verba and Pye (1965) gave more momentum to the concept of political culture.

According to Almond, "every political system is embedded in a particular pattern of orientations to political action, its...*political culture*" (quoted in Gendzel 1997, 227). Defined as "orientation toward politics," political culture came to include such loosely conceptualized terms in Comparative Politics as *attitudes, values, ideology,* and *socialization* (Gendzel 1997, 227). Close to Weber's theory of Protestantism (1958) as the cultural engine of modernization, political culture had not only become the main gauge of different political systems, but more specifically of a democratic system. However, the concept met some early challenges, including the question of how to identify, measure, and compare "the pattern of orientations" of nations. Relying on what was known as *psephology*, or the study of voting behavior, Almond and Verba, in their *Civic Culture* (1963), vowed to engineer "a scientific theory of democracy" by "codifying the operating characteristics of the democratic polity itself" (Gendzel 1997, 228).

However, political culture, or the part of culture relevant to politics, suffers from both poverty and riches: it is cursed with many data and fragments of theory but little agreement on concepts and paradigms (Barnes 1994, 45). Several critics rejected the notion of political culture for its failure to meet the measurement challenge, which left it useless for separating democracies from dictatorships. As a matter of fact, some even saw in the concept the chicken-egg conundrum of cause and effect: Did civic culture create democracy, or did democracy generate civic culture (Gendzel 1997, 229)? Doubting the effectiveness of political culture, Wildavsky (1988) also asked some fundamental questions: what sorts of people, organized into what kind of culture, sharing which values, legitimating which practices, would want to behave in certain way to keep their people together and discomfort their opponents?

As these questions indicate, the attempt to incorporate the idea of culture as a resource into political culture theory has not been linear. The behavioral definition of political culture as mass attitude towards politics and political symbols might be regarded as a means of investigation of the success of claims of nominal national identity (Welch 1993, 135). However, other scholars trace political culture to the discretionary activities of the political élite, arguing that culture is a resource exploited by the élite (Laitin and Wildavsky 1988, 592). The concept remains controversial, and Geertz summarizes well the debate surrounding it:

> There is widespread skepticism among social scientists about the role of culture in politics. For some, it is a general concept similar to system or civilization, useful in discussion but devoid of utility in empirical work. For others, culture is a residual category, the black box into which are poured all the variables that cannot be identified and operationalized. Yet, culture can be an important independent or explanatory variable. It has an influence on behavior that cannot be accounted for by the impact of coercion, structures, laws, economic rationality, and other such influences. At the very least it provides a useful vocabulary for describing societies. There is substantial agreement that the anthropologist's "thick description" – detailed and theory-guided analysis that makes no claims to universalism – is possible. (1973, 3-30)

However, despite its shortcomings, political culture, as an explanatory model has been exported into Third World politics in general, and Africa's in particular.

In Africa, the concept of political culture emerged with the need to explain political change on the continent after independence. As the set of values supposed to govern political behavior, political culture was thought to play a key role in the political process. Political culture can, sometimes, help define political roles, expectations, and objectives, thus giving overall contextual coherence to the political system and its relationships with the general population (Kamrava 1993, 139). In her assessment of African political culture, Chazan maintains that:

> African political cultures have developed along two discrete lines in the contemporary period. The first, élite, strand of African political cultures has been formed by individuals and groups linked to the formal political apparatus and has revolved around the state. The second, popular, brand of African political cultures has its base in the social order. Although it addresses issues related to the pub domain, it focuses more explicitly on questions of economic survival, the maintenance of autonomous social relations, and meaningful participation. Each of the dimensions of African political cultures has developed an institutional, normative, and symbolic structure of its own since the waning years of the colonial era. (1994, 68)

Through its use of symbolism and its role as legitimator of the polity, political culture helps bind together political systems that are otherwise torn by parochial allegiances, rapid social change, geographic space, and nationalist sentiments (Pye 1971, 111-112). In countries lacking tangible or perceptual symbols of national identity are lacking or where political regimes have little popular legitimacy, political culture strengthens prevailing political institutions and their links with the larger society (Kamrava 1993, 139). Depending on the degree of consensus within society, a political culture is either integrated (high degree) or fragmented (low degree). Although Chazan (1994, 59) maintains that political cultures are endogenous to political structures and are consequently found within political life, most political cultures in Africa are believed to be fragmented and therefore prone to political instability and disruption (1982, 119-120).

There is also a difference between the political culture of the masses and that of the élites. While the former has to do with the population as a whole, the latter concerns the leadership more. In African politics, the dichotomy between the two can undermine the masses' support for the leadership, since they are not on the same cultural wavelength (Kamrava 1993, 140).

Political cultures can also be divided into three variations: parochial, subject, and participant. In parochial political cultures, political orientations toward political roles are the same as religious or social ones. In subject political cultures, the individual is merely subject to the government's administrative output, with no input on his/her part. In participatory political process, in the contrary, social classes play a key role in the political process, whether in its support or its defiance (Kamrava 1993, 142). While most African countries are characterized by subject political cultures, some are "less" subject than others.

From the attitudes of the populations of both Togo and Benin towards colonialism, to their behavior since independence, and the politicians' conception of political opposition in both countries, it seems that Beninese's awareness of and participation in the political process made a difference in the opposite result these two countries reached during their processes of democratization. If "change begins with culture" (Sahlins 1976, 22), the different political outcomes of the democratization process in both countries could also be attributed to their cultures.

Endnotes

[1] This meaning of democracy is posited by Professor Jack Donnelly in a lecture on *Democracy and Democratization*, at the Graduate School of International Studies (University of Denver, February 1995).

[2] Both Frantz Fanon (*The Wretched of the Earth*, New York: Grove Press, 1968) and Albert Memmi (*The Colonizer and the Colonized*, Boston: Beacon Press, 1967) described the impact of colonialism on African societies.

[3] In his March 1998 tour of Africa, the US President William J. Clinton made a similar suggestion when he declared that there is no blueprint for democracy, and that each country can have its own version of democracy.

[4] According to Carol Pateman, participatory democracy denotes the existence of a reciprocal relationship between democratic political institutions and participative social institutions, with particular emphasis upon the educative effects of democratic participation in the workplace.

[5] The Partition of Africa took place in a Conference chaired by Bismarck (German Chancellor) in Berlin from December 1884 to January 1885.

CHAPTER THREE

BENIN AND TOGO THROUGH HISTORY

Squeezed between two giant Anglophone countries, Nigeria and Ghana, Benin and Togo, are two relatively tiny neighboring Francophone states in West Africa. They share a great number of similarities: climate, cultural composition, and pre-colonial histories (Cornevin 1968, 1981, 1988; Decalo 1995, 1996). If not for their different political mores, Benin and Togo could have been one entity, and their background lends itself to such an interpretation. These similarities make their political differences all the more striking. These differences result from the diverging role played by the military in the process of democratic transition.

Political Development of Benin

The Republic of Benin formerly known as the Republic of Dahomey between 1960 and 1975; and People's Republic of Benin between 1975 and 1991, is one of Africa's tiniest countries with an area of 112,655 square kilometers. Its borders extend from a 181-kilometer Atlantic Ocean coastline to the Niger River 675 kilometers to the North. Squeezed between the Republic of Togo in the west and the Federal Republic of Nigeria in the east, Benin's other neighbors are Burkina Faso (former Upper Volta) in the northwest and the Republic of Niger in the north (Decalo 1995, 1).

Benin consists of five geographical regions: (1) the coastal region, which is a flat lagoon area (with sea outlets only at Grand-Popo and

Cotonou) dotted with coconut palms; (2) the fertile clay barre region reaching to Abomey; (3) the plateaus of the center of Benin (Abomey, Zagnanado, Kétou and Aplahoué); (4) the northern region, composed mainly of the Atakora mountains in the west (654m) stretching into Togo; and (5) the Niger river drainage plains in the northeast (Cornevin 1968, 13; Decalo 1995, 1)

In addition, Benin possesses two climatic zones. The north experiences two seasons: a rainy season between July and September, and a hot, dry season between October and April. The south has four seasons: a heavy rain season between March and July, following by a short dry season (through mid-September), a short rainy season that falls between September and November, followed by the main dry season between November and March (Decalo 1995, 1). The natural drainage system includes the Niger River and its tributaries in the north, and the Mono, Ouémé and Couffo rivers that flow southward. Benin's vegetation consists of palm plantations, light forests, and savanna land (Cornevin 1981, 17).

With at least forty-six ethnic groups, Benin has a population of over five million, more highly concentrated in the south. The most prominent ethnic groups are the Fon, the Adja, the Yoruba, the Goun, and the Bariba. The majority of people in Benin follow traditional religions, although, officially, there are twenty percent of Christians and twenty-five percent of Muslims (Decalo 1995, 2). Although the administrative capital is Porto-Novo, most government offices, the presidential palace, and state companies reside in Cotonou, the economic capital (Eades and Allen 1996, xviii-xxiv).

The pre-colonial history of Benin is that of the once-powerful kingdom of Danhomê. From Adja Tado, in contemporary Togo, the Agasouvi dynasty founded the traditional kingdoms of Abomey, Allada, Adjatchê (Porto-Novo), and Savi (Decalo 1995, 2). Although they were all settled in Allada initially, rivalries split the brothers. Tê-Agbanli migrated to Adjatchê, Do-Gbagri to Abomey, while Adjahouto remained in Allada (Lombard 1958, 72).

Of all three brotherly kingdoms, Abomey, later known as Danhomê, exhibited more power. Having conquered Allada in 1724, and the port city of Whydah (Ouidah) in 1727, the kingdom of Danhomê gained direct access to the European market (Decalo 1995, 2). To maintain its status as a major power in the region, Danhomê engaged in slave trade to get more guns (Eades and Allen 1996, xxviii-xxix). With the permanent threat of the Oyo Empire in Yorubaland, Danhomê had to build a strong army. As a matter of fact, Danhomê was the first kingdom to establish a military school, and to create an élite women's military unit, known as the *"Amazones"* (Amazons) (Lombard 1958, 87). However, growing military power and the refusal to curtail the slave trade, would put Danhomê and European powers at loggerheads. Both the British, from their protectorate in Lagos (Nigeria), and the French vowed to defeat Danhomê, and the repudiation of the treaty ceding Cotonou to the French became the bone of contention that flared up a serious conflict between France and Danhomê (Decalo 1995, 3; Conklin 1997, 33). Through the duplicity of Porto-Novo, its arch-enemy, Abomey, the capital of Danhomê was captured by France in 1893. The following year, King Behanzin surrendered and was sent to exile in Martinique (Eades and Allen 1996, xxxi). He was later on transferred to Algeria where he died of pneumonia in 1906. His brother, Agoli-Agbo, who assumed the throne, was first basically a puppet king whose strings were in French hands (Akinjogbin 1967). However, he ended up disagreeing with the French policies, and was consequently deposed in 1900, leaving the throne vacant and allowing the French to have full control of the kingdom.

By joining the newly formed *Afrique Occidentale Française* (A.O.F.)—French West Africa— in 1904, Danhomê became a formal French colony until 1958, when it became a self-governing republic within the *Communauté Française* (French Community). Upon gaining its independence on August 1, 1960, Danhomê possessed a weak economy, a poorly integrated society rife with ethnic and regional cleavages, and a splintered political élite (Decalo 1995, 5). Alluding to ethnic cleavages and their impact on Dahomean politics, Decalo notes that:

> Dahomean social and political life has traditionally been marked by a high degree of fragmentation and strong regionalist sentiments that have persisted to this day. These cleavages have their origin in the pre-colonial period and were further solidified and perpetuated by the French administration and the rise of nationalist leaders and political parties. In the South, the two dominant entities in the 18th and 19th centuries were the kingdoms of Abomey and Porto-Novo, established following the succession dispute between the three sons of King Kokpon of Allada in the seventeenth century. A state of intense competition, friction and semi-permanent warfare prevailed between these two rival kingdoms, their last major clash occurring as recently as 1891. Though Porto-Novo was never vanquished, and indeed frequently came out the better in these perpetual clashes, Abomey was the more powerful and unified of the two. With the pacification of the south by the French, the perennial

conflicts abated, though mutual suspicion and jealousy remained, sublimated into less violent forms of competition. (1968, 6)

After the first presidential elections of 1960, the leader of the *Parti Dahoméen de l'Unité*, Mr. Hubert C. Maga, became the first President (Eades and Allen 1996, xxxiii). But as a northerner, he upset the Adja-Fon majority of the south, triggering the intervention of the army after only three years. General Christophe Soglo, Chief of Staff of the Army, from Abomey, took over for a brief period. In January 1964, two southerners, Apithy and Ahomadégbé, were elected respectively President and Prime Minister (Glèlè 1969), with the hope of resolving Dahomey's political and ethnic problems.

In 1965, a series of political crises forced the resignation of both Apithy and Ahomadégbé. The provisional government that was formed could not hold the country together, and Soglo once again assumed power (Decalo 1995, 6). In 1967, another coup led by Major Maurice Kouandété, sent Soglo into retirement. However, Kouandété himself was replaced by Soglo's popular Chief of Staff, Major Alphonse Alley (Cornevin 1981).

In 1968, there was an attempt to return to civilian rule. A referendum approved a new constitution, and a presidential election took place in May. With former leading politicians banned from contesting, the population boycotted the elections and the high abstention rate (up to 99% in the north) forced the military leadership to declare the elections void (Decalo 1970, 79). In that vacuum, Dr. Emile-Derlin Zinsou was chosen as President by the military, confirmed later on by a referendum.

Once again, Kouandété deposed Zinsou in 1969, and a three-member military Directory was put in place (Onwumechili 1998, 43). In 1970, a presidential election could not clearly separate the three main candidates: Ahomadégbé, Apithy, and Maga. The Directory decided to cede power to all three under a triumvirate formula that grants the presidency in rotation to the three personalities (Heilbrunn 1994; Decalo 1995, 8-9). But while Maga's tenure was flawless, Ahomadégbé's was interrupted by a military coup that brought Major Mathieu Kérékou to power.

When a group of young officers led by Kérékou took over in 1972, there was a widespread sense of relief because civilian leaders seemed incapable of resolving their differences. The early days of the October 26, 1972 *Révolution* saw a high degree of support (Decalo 1995, 10). The military led the population to believe that equal representation and unity would be their motto, and that their advent was a chance to renew Benin.

However, a series of mistakes and miscalculations led the country into an economic and political *cul-de-sac* (Adjaho 1992).

Describing the combination of economic decline, donor concern and criticism Benin experienced up to the early 1980s, Allen states that:

> The intensifying economic crisis affected both the state and civil society. Some parts of the state had never been effective, notably the party and its associated institutions for youth, women and workers. The size of the single party seems always to have been small, and party membership to have been more a recognition of a member's existing power or status than a means of recruiting and training able and loyal cadres. Although some of the auxiliaries did function with some efficiency in the 1970s, by the early 1980s there were continual complaints from the leadership at the sloth and incompetence of all party organs below national level. (1989, 67)

In the same vein, Westebbe attributes the roots of Benin's economic and social malaise to Kérékou's regime in asserting that:

> Government programs had created protected havens for officials who, not being subject to the pressures of economic competition, of performance-based promotions, or of the scrutiny of a democratically elected parliament and a free press, used their positions for personal aggrandizement. These activities slowed economic growth and caused "the few" instead of "the many" to benefit from growth and to have access to the assets of the public sector. (1994, 80)

The Marxist policy of 'Scientific Socialism' clearly dictated the nationalization of important sectors of the economy (Decalo 1995, 10), expanding opportunities for corruption. Benin embarked on a path of mismanagement, embezzlement, corruption, nepotism, which only ended when a bankrupt Kérékou regime was forced to convene a national conference, the original mission of which was to attend the economy of the country. In Allen's assessment (1989, 68), "public realization of the true extent of corruption helped shape political consciousness in 1989, as well as giving rise to the local phrase 'laxisme-béninisme' to describe the regime's true ideology." Eventually, in a peaceful democratic transition, Benin was given another chance to right its wrongs (Decalo 1997).

The transition government that followed the national conference succeeded in reversing years of corruption and economic mismanagement, breathing new life into political reforms. These successful reforms included such rudimentary tasks as paying salaries on time and re-opening schools shut down earlier because of teachers and students' strikes. The transition government's more remarkable accomplishments included trimming the bloated civil service and revamping the educational system, especially the university curriculum (Westebbe 1994, 96).

In a two-round presidential elections, March 10 and 24, 1991, Nicéphore Soglo, a former World Bank official defeated Kérékou. Inaugurated on April 4, 1991, President Soglo embarked on the Herculean tasks ahead (Mayrargue 1996, 126-127). Having been the interim Prime Minister, he continued to redress the economy, intensifying efforts at economic liberalization. He also followed the recommendations of the national conference by instituting criminal proceedings against corrupt former state officials (Eades and Allen 1996, xl-xli).

But, his endeavors were not without difficulties. In his very first year in office, civil servants claiming their salary arrears accumulated under the Kérékou regime undertook intermittent strikes to make their point (Mayrargue 1996, 127). In May of the following year, a group of disgruntled soldiers who were, supposedly, plotting a coup, were arrested (Clarke 1995, 236). They subsequently managed to escape from custody, and most were sentenced *in absentia* (Englebert 1999a, 179). Because the majority of the "coup plotters" were from the north, Soglo was perceived by northerners as someone bent on bringing back into Benin the north-south dichotomy.

Besides his troublesome relationship with the military, and the northerners, Soglo's government style also created a great deal of resentment among the general population. His leadership was called into question several times, as he displayed what many *Béninois* regarded as sheer arrogance (Eades and Allen 1996, xli). Although he was successful at revamping the economy, he created friction between himself and other political leaders who initially had contributed to his victory. He failed to take into account the fact that he came to power with no formal political party's support (Englebert 1999a, 180).

By the time, *La Renaissance du Bénin* (RB), the party formed by his wife in 1992 came to his rescue, the damage was done. Despite a pro-Soglo majority in the parliament, the anger of former allies of Soglo's made passing some legislation very difficult (Eades and Allen 1996, xli). His lack of courtesy *vis-à-vis* the National Assembly continued to haunt him, and dissent within the RB, did not help his case. In October 1993, when fifteen members of the coalition withdrew their support, Soglo lost his majority and his "descent to hell" began (Englebert 1999a, 181). Earlier in the year, civil servants had already conveyed, in a three-day strike, their disapproval of the ten percent reduction in salaries. But, with the fifty percent devaluation in January 1994 of the *CFA* franc, Soglo had to face social unrest (Decalo 1995 17). Salaries were rather increased by ten percent, as well as the reintroduction of housing allowances (abolished in 1986 by Kérékou's regime), and an end to an eight-year freeze on promotions within the civil service. But, in 1994, when the parliament approved increases in wages and student grants beyond the government's projections, a constitutional crisis emerged (Clarke 1995). When the matter was referred to the constitutional court, Soglo prevailed. Unfortunately, that legal victory contributed to his downfall, because several politicians realized that only a united front could weaken Soglo's determination.

Another incident with the parliament occurred in January 1996, when the National Assembly rejected the government's budget (Mayrargue 1996, 127). In a defiant act, Soglo issued an edict enacting the budget, claiming that failure to implement his plan would jeopardize the country's finances, by blocking a loan of $500,000,000 pledged by the international community (Englebert 1999a, 182).

Clearly, Soglo earned the respect of the international financial community for his handling of Benin's economy (Clarke 1995, 236), but there was disquiet within Benin that strong economic growth had been achieved at the expense of pressing social concerns. Moreover, criticism was increasingly leveled at what was termed the regime's "authoritarian drift" and alleged nepotism (Eades and Allen 1996, xlii). In the wake of a very poor relationship between the executive and the legislative, Kérékou, who emerged as the only challenger, gathered enough momentum to upset President Soglo. The latter's strict adherence to an IMF/World Bank structural adjustment program, alienated him from parliamentarians (*députés*), civil servants, and the poor, despite some economic gains for Benin as a whole (Decalo 1997, 59).

In an ironic mirror image of Kérékou's downfall in March 1991, Soglo had become the target. Having secured a slim lead over Kérékou in the first round of March 3, 1996 presidential elections, Soglo fell to a "uniting for democracy" policy by the opposition.[1] Thanks to the support of all the other defeated candidates, Kérékou won the second round of the balloting. Despite allegations of vote rigging, intimidation, and calls for cancellation of the results, the constitutional court confirmed the outcome of the elections, allowing Kérékou to return to power (Englebert 1999, 182).

Unfortunately, "Kérékou II," as his return is dubbed in Benin, did not differ from his first experience with power in the country. Although, he is now a "born again" in political, economical, and religious matters, his true self took over some practical and pragmatic decisions. Kérékou's government stated priorities were to strengthen the rule of law, to promote economic revival and social development and to strive for national reconciliation (Englebert 1999a, 182). However, his first efforts of acknowledgement of the opposition's support through a government of national reconciliation, led by a *de facto* Prime Minister[2] Adrien Houngbédji, lasted only a few months. Due to diverging views on how to manage civil servants' strikes, Houngbédji resigned in 1998, taking with him his support for Kérékou (Europa 1999, 636).

Since then, Kérékou has named a new government with the return of several former "comrades," who previously helped him, to despoil the country. However, the rehabilitation of former "associates" is generating a great deal of anxiety within the population in general, and among civil servants and students, in particular (Decalo 1997, 60). In fact, Benin seems to have renewed with frequent strikes and social unrest since the return of former "comrades." Relations between the government and civil servants remained strained because of the lack of governmental political will to satisfy the workers' demands. Given the declining living conditions in Benin, it will take more than coalition and reshuffling of government to tackle the severe economic problems facing the country (Decalo 1997, 59).

Political Development of Togo

Togo is also a small West African country, forming a narrow strip stretching north from a coastline of 32 miles, and 320 miles inland. Nestled between Benin to the east and Ghana to the west, Togo's northern neighbor is Burkina Faso (Cornevin 1959, 13). Six natural geographical regions exist in Togo: (1) sandy beaches, estuaries, and inland lagoons; (2) the barre-soil Ouatchi plateaus in the immediate hinterland; (3) the higher Mono tableland drained by the mono river and its tributaries; (4) the *Chaîne du Togo* mountains which is a continuation of *Atakora* of Benin; (5) the northern sandstone *Oti* plateau; and (6) the northwestern granite regions in the vicinity of Dapaong (Decalo 1996, 1; Cornevin 1988, 7).

The climate in the coastal region is hot and humid, with a heavy rainy season between May and October. In the central region, rain is the heaviest in May-June and in October. In the north where the average temperature is 30°C (86°F), there is a rainy season between July and September (Cornevin 1959, 15). With approximately 30 ethnic groups, of which the main ones are the *Ewe*, the *Kabiyè*, and the *Mina*, Togo's population is 4 million. The official languages are French, Ewe, and Kabiyè. About half of the Population worships traditional gods, while 35% are Christians, and 15% Muslims. Lomé is the capital of Togo (Englebert 1999f, 1089).

Although first sighted by the Portuguese, the Togolese coast became a bone of contention among the French, the British, and the German empires. The Danes who were also involved in trade on the western part of the coast, withdrew with the sale of Kéta to Britain in 1850 (Decalo 1996, 5). Togo got its name from a small coastal village by the same name (*To*=water, *Go*=coast) where on July 4, 1884, German Imperial Commissioner Gustav Nachtigal signed the first protectorate agreement with Chief Mlapa III. From the coast, Germany tried to move towards the north despite strong resistance (Decalo 1996, 5). As Togoland, the territory became a German colony in 1894. The definitive boundaries of Togo were finally fixed in a series of conferences with the other colonial powers, and ratified in a Treaty in Paris in 1897 (Cornevin 1988, 21).

Although the German colonial era was brief (only thirty years), and was very authoritarian, it provided the basis for Togo's infrastructure. Besides a good road system, Lomé's breakwaters and wharf, along with a railroad system, were all built by the German administration (Decalo 1990, 209). Despite advances in education and agriculture, however, a considerable opposition demonstrated their resentment to the harshness of the German administration (Englebert 1999f, 1089).

Shortly after the outbreak of World War I, Togo was occupied by French and British forces. With the help of the *Ewe* who migrated earlier to the Gold Coast, the allied troops overthrew the German administration. At the end of the war, Togoland was divided into zones of occupation, with France controlling the larger eastern section, while the British took over the west (Decalo 1996, 126). With the two sides administered by different powers under the League of Nations, the homeland of the *Ewe* people was split, raising the very pertinent and lingering issue of "*Ewe* reunification." After the Second World War, Togoland joined the United Nations Trust Territories (Agblemangnon 1966, 16).

In 1956, the *Ewe* problem became so important that a UN-supervised plebiscite was held. Despite *Ewe* opposition, the majority of British Togoland supported a merger with the neighboring territory of the Gold Coast. The other half of Togoland also held a plebiscite in October of the same year to become part of the French Community (Decalo 1990, 208-209). While British Togoland became independent with Ghana in 1957, French Togoland, after self-government, became independent on April 27, 1960, as the Togolese Republic, or simply, Togo (Englebert 1999f, 1089; Decalo 1996, 6).

Before independence, there were two main political parties in Togo: the *Comité de l'Unité Togolaise* (usually known as *Unité Togolaise*-UT), led by Sylvanus Olympio, and the *Parti Togolais du Progrès* (PTP), led by Olympio's brother in-law, Nicolas Grunitzky, who was the first Prime Minister in the autonomous government. In 1958, Olympio, an *Ewe* reunification advocate, won the UN-supervised election, and led Togo to independence (Cornevin 1988, 22; Decalo 1996, 6).

In the 1961 elections, Olympio became Togo's first President, elected for a seven-year term, while his UT party won all 51 seats in the National Assembly after opposition candidates were disallowed (Decalo 1990, 212). A new constitution was approved through a referendum, and Togo seemed headed for a brighter future. Unfortunately, Olympio's regime became increasingly authoritarian by 1963, and a fatal military coup ended his rule (Decalo 1996, 7). At the insurgents' request, Grunitzky returned from exile and assumed the presidency on a provisional basis, before being confirmed by another referendum. In the hopes of uniting the country, Grunitzky banned both the UT and the PTP, and created the *Union Démocratique des Peuples Togolais* (UDPT) (Decalo 1996, 283). However, the new regime encountered opposition from UT supporters who staged an unsuccessful coup in November 1966 (Cornevin 1988).

During all these years, the newly formed Togolese army experienced some internal problems, and an obvious rift within the armed forces triggered a bloodless coup on January 1967 (Decalo 1990, 213). The constitution was abrogated, the assembly dissolved, and all parties banned. Lieutenant-Colonel (later General) Étienne Gnassingbé Éyadéma, a Kabiyè, and a suspect in Olympio's assassination, took over. In November 1969, a new party, the *Rassemblement du Peuple Togolais* (RPT) was set up by Éyadéma to rule Togo (Heilbrunn 1997, 230). Civilian leaders, unhappy with the military second take-over looked for ways to replace Éyadéma's government. In 1970, a foiled coup attempt sent several of Olympio's supporters to jail (Decalo 1973b). Having assumed power through a coup, Éyadéma searched for ways to become legitimate. In January 1972, a referendum gave him that opportunity when a massive vote confirmed his support. For several years, his alleged intention to cling to power was met through staged demonstrations and support for the continuation of his rule, and the 1977 government reshuffle gave him full control over the army (Englebert 1999f, 1090). When, in that very year, a plot was alleged, once again, Olympio's exiled supporters were sentenced *in absentia*, although the sentences were subsequently repealed by Éyadéma (Decalo 1990, 236).

On December 30, 1979, Éyadéma, the sole candidate, was, of course, elected for a seven-year term, with a brand new constitution, and an RPT National Assembly. On January 1980, he proclaimed the "Third Republic," in the hopes, once again, to convince the opposition. But, even his attempt to "democratize" by allowing independent candidates to stand for legislative elections, failed to calm the opposition (Englebert 1999f, 1091). As a matter of fact, the opposition's activities, genuine and alleged, provoked in 1985 a wave of massive arrests, following a series of bombings in Lomé and elsewhere (Decalo 1996, 9).

In the midst of alleged terrorist attacks and plots, torture of political prisoners, Éyadéma was re-elected in 1986, for another seven-year term, reportedly obtaining 99.95% of the votes cast (Europa 1999, 3458). In that same year, flagrant violations of human rights demanded the establishment of a human rights commission: the *Commission Nationale des Droits de l'Homme* (CNDH) (Heilbrunn 1997, 230). Notwithstanding that commission, political demonstrations were met with systematic and brutal abuses of human rights, arbitrary and mass arrests, imprisonment without trial, torture, and liquidation while in prison (Heilbrunn 1994; Decalo 1996, 9; Englebert 1999f, 1090).

Although the National Assembly was renewed in 1990, with only RPT members, the call for reforms became apparent, and a national council of the RPT considered the restitution of multipartyism, and greater freedom of expression. While several opposition movements were being formed, the ban on political parties was reiterated (Decalo 1990, 224-225). This triggered a new wave of protests and demonstrations, which saw professors, teachers, and students join the "liberation struggle." Clemency measures and amnesty for all political dissidents fell short of the opposition's expectations, and the pressure to really democratize continue (Englebert 1999f, 1089). It took a serious economic crisis, global winds of change, and external donors to force Éyadéma to convene a national conference for the introduction of political and economic reforms (Heilbrunn 1993, 1994; 1997).

Éyadéma has always displayed a lavish and patrimonial style of ruling, well described by a former U.S. ambassador to Togo (1986-1988). According to David Korn, Éyadéma ran Togo,

> as his own private fiefdom...while most Togolese struggle in poverty, he had a luxurious palace built for himself near his hometown. He kept a fleet of airplanes for his personal use, dressed up spiffily in expensive French suits, and threw huge gala dinners at which visiting dignitaries gorged on Norwegian smoked salmon and Chateaubriand steaks flown from Paris, all washed down with the best French wines. (1991)

It is against this background that the opposition demanded and won a forum to redress past wrongs. At the end of the national gathering, Éyadéma agreed to transfer power to a Prime Minister, chosen by the national conference. He also accepted the replacement of his RPT dominated National Assembly with an interim *Haut Conseil de la République* (High Council of the Republic) (Englebert 1999f, 1091). But, when the new Prime Minister, Joseph Koffigoh, attempted to assume the responsibilities of the Defense Ministry, according to the provisions of the conference, Éyadéma and his cronies denounced that move and threatened to take actions. In mid-October 1991, the High Council took concrete steps to oust Éyadéma and to ban the RPT. These decisions were followed by military coup attempts suspended only by Éyadéma's public appeals to the rebels (Heilbrunn 1997, 238).

On October 22, the army seized the National Assembly building, demanding the release of frozen RPT funds in return for the release of forty legislative "hostages." In November, the loyalist soldiers surrounded the residence of the Prime Minister, and in December, they announced that they had "reclaimed" strategic points throughout Togo (Heilbrunn 1997, 239). They also called upon Éyadéma to name a new Prime Minister, and dissolve the High Council. At gun-point, Koffigoh was summoned to form a national unity government, which was announced on December 30, 1991 (Decalo 1996, 10).

From then on, it became apparent that Togo's democratization process was doomed. Several subsequent general strikes organized by the opposition failed to bring Éyadéma in compliance with the decisions of the national conference. Several incidents and rumors of coups or plots, both real and imaginary, marred the political scene in Togo. All the attempts to reduce the gap between Éyadéma and the opposition have failed, and gradually, Éyadéma recovered his power, authority and privileges (Marchal 1998, 358). With the opposition on the run, "democratic" Togo closely resembles the one-party Togo before 1991. "Pluralistic" elections, with no important opposition candidates have been 'won' by Éyadéma and his RPT (Decalo 1996, 10).

The results of the June 1998 presidential elections, showed Éyadéma as the winner over protests, and he went ahead with parliamentary elections, with no opposition candidates. Both presidential and legislative ballots have been challenged by the opposition, and also denounced by some European countries whose representatives monitored the elections.[3] The crisis in Togo's democratization process seems to be far from over, and the hardening of positions from both sides is not a good omen for Benin's sister republic.

Economic Development of Benin

The developing nations or former colonies do not seem to have been adequately incorporated into a more dynamic global economy, and in most places colonial rule did not transform the traditional economies into progressive capitalist societies along the lines of European industrial or agricultural development (Conteh-Morgan 1997, 47). In Benin, as elsewhere in Africa, the muted effects of colonial economic policies on traditional African economies and created an economic nightmare (Glèlè 1969, 1974).

By the middle of the 19th century, the coast of Dahomey exported as many palm products as it would on the eve of independence after seventy years of colonial rule (Cornevin 1981). Although, some argue that colonization endowed African countries in general, and Dahomey in particular, with "modern," or "European," economy, it clearly failed to bring about genuine economic development (Adjaho 1992). Rather, colonization has caused an economic decline that, owing to bad leadership on the continent, lingers till today (Houngnikpo and Kyambalesa 2001).

In pre-colonial Dahomey and the early days of independence, the economy was very traditional. While farmers cultivated maize, manioc, and yams in the south and the center, millet and sorghum were the crops of the north. Fishing, the most valuable source of protein, was also heavily practiced by several households despite the slowdown occasioned by the new port of Cotonou (Dossou 1993). Dahomeans also participated in livestock farming, which included cattle, sheep and goats in the north, while the south specialized in pigs. But, given the high consumption, Dahomey had to import meat from neighboring Niger (Godin 1986, 39). The country's main exports came from palm plantations, which got a boost in 1962 from France and the European Economic Community (EEC), through a selected industrial palm plantations, carried out by the *Société Nationale pour le Développement Rural* (SONADER). Between 1960 and 1970, Dahomey's principal industries relied on palm oil and its derivatives (Decalo 1995; Hodgkinson 1999a 182). Other less important export products included groundnuts, cotton, *karité* (almond nuts), and cashew nuts. In spite of the presence of these products, and the existence of mineral potential, Dahomey's economy remained rudimentary until the 1970s (Cornevin 1981, 231).

By late 1970s, it became apparent that Benin's dual economy depended heavily on Nigeria. The dualism of Benin's economy lay in the existence of an official, government-documented section, and an unofficial, largely unrecorded sector, consisting of basic food production and cross-border trade with Nigeria. The *secteur parallèle*, or underground economics, (Godin 1986; Adjaho 1992) is so important that economic trends in Nigeria determine the pace of economic growth in Benin. The influence of the Nigerian economy is also clearly demonstrated when Benin suffered an economic depression in 1985, due to the closure of the border with Nigeria between April 1984 and March 1986 (Heilbrunn 1999; Hodgkinson 1999a, 183).

Benin's economy still depends on the agricultural sector, which accounts for about two-fifths of GDP and occupies some fifty-six percent of the working population, according to 1992 census. Output of the major food crops has been rising strongly since the drought of 1981-1983, reflecting both improved climatic conditions and a transfer of emphasis from cash crops to the cultivation of staple foods (Adjovi 1993). Benin is now self-sufficient in staple foods, and exports its surplus to neighboring countries, particularly Nigeria. Palm oil and its by-products continue to be the major cash crop. The output has fallen however, because of the decreasing world price.

Exploitation of timber resources is rising. A reforestation program designed to counter desertification seems to be succeeding. Livestock farming is improving thanks to Europe-funded animal husbandry. However, traditional fishing is in decline due to the salination of the lagoons, as a result of the extension of the port of Cotonou (Europa 1999, 637).

Interestingly, cotton is becoming a valuable commercial crop (Hodgkinson 1999a, 183). By the late 1980s, cotton turned out to be by far the most important export commodity. From 9,000 tons in 1966-1967 to 50,000 tons in 1972-1973, output declined to an annual average of around 14,000 tons in the late 1970s and early 1980s. That overall decline was partly due to the departure of a French cotton company, and partly to poor marketing and smuggling to neighboring countries. But with new investment and favorable climatic conditions, output improved consistently, to reach its zenith in 1995/1996 with 365,000 tons (Adjaho 1992; Hodgkinson 1999a, 184). While cotton, which needs little water, prospers in the north, the rainy south, allows the production of coffee, cocoa, groundnuts, and *karité*. However, low government purchase price is forcing farmers to switch to subsistence food crops, since they could sell their harvest to neighboring through "black market," at higher prices (Adjaho 1992, 54).

Although phosphates, kaolin, chromium, rutile, gold and iron ore have been found in the north, the minerals currently being exploited are limestone, marble, petroleum and natural gas (Hodgkinson 1999a, 183). Manufacturing activity is still small-scale and, apart from the construction materials industry, confined to the processing of primary products for export (cotton ginning, oil palm processing), or import substitution of simple consumer goods. Two joint ventures with Nigeria – the cement plant at Onigbolo and the sugar complex at Savé, which came into operation in the early 1980s – gave the industrial sector a short-lived boost (Decalo 1995, 321-330). At Onigbolo, plans to sell one-half of the schedule annual output of 600,000 tons to Nigeria did not materialize simply because of Nigeria's bad economy and the overproduction in West Africa. Forced to operate at half capacity, the cement plant became a losing deal (Decalo 1995; Heilbrunn 1999; Hodgkinson 1999a, 183).

A similar fate struck the sugar complex at Savé. Following its commission in 1983, with an annual capacity of 45,000 tons, the complex operated only intermittently at a small fraction of its capacity. Once the world sugar prices plummeted, the complex became unprofitable and ceased operation in 1991. In the end, both enterprises joined others designated for the privatization program designed by the Soglo government to improve Benin's troubled economy (Adjaho 1992).

Since the early 1980s, Benin has been struggling to reduce the chronic deficit on its budget. For a country with budgetary revenue heavily dependent on customs duties, the closure of the Nigerian border, seriously undermined Benin's economy (Heilbrunn 1999, 52-53). But, while the country suffered hard financial times, nationalized companies continued to inflate Benin's deficit. When the deficit reached a peak of 7.3 percent of GDP in 1986, a wide-ranging austerity program became unavoidable (Godin 1986; Adjaho 1992).

In 1987, failing enterprises were transferred to private ownership, liquidated or rehabilitated. The salaries in the public sector were frozen in 1987 before being reduced the following year. Despite the retrenchment of the socialist state, Benin's finances continue to worsen until the 1990s. As a matter of fact, the incapacity of Kérékou's regime in light of the economic conditions contributed heavily to that government's downfall (Nyang'oro 1994; Heilbrunn 1994; Clarke 1995; Decalo 1997).

Thanks to the generosity of Benin's creditors, Soglo managed to reduce the deficit. From a deficit that surged to 10.7 percent of GDP in 1989, the Soglo administration brought it down to 3.1 percent in 1993, owing to higher revenues, to the privatization program, and to lower interest payments. Unfortunately, the devaluation of the CFA franc in 1994 took the deficit back to 6.6 percent. Throughout 1995, 1996, and 1997, the deficit continued to rise, although at a lower pace (Hodgkinson 1999a, 184).

Pressure from the international financial organizations forced Benin to reduce its state payroll to less than forty percent of domestic revenue through a substantial reduction in numbers of civil servants and an end of automatic pay rises (Adjaho 1992). However, the new policy is generating a great deal of polemics, because civil servants are refusing to be the scapegoats of previous regimes' failed policies (Decalo 1997, 50). The hope is that France and other generous countries will come to the rescue and help save Benin's economy, the only gauge of a successful political Benin.

Economic Development in Togo

There are three distinct periods in the growth of Togolese economy: the first during the German colonial era, the second after the end of the Second World War, and the third sparked by the boom in phosphate prices (Decalo 1996, 2).

During the colonial era, German efforts to transform their new possession into a self-sufficient model colony (*Musterkolonie*) brought economic advances to the southern part of the territory (Decalo 1990, 208). Thanks to a plantation economy that took advantage of the new railway lines, the colony developed export products like coffee, cocoa, palm oil, and cotton, and maize, millet, cassava (manioc) and sweet potatoes for local consumption (Heilbrunn 1994). There were both German and native-owned plantations, facilitated by private ownership of the land. But following the partition of the territory, French Togo entered a long period of stagnation aggravated by the great depression (Coleman 1956; Cornevin 1959).

At the end of World War II, Togo's economy continued to struggle until the French government decided to come to its rescue. As a result of French investment, Togo's economy started to improve. Former German plantations were distributed to local farmers, who received adequate training to improve their methods (Cornevin 1988). With agricultural schools in place, and farmers eager to implement their knowledge, agriculture became a more important sector of Togo's economy until the mid-1960s when the country's phosphate industry came of age (Hodgkinson 1999c, 1096).

By the time of independence, agricultural exports had ceased to play a major role in Togo's finances. There were still cash crops such as cocoa, coffee, palm nuts, and cotton. But, their size diminished greatly. In 1974, a massive, albeit temporary, global price increase for phosphates quadrupled state revenues, ushering the country into a period of economic boom (Decalo 1996, 2). Togo's phosphate deposits are the richest on earth, with a mineral content of 81 percent. Exports of phosphates from the reserves at Akoupamé and Hahotoé by the *Compagnie Togolaise des Mines du Bénin* (CTMB), later on by the *Office Togolais des Phosphates* (OTP), rose from 199,000 tons in 1962 to 2.6 million tons in 1974 (Europa 1999, 3462).

After several incidents and misunderstandings, a desire to control the phosphate industry prompted the Togolese government to nationalize the company in 1974. In the following year, phosphate prices slumped, due to an energy crisis and a fall in world demand. Since then, the phosphate industry in Togo has been going through a "yo-yo" development (Heilbrunn 1997, 226). After lengthy negotiations with creditors, the government agreed to open the phosphate industry to private ownership in 1997, and thirty-eight percent of the company's capital was offered for sale (Hodgkinson 1999c, 1097).

In the meantime, the instability of the phosphate industry incidentally boosted agriculture. Having slowed down in the 1970s, and suffered from the drought of the 1980s, agricultural output recovered in the 1990s. Cotton is again the country's main export crop. Coffee is also recovering. Owing to improvement in climatic conditions, to the impact of replanting programs, and to higher prices, coffee production is contributing to Togo's economy (Decalo 1996). Other cash crops gradually helping Togo are cocoa and groundnuts productions which are getting a great deal of assistance from the European Development Fund, and France's *Fonds d'Aide et de Coopération* (FAC), hoping to improve the overall performance of Togo's finances (Chafer 1992).

In the past, Togo's official investment targets have been attained or even exceeded. But during the late 1970s, development spending was reduced, and a government austerity program had to be put in place because of economic difficulties (Cornevin 1988). Both the 1976-1980 and the 1981-1985 economic plans were leaner, taking into account not only the fluctuation of the prices of phosphate and those of the cash crops, but also the fact that foreign aid might not come (Chafer 1992). Reflecting the influence of the IMF, the 1985-1990 development plan involved relatively modest targets: an average rise in real GNP of 1.9 per year and an absence of new investment projects in favor of the maintenance and rehabilitation of existing ones. The fiscal austerity plan imposed higher taxation, further spending reductions, and a five-year "freeze" on public-sector salaries (Hodgkinson 1999c, 1097).

By 1987, when these measures were relaxed and the salary "freeze" was lifted, the budget deficit doubled, to 6.8 percent of GDP. The deficit has been growing since, and the general strike of 1993 and the CFA franc devaluation did not help it. The seven-month social unrest impacted both generation and collection of revenues (Heilbrunn 1997, 227). Although the government reduced its forecast budget from 90,000 million to 50,000 million CFA francs, the actual revenue was evaluated as 38,220 million CFA francs, forcing the government to rely on foreign reserves (Decalo 1996).

Given the tense situation between the government and civil servants, and after the promise to pay the civil servants' arrears, the government designed more creative means to fight the budget deficit. Besides improved methods of tax collection, the government introduced value-added tax to replace general business tax. Since 1995, the budget deficit has been shrinking consistently (Heilbrunn 1997, 228).

The government's economic program for 1997-1999, supported by the IMF and the World Bank, is aimed at achieving sustained and diversified economic growth and a viable external position (Hodgkinson 1999c, 1098). By downsizing the bloated economy and civil service, and by controlling the staggering national debt, Togo might be on the right track. Éyadéma's rule and his northern and military origins continue to be rejected in the south. Although the presumed final eclipse of Éyadéma anticipated by the National Conference never materialized, the pressure is definitively on for both economic and political reforms, in order for Togo to reclaim its former nickname: the Switzerland of Africa (Decalo 1996, 4).

Endnotes

[1] According to an informant (an opposition political leader), by 1995, it became clear that Soglo had abandoned his basis and secret meetings and dealings had already sealed his fate before the elections (Cotonou, December 1996).

[2] Provision for the post of a Prime Minister is not stipulated in the 1991 Constitution.

[3] Germany, Italy, Sweden and Norway are among European countries that expressed doubt about the transparency of the 1998 presidential elections in Togo.

CHAPTER FOUR

NATIONAL CONFERENCE AND POLITICAL TRANSITION IN AFRICA

Nearly every African traditional culture has some kind of mechanism for the peaceful resolution of disputes within the group and with neighboring societies, and for many Africans the national conference is clearly compatible with the traditional consensual methods of solving problems.

Clarke 1995, 228.

After several decades of political turmoil and dashed hopes, Africa emerged as a continent willing to change the course of its history. Owing to both exogenous factors, such as the democratic wind from Eastern Europe and pressure from donors, as well as endogenous factors, including civil society's endurance and the military's willingness, Africa embarked on a democratic path (Boulaga 1993; Monga 1995). But while leaders on the continent realized that change was inevitable, how to proceed remained unsure. Ideally, most leaders preferred to reform their economic and political systems without having to give up their power (Dowden 1993, 609).

Soon after political independence, most African countries degenerated into one-party authoritarianism, dictatorship, or military rule. One-party rule was justified or rationalized on the basis of national unity or economic development. Some alleged that single parties reflected African forms of democracy and consensus-building (Nyang'oro 1994, 133). In an outburst of frustrations, Africans demanded and, in most cases, succeeding in achieving a national conference, more accurately reflecting the politics of ancient Africa.

To the amazement of incumbent leaders who hoped to remain in power, events evolved so rapidly and unpredictably, that the wind of democratization swept away Africa's authoritarian regimes (Baynham 1991a). Through national conferences, African leaders and their opposition gathered to find cure for the diseases of their countries (Clark 1997, 98). Although, viewed as a means for peacefully transforming the political and economic environment, the national conference failed to deliver in some cases (Ihonvbere 1998, 3-26). While some countries renewed with hope through their national conference, others sank further in their political nightmare despite their gatherings.

National Conference as a Political Phenomenon

The idea of gathering people from all categories to resolve a national crisis finds a precedent in pre-colonial Africa. Traditional African cultures often possessed mechanisms for the peaceful resolution of intra-group conflicts, which closely resemble the national conference model (Clarke 1995, 228). Participatory and inclusive, pre-colonial political systems represented a democratic tradition on which Africa could have modelled post-colonial politics (Bratton and van de Walle 1998, 38). The struggle to democratize following one-party rule re-discovered this political heritage. So, when Benin came up with the concept of national conference the leadership was simply going back to history. The national conference replicated on one hand, what was known as *sous l'arbre à palabre* (Boulaga 1993) in Francophone Africa, *palaver* in Anglophone Africa, and *kgotla* in Botswana (Molutsi and Holm 1990), and on the other, the political events of 1789 in France: the Estates-General (*les États-Généraux*) (Laloupo 1992-1993).

Despite the age of enlightenment and the advent of so-called "enlightened despots," progress was very slow to come about in France. The Old Regime was still equated with legal aristocracy and feudalism (Fitzsimmons 1994, 3). Everyone in France belonged to an "estate" or "order" of society. The First Estate was the clergy, the Second Estate was the nobility, and the Third Estate included everyone else—from the wealthiest business and professional classes to the poorest peasantry and city workers. These categories were important because they determined an individual's legal rights and personal prestige (Palmer and Colton 1975, 376).

But the threefold division of society gradually waned as the boundary between the clergy and the nobility began to blur out. The church, which was at the root of the prevailing social system, started courting the higher tier of nobility. Revenues from vast church properties went to the aristocratic occupants of the higher ecclesiastical offices (Maurois 1956, 268-273). The duplicity or complicity between the clergy and the nobility, or the higher ladder of nobility, was becoming evident. In order to control a wider audience, the clergy was bent on including the new and widening category of aristocrats. Government service, higher church offices, army, parliaments, and most other public and semi-public privileges received aristocratic titles (Palmer and Colton 1971, 377).

Repeatedly, through parliaments, Provincial Estates, or the assembly of the clergy dominated by the noble bishops, the aristocracy had blocked royal plans for taxation and shown a desire to control the policies of the state. At the same time, the bourgeoisie, or upper crust of the Third Estate, had never been so influential (Fitzsimmons 1994, 4). An increase of French foreign trade between 1713 and 1789 gave more power to the merchant class. With the growth and the strength of their class, the bourgeois started resenting the distinctions enjoyed by the nobles. Besides the nobility's huge tax breaks, the bourgeois resented their superior attitude and arrogance. What had formerly been customary respect turned into a humiliation. The bourgeois felt that they were being shut out from office and honors (Brinton 1963, 26).

In the meantime, the common people were becoming worse off economically. Wage earners failed to share in the wave of business prosperity. Between the 1730s and the 1780s, the prices of the consumers' goods rose about sixty-five percent, whereas wages rose only twenty-two percent (Fitzsimmons 1994, 6-7). That situation generated the commoners' hatred towards the clergy, the nobility and the bourgeoisie. At the same time, relations between the peasants and the Lords were getting sour. The former began to resent the latter's privileges. Upset by the "feudal dues," the peasants displayed their anger at the nobility. Like the wage earners, the peasants were not benefiting from the overall prosperity (Maurois 1956, 267).

While resentment was mounting, France's finances suffered serious difficulties. By 1788, costs for the upkeep of the army and the navy, and the burden of public debt, put a great deal of stress on France's budget. Taxes and other revenues fell short of necessary expenditures (Maurois 1956, 270), due to the tax exemptions and tax evasions by the nobility and the clergy. Thus, although the country was prosperous, the government coffers were empty. The social classes that enjoyed most of the wealth of the country did not pay taxes corresponding to their income, and, even worse, they resisted taxation as degrading (Fitzsimmons 1994, 4).

To resolve France's financial crisis, a sweeping decision was taken. A general tax on all landowners, was created. A lightening of indirect taxes and the abolition of internal tariffs to stimulate economic production were suggested. The confiscation of some properties of the church was also proposed (Fitzsimmons 1994, 18-19). But, the biggest novel idea was the suggestion that all landowners, noble, clerical, bourgeois, and peasant should be represented in provincial assemblies without regard to estate or order (Maurois 1956, 278-279).

These drastic proposals by the Finance Minister were designed to solve the fiscal problem and avert any potential social unrest. But, they struck not only at privileges in taxation, but also at the threefold hierarchic organization of society. Aware that the parliament of Paris would not share his views, Finance Minister, Calonne, convened an "assembly of notables," hoping to win its endorsement. But the insistence of the notables to share in control of the government created an unforeseen deadlock (Maurois 1956, 281). King Louis XVI dismissed Calonne and replaced him with the archbishop of Toulouse, Loménie de Brienne. The new Finance Minister tried in vain to push the program through the Parliament. The program was rejected on the basis that only the three estates, assembled in Estates-General, could authorize new taxes (Fitzsimmons 1994, 22-23).

Fearing that Estates-General would be dominated by the nobility, the King and his Finance Minister refused to give any thought to the idea. Rather, they attempted to break the provincial parliaments by creating a new judicial system with no influence over policy. Evidently, this led to a serious revolt of the nobility (Maurois 1956, 280). All the parliaments and Provincial Estates resisted, army officers refused to take orders, and the nobility began to organize political movements. The government was brought to a standstill, unable to borrow money or collect taxes, forcing the king to call Estates-General. The various classes were invited to elect their representatives, and also to come up with their list of grievances – *cahiers de doléances* – (Brinton 1963, 46).

While the last Estates-General in 1614 were held in three separate orders this time, the king wanted one general gathering to tackle the most serious issues France had to deal with. The king called for suggestions on how to organize such an assembly under modern conditions. Several political pamphlets and other leaflets surfaced, with all kinds of recommendations (Maurois 1956, 173-175). While the Parliament of Paris, restored to its functions, continued to demand a meeting in three different orders, the nobility's position remained unclear. The nobles did, however, surprise many with their liberal program, which included constitutional government, guarantees of personal liberty for all, freedom of speech and press, freedom from arbitrary arrest and confinement. But, while they were now prepared to pay some taxes, they also hoped to be given a preponderant role in the politics of the state (Fitzsimmons 1994, 26-27).

By May 1789, when the actual meeting convened in Versailles, a debate lingered over the role of each of the three Estates. Both the clergy and the nobility wanted to control the gathering on a class basis. The Third Estates, most of whose representatives were lawyers, boycotted the organization in three separate chambers. It insisted that deputies of all three orders be seated as a single house and vote as individuals. After a six-week stalemate, a few bold priests left the First Estate to join the commoners in the Third Estate, thus creating a new dynamic (Maurois 1956, 281-282).

On June 17, the Third Estate declared itself the "National Assembly." A state of confusion and apprehension, and pressure from the nobility, forced the king to halt the proceedings. But he met the resistance of the "new deputies," who refused to give up their overnight proclamation of sovereign power. Outraged, the king summoned the Army to "normalize" the situation. The commoners, having realized that their king was siding with the nobility, became more determined to transform French society for good (Palmer and Colton 1971, 383).

In a courageous move, the new National Assembly took some sweeping reforms, which affirmed the principles of the new state. The rule of law, equal individual citizenship, and collective sovereignty of the people, were the new credos by which France will be governed (Fitzsimmons 1994, 28). The "Declaration of the Rights of Man and Citizen" issued on August 26, 1789, stated that "Men are born and remain free and equal in rights," and that man's natural rights included "liberty, property, security, and resistance to oppression." Two centuries later, several former French colonies would try to repeat the experience of 1789 France (Boulaga 1993; Robinson 1994).

National Conference in Benin

For several years, General Kérékou maintained a firm control over Benin. Thanks to his "Marxist" stance, he received foreign aid and military assistance from the Soviet Union and other Eastern European countries (Decalo 1995, 11-12). Through his cronies and thugs, Kérékou transformed Benin into a police state, sending the opposition underground. But, with the thaw of the Cold War that culminated with the fall of the Berlin wall, strategic assistance to countries like Benin lost its importance (Berton 1992; Banégas 1997, 25-26). Taking advantage of the new dynamic, civil society rekindled its demands for better living conditions. Kérékou remained unmoved until Western donor countries made any aid conditional on political and economic reforms, opening up the way for a national conference (Bourgi and Castern 1992).

To understand the rationale of a national conference, one needs to grasp the economic, political, and social conditions in the country up to February 1990 (Banégas 1997, 26-27). A few years after Kérékou became the head of state, his plans started falling apart, due to his civilian advisers who had their own agendas. Behind the rhetoric of revolution, stood a group of frustrated intellectuals who awaited an opportunity to improve their standing in society (Fatton, Jr., 1992, 104). When called upon to help Benin "take off," these intellectuals took off financially without Benin (Adjaho 1992). By the early 1980s, it became obvious that Benin was losing its development war. But, by that time also, the deliberate blurring of the public and the private spheres made embezzlement an unimportant issue (Houngnikpo and Kyambalesa 2001).

Describing the conditions of Benin on the eve of the conference, Westebbe posits:

> The immediate cause of the political crisis that erupted in late 1989 was the failure of the regime to pay civil service workers' and teachers' salaries. Three months of salary arrears had been incurred by May 1989, just after the SAL [Structural Adjustment Loan] to Benin was launched. Teachers were already on strike, and civil servants joined then intermittently, beginning in December, when arrears reached six months. The administrative apparatus was at a standstill;

an entire school year had been lost, and another one was at risk. (1994, 93)

The crisis worsened as banks became insolvent, because of unsecured loans to Benin's commercial élites (Dossou 1993, 192). The banks' scandal directed *Béninois'* anger at Kérékou's regime for allowing such a thing. While civil servants, teachers, and students struggled to make ends meet, the *apparatchiki* of the government continued to display a lavish lifestyle (Adjaho 1992; Adjovi 1993). To make matters worse, the recently-imposed SAP called for a leaner government, requiring all kinds of cuts. In Westebbe's words (1994, 88): "... the Benin government embraced a radical program of structural reform that represented a fundamental shift in development strategy. It moved toward economic liberalization and private sector development while substantially reducing the role of the public sector." In a nutshell, the SAP seeks to "reform the current [Benin] budget and general public sector management, impose investment programming, deepen public enterprise reforms, restructure the banking system, reform trade policy, and deregulate markets' (Westebbe 1994, 89).

Given their already depressed living standards, the population's anger became evident. Trade unions and students denounced the World Bank and the IMF recommendations (Banégas 1997, 28-29). With the only trade union in Benin under the aegis of the government, with influential members of the board co-opted by the only political party, its ability to voice popular dissatisfaction was limited. Three renegade trade unions, the *Syndicat National de l'Enseignement Supérieur*—SNES— (Higher Education National Trade Union), and the public administration workers' union, and that of the postal workers, declared independence and started challenging the government (Dossou 1993). Aware of both the social mood within the country and the condemnations leveled against his power from outside, Kérékou started moving towards a loosening of his economic and political system. The "autonomous" trade unions had "pledged" to make Benin "ungovernable," and ignoring such a warning would have been tantamount to political suicide (Boulaga 1993; Adjovi 1993; Heilbrunn 1994; Decalo 1997).

In the absence of legitimate opposition, accountability became practically impossible and corruption unavoidable, leaving the country in a state of permanent instability. A persistent economic and political crisis forced Kérékou to alter his stance on the future of Benin, and

Magnusson's evaluation of what led to the national Conference is quite accurate:

> The military-authoritarian solution to political instability became the seedbed of rampant corruption and increasingly untenable repression in the 1980s. The financial restrictions of structural adjustment, the looting of state coffers, and the collapse of the banking system destroyed the regime's ability to finance civil peace. In the years prior to the transition, corruption, lack of paychecks, and broad human rights abuses transformed resentment into more active opposition. Under duress, President Kérékou presided over the dismantling of a bankrupt, patronage-based banking system, as well as the dissolution of the one-party state, the official burial of Marxism-Leninism, dispensations offering freedom of the press and political organizations, and a grant of amnesty to political prisoners and exiles. (1999, 219)

Having tried his traditional dilatory methods, without success, Kérékou finally approached two university professors, René Ahouansou and Robert Dossou, to help turn the tide (Heilbrunn 1994, 665). Reluctantly, Ahouansou and Dossou accepted the offer, on condition that serious and genuine efforts be put into resolving the looming social unrest. After several meetings with the leaders of the independent trade unions, it became crystal clear that nothing short of fundamental economic and political reforms was going to halt the *mouvement* (general strike) (Pollard 1992, 28-29).

When, by December 1989, desperate civil servants, teachers, and students issued an ultimatum for payment of arrears of salaries and stipends, in the harshest possible tone, Kérékou and his clique took notice. A two-day "*consultations*" meeting of the Central Committee of the *Parti de la Révolution Populaire du Bénin* (PRPB), was convened to appease the population. During that important meeting of the political and military leadership, Kérékou, according to Westebbe,

> posed four rhetorical questions for discussion and resolution: (1) Is Marxism-Leninism consistent with economic liberalization and private sector promotion? (2) Do the principles by which the party controls the state guarantee the effective participation of those Beninese who do not share the Leninist ideology? (3) Do the structures and operation of the state safeguard efficiency in the conduct of public affairs? (4) Do the constitutional principles allow for initiative and harmonious development in the private sector? The President asked the assembled representatives to consider the political

changes necessary for people to accept the order and discipline required by "our" structural adjustment program. (1994, 94)

The high-level gathering yielded unexpected conclusions: it officially renounced Marxism-Leninism, and called for a national conference (Dabezies 1992, 30-31). A preparatory committee composed of the ministers of interior, information, justice, labor, education, and commerce, was set up to recommend the logistics of the meeting, the participants, and the agenda of the conference (Heilbrunn 1993, 1994). First believed by many to be a diversionary tactic, a sudden political change began to take hold in the country.

In the wake of the tense political atmosphere, Kérékou made an important first move, by allowing the formation of political parties. Like King Guézo, who asked "all the sons of the country to plug the holes of the punctured calabash [jar] with their fingers in order to save the fatherland" (Fatton, Jr. 1991, 88), when faced with both economic and political difficulties, Kérékou called on "all the living forces of the nation, whatever their political sensibilities," to help steer Benin through its problems (Robinson 1994, 575). However, many doubted the sincerity of such an ideological shift, arguing that Kérékou was seeking an economic renewal with only cosmetic political change. Consequently, threats of strikes were persisted, until the national conference was actually convened.

On February 19, 1990, a very important chapter in Benin's history began. The Hotel PLM-Aledjo of Cotonou became the locus of what Beninese thought impossible a few months earlier (Decalo 1997, 54). Although invitations were extended to all strata of Benin's populations, and even to Beninese abroad, the government still hoped to welcome only a token representation of the people, in order to avoid fundamental alterations (Robinson 1994; Eades and Allen 1996, xl). Unfortunately for the government, but fortunately for the country, not only did the invited guests show up, but also did organized political groups that demanded and obtained representation (Decalo 1997, 54).

Participants included members of the ruling party, trade unionists, civil servants, "political tendencies" (emerging political parties), students, religious leaders, farmers, and the military (Dossou 1993; Heilbrunn 1994; Clarke 1994, 234). All former heads of state of Benin, including one sentenced *in absentia*, for "subversive activities against the state," were also invited. To grant an international status to the conference, the entire diplomatic corps gratified the gathering with its presence (Laloupo 1992-1993).

It was in a tense atmosphere that Kérékou took the floor that morning of February 19, laying down, in his traditionally verbose style, his expectations for the conference (Decalo 1997, 54). Given the solemnity of the audience, his anxiety became apparent when he reiterated his guidelines to the conference: to "fix" the economic structure of Benin with no substantial change to the political system (Nzouankeu 1993, 45). Although he called for political renewal, and pledged to implement the IMF's Structural Adjustment Program, his focus clearly remained on the country's critical economic crisis.

In his address, he asked participants to draw up a list of economic problems to solve (Gbado 1991). Through an elaborate round of applause, more out of courtesy than anything else, the participants gave the impression of appeasing Kérékou, who left the audience filled with confidence (Decalo 1997, 55). But the participants had their own agenda. After so many years of unshared power and mismanagement they were determined to use this golden opportunity to settle, indirectly, a few scores (Adjovi 1993).

From a great start, the conference seemed to be proceeding smoothly under the leadership of the Archbishop of Cotonou, Monsignor Isidore de Souza, until its third day. On February 21, aware that the profound changes they had in mind could not be suggested under the old regime, the participants, after long deliberations, declared the conference 'sovereign' (Clarke 1994, 234; Decalo 1997, 54) That move would have ruined the gathering, if not for the extraordinary negotiation skills displayed by the Chairman of the conference (Heilbrunn 1994).

The declaration of sovereignty by the delegates shocked Kérékou to the point where he was willing to disband the meeting. Open threats of a military coup came from the abrasive and arrogant Kouandété, who urged his fellow northerners in the armed forces to take over if Kérékou were to be removed from office. Only De Souza, and pressure from France, saved the conference, and, consequently, Benin (Nzouankeu 1993, 45).

Gaining strength from their self-proclaimed sovereignty, participants embarked on a series of political transformations. The 1977 Constitution (*Loi Fondamentale*) and its institutions were abolished. Several ad-hoc committees were formed to look into different aspects of the crisis in Benin. After ten days of proceedings, the delegates agreed on sweeping reforms (Laloupo 1992-1993). Pending national elections of a new legislature, the functions of the former *Assemblée Nationale*

Révolutionnaire (ANR) were to be assumed by an interim *Haut Conseil de la République* (HCR), which included the main opposition leaders (Clarke 1994, 235). For having allowed the conference to continue, Kérékou was allowed to remain in power during a transition period. He was, however, stripped of most of his power and executive authority (Robinson 1994, 576).

As a "sovereign and executive" body, the conference's decisions superseded all existing laws, regulations, and provisions. After a severe critique of Kérékou's tenure, live on radio and television, from which the participants drew the necessary lessons, appropriate actions were taken (Decalo 1997, 55). The conference set dates for the election of a president, who would have a five-year term, which would be renewed once. The conference also elected an interim Prime Minister, Mr. Nicéphore Soglo to guarantee the implementation of its decisions during the transition (Clarke 1994, 234). According to Robinson:

> Soglo's mandate was to restore the structural adjustment process and create a consensus for its implementation. Soglo was committed to cleaning up correction and introducing institutional reforms. His was a government committed to morality in public life, the rule of law, efficient use of public resources, and raising revenues to finance vital expenditures. (1994, 96)

However, the scariest part was to come, since the decisions still needed Kérékou's approval after he had blamed the conference for staging a "civilian coup" (Nzouankeu 1993, 45).

The atmosphere was unbearable that morning of February 28, 1990. A great deal of rumor and speculation did not help the situation. According to what is known in Benin as rumor and speculation, or *radio trottoir* (Nzouankeu 1993, 45), predicted that Kérékou, under pressure from his fellow northerners and his Marxist clique, would not approve the decisions of the conference (Laloupo 1992-1993). All along, that fear had been present. But, on the last day, it became real, to the point where, the president of the conference, Archbishop de Souza, urged the audience to invoke God's blessings (Fondation Friedrich Naumann 1994).

Surprisingly, Kérékou, in a very brief address to the delegates, expressed his willingness to comply with all the decisions reached by the conference. Both the advocates of reform and the diehard supporters of Kérékou's shared amazement. Apparently, Kérékou was supposed to reject some, if not all, of the decisions in a long diatribe submitted by the Central Committee of the former only party (Dossou 1993; Decalo 1997,

54). However, for whatever reasons, Kérékou decided to give democracy a chance.

Magnusson aptly captures Kérékou's contribution not only to the success of the national conference, but also, and foremost, to the future the fragile democratic transition in Benin, when he states:

> He [Kérékou] admitted that the Marxism-Leninism option had been a divisive failure, rather than the unifying, developmental ideology that he had envisioned. In local culture, the regurgitation of the sorcerer's wares must be accompanied by an admission of culpability in order for the victim to be freed from its power. Kérékou's admission, his acceptance of the National Conference decision as binding, and his 1991 acceptance of his electoral defeat proved to be the basis for his national rehabilitation among many people as a heroic figure who had paved the way for African democracy. (1999, 222)

Indeed, Kérékou's acceptance of the resolutions of the gathering did usher in Benin a truly new political environment. A new constitution was approved through a national referendum. Basic civic and political rights, restricted or banned for several years, became realities (Laloupo 1992-1993; Clarke 1994, 234). A new legislation was promulgated permitting the registration of political parties. Independent newspapers and journals flourished (Adjovi 1993; Dossou 1993; Clark 1998). However, while Benin's national conference allowed for political renewal and hope, Togo's was full of uncertainty from start to finish.

National Conference in Togo

Until recently, Togo was viewed as a haven of peace. Despite Éyadéma's tight grip on power since 1967, the country seemed to enjoy a relative stability owing to phosphate revenues (Decalo 1996, 2). Togo was not, and has never been without political and social problems, but the tolerance of these problems was facilitated by economic comfort (Cornevin 1988). Gradually, however, things started to fall apart, and Éyadéma started to feel the heat. With the degradation of the economic shield, political and social issues became more acute and generated an unprecedented level of resentment that would lead to a national conference (Heilbrunn 1993, 1994).

Although Éyadéma has never enjoyed full legitimacy because of his alleged role in the death of the first President of Togo, he managed to subdue open opposition through the traditional means used by most

African leaders: clientelism (Chabal 1986, 1994). By "buying off" some of the leaders of other unhappy ethnic groups, with a strategic distribution of political posts, Éyadéma warded off any serious dissent. At different times, several non-*Kabiyè* dignitaries contributed, willingly or unwillingly, to Éyadéma's authoritarian regime. Personalities like General Yao Mawulikplimi Amegi, Atsu-Koffi Amegah, Tete Tevi-Benissan, Kpotivi Tevi Dzidzogbe Laclé, Yao Kunale Ekloh, and Edem Kodjo, all assumed important functions in Togo under Éyadéma (Decalo 1996). But by the 1980s, the honeymoon between Éyadéma and the non-*Kabiyè* élites was coming to an end (Heilbrunn 1997).

In 1985, Lomé experienced a series of bombings, unheard of in Togo's history. That was the beginning of a new era, in which the opposition was prepared, by any means available, to make its points: either Éyadéma reforms the political system peacefully, or he would be forced to leave power. In 1986, another event sent a stronger message. A "terrorist commando unit" briefly occupied the main military barracks, the RPT headquarters, and the national radio station (Englebert 1999f, 1091). Ghana and Burkina Faso were accused by the government for supporting and providing weapons to the "mercenaries" (Legum 1999, 916). To lend their backing to Éyadéma's regime, President Mobutu of Zaire and Mitterand of France sent troops to Togo. Nevertheless, the bombings and the aggression marked a fundamental change in Togo's political culture (Decalo 1993, 1994, 1996).

By 1989, Éyadéma started shifting his position. He was now willing to assent to multi-party politics, "if that is the will of the people" (Heilbrunn 1997, 228). At the same time, hard-liners within the RPT rejected any idea of multipartyism. While the pressure was clearly coming from outside of Togo, political and economic demands ignited from within. Civil society, and specifically students, became more vocal in their protest (Heilbrunn 1993, 1994). In August 1990, an independent *Ligue Togolaise des Droits de l'Homme* (LDTH) was formed in direct challenge of the government *Commission Nationale des Droits de l'Homme* (CNDH), because of the impression that the CNDH was not doing enough to uncover the numerous abuses of human rights in Togo (Heilbrunn 1997, 238). Several people, including Logo Dossouvi and Doglo Agbelenko, were detained on suspicion of distribution of anti-government leaflets (Press 2000, 88-89). During their trial, violent demonstrations erupted in Lomé, resulting in four deaths (Englebert 1999f, 1090).

In October, a commission was established to draft a new constitution geared at easing the political situation. Although that constitution, which called for a multi-party political system, received approval from the Togolese people, social unrest continued (Heilbrunn 1997, 239). In January 1991, Éyadéma granted an amnesty to all those implicated in political offenses. The sentences of criminal offenders were also reduced. Even mandatory contributions to the single party, the RPT, were abolished in a show of genuine desire of change (Nwajiaku 1994).

Unfortunately, a boycott of classes by university students and secondary school pupils in March 1991 demonstrated that stability would not come easily. In April, further student unrest ensued, prompted by a demonstration in Lomé by pupils at the Roman Catholic mission schools in support of their teachers' demands for wage increases (Englebert 1999f, 1091). The opposition was willing to consider no concession other than the convening of a national conference. As a matter of fact, several opposition movements joined their forces in the *Front des Associations pour le Renouveau* (FAR) to press for immediate political overture (Heilbrunn 1997, 232-233).

Finally, Éyadéma decided to talk to the opposition, and the leader of CAR was invited for a *tête-à-tête*. As a result of these talks, Éyadéma consented to an amnesty for all dissidents, agreed to the legalization of all political parties, and approved the organization of a national forum to discuss the country's political evolution (Decalo 1996). But, due to renewed social and labor unrest, the preparation of the conference proved extremely difficult. Any attempt by the opposition leaders to design a strategy with which to handle the conference was disrupted by supporters of the incumbent regime. The sheer fear that the term "national conference" might imitate events in Benin delayed the actual opening for several days (Heilbrunn 1997).

Initially scheduled to open in late June, the conference became reality on July 8, 1991. In attendance were the government representatives, the newly legalized political parties, workers' leaders, students' representatives, and religious delegates. Despite the tense mood, things seem to be going well, until, like in Benin, and confirming Éyadéma's concern, the conference declared itself "sovereign," suspended the 1979 constitution, and dissolved the national assembly (Nwajiaku 1994). All these acts clearly violated a June 12 agreement that the opposition has entered into with the government.

However, at that point the opposition felt it had nothing to lose and took a huge risk that turned out to be the biggest political miscalculation of Togo's history (Heilbrunn 1997, 236-237). Furious over those steps taken "illegally" by the conference, the government representatives simply walked out and boycotted the proceedings for a week. Upon their return, they presented the gathering with a caveat, stating that they may reject any or all of the conference resolutions. That preemptive strike simply demonstrated Éyadéma's determination to cling to power (Heilbrunn 1994, 1997; Decalo 1996; Clark 1998).

Almost to prove their resolve, the delegates insisted on sequestering the assets of the RPT and the *Confédération Nationale des Travailleurs du Togo* (CNTT—the Labor Union) in defiance of the government. The conference also decided to create a commission to look into the financial dealings of these organizations, together with an authority to take steps to prevent illicit flight of capital during the national gathering (Heilbrunn 1993). The representatives even imposed an exit visa on any government official traveling abroad. These clear signs of frustration for Éyadéma's side made the political situation more complex (Saga 1991).

Meanwhile, during the proceedings, which were relayed by the media, renewed allegations of human rights violations resurfaced. Within an environment almost surrealistic, witnesses, among which, agents of Éyadéma's regime, exposed instances of tortures and murders, in "death camps" (Heilbrunn 1997, 238). Following these horrible allegations, Éyadéma, already upset for having been deprived of most of his powers, abruptly suspended the national conference. That bold act called for a bolder one on the part of the delegates: they proclaimed a provisional government under the leadership of Joseph Koffigoh (Heilbrunn 1994, 687).

Although, in the end, Éyadéma, reluctantly confirmed, the transitional government of Koffigoh, the conference ended on August 28, 1991, without a clear sense of purpose and achievements. Unlike other African countries where a national conference brought some sense of renewal and reconciliation (Clarke 1994; Clark 1998), the national gathering in Togo was more of a distraction. In Wiseman's words (1996, 69), "In Togo, it would appear that, for [a] moment, those struggling against democracy have the upper hand over those struggling for democracy."

Decalo's assessment also reveals Éyadéma's new status since the end of the national conference in Togo:

> In Togo, General Éyadéma, in 1990 on the verge of being consigned to the dustbin of history by a resurgent national conference in Lomé brutally clawed his way to an officially 'competitive' presidential election victory (most opposition leaders boycotted an exercise marked by intimidation, murder and terror). He then mobilized the

Kabre [Kabiyè] ethnic vote in the 1994 legislative elections,
transforming himself into the only viable political leader in the
country, and technically a democrat to boot! (1994, 989)

Despite the apparent failure of Togo's national gathering, other African
states continued to look for peaceful means of altering their faltering
political and economic systems. Following the Benin's example then,
several African countries, including Gabon, the Congo, Mali, and Niger,
also held national conferences with varying degrees of success (Pérennès
and Puel 1991, 11). Benin's fellow Francophone African nations were
similarly influenced by the French experience. After witnessing Benin's
national conference, they attempted to replicate that success. In their
explanation of the rationale behind the emulation of the Benin case by
other Francophone African nations, the editors of *West Africa* contend
that:

[The French revolutionary] precedent seems to have influenced the
political movements in Benin in their campaign for a national
conference, and, when they called it, in their immediate capture of
sovereignty. In Francophone Africa, where there are many weak,
interdependent mini-states, there is also often a knock-on effect
relating to language, media, class and age networking, and other
channels of communication. Political events in one are picked up in
another, as has been seen in the past with both student agitations and
military coups. (*West Africa* 1991, 1313)

National Conferences in Other African Countries

Although the first national forum to bring about political and
economic reforms in Africa did not occur in Benin, but rather in the
archipelago of Sao Tomé and Príncipe (Clark 1998, 100), the
accomplishments of the events in Benin made that country *the* example of
smooth democratic transition. Benin had hardly concluded its conference
when a whole set of countries embarked on national gathering to "fix"
their political systems (Clark and Gardinier 1997).

Sao Tomé and Príncipe

The tiny islands of Sao Tomé and Príncipe lie in the Gulf of Guinea
about 150 miles off West Africa. Discovered by the Portuguese navigators
in 1471, the islands became in the 17th century, a major producer of sugar
thanks to intensive slave labor (Hodges and Newitt 1988, 2). However, by

the 19th century, the introduction of coffee and cacao brought new prosperity. In 1908, the island of Sao Tomé was the world's largest producer of cacao, and the crop remained an important commodity after independence in 1975 (Legum 1998, B236; Hodges and Newitt 1988, 95). Nationalist activities by an exiled liberation movement and a revolution in Portugal,[1] prompted a transfer of political power to Manuel Pinto da Costa, an economist trained in the German Democratic Republic, with leftist tendencies (Hodges and Newitt 1988, 97). In 1978, three months after independence, President Pinto da Costa declared the ongoing "national revolutionary democracy" a transitional socialist phase, and a "non-capitalist" road to development (Hodges and Newitt 1988, 104). Despite opposition by the majority of the leadership, the formal adoption of Marxism-Leninism led to a wave of nationalizations (Seibert 1999, 879).

That program of large-scale nationalizations rapidly undermined the economy and intensified factional strife within the leadership. After that, serious disturbances, periodic riots, and social unrest, marred the political scene of Sao Tomé and Príncipe. Even close associates left the country out of disgust over their country's direction (Hodges and Newitt 1988, 105). However, like in other African countries, harsh measures against opposition leaders or dissenters, allowed President Pinto da Costa to remain on his "non-capitalist" path until 1985.

As a total economic collapse became imminent, President Pinto da Costa shifted his strategies (Legum 1998, B236). Through the dismissal of government hard-liners, he initiated a whole new series of dramatic changes: the state withdrew from several economic sectors, the state-controlled import and export organizations lost a substantial part of their monopoly trading rights, and the government encouraged foreign management of state agricultural enterprises (Europa 1999, 3051). There was even a new investment code to attract foreign investors and improve the economic situation.

Political moves followed economic ones, although, to a lesser extent. Despite the election of new members of the national assembly, Manuel Pinto da Costa was confirmed as President. But, the new atmosphere of national reconciliation did not last (Seibert 1999, 876). The opposition still used violence to call for genuine and true political reforms. Shaken by a failed coup attempt in late 1989, President Pinto da Costa convened a national gathering, without the opposition, to seek fundamental political changes (Legum 1998, B236). During the conference, he announced a profound constitutional revision, his support for a full multi-party democracy, the complete guarantee of all human rights, and the abolition of the death penalty (Europa 1999, 3051).

These unilateral reforms allowed a former Prime Minister and dissident, Miguel Trovoada to be elected as President of Sao Tomé and Príncipe in March 1991 setting the country on a democratic path since.

The Republic of Gabon

In contrast to Benin where economic issues motivated a national conference, Gabon is a well-endowed country (timber, manganese, oil) that has one of the highest *per capita* incomes in Africa (Barnes 1992, 95-101; Messone and Gros 1998, 135). But, two main problems have always threatened Gabon: great disparities in income distribution, and ethnic rivalry for political power (Barnes 1992, 112-115). Messone and Gros give a good picture of Gabon on the eve of the national conference:

> At independence in 1960, Gabon possessed one of the greatest economic potentials in Sub-Saharan Africa and was until 1986 presented to international investors as an acceptable investment risk. Gabon's small population of about one million or less, allowed the country to boast the highest per capita GNP of the region in the 1970s at $4, 250. Gabon's prosperity was made possible by the oil boom of the 1970s, considerable mineral wealth in uranium and manganese deposits, and a forest rich in various hardwoods. Yet, the country was not spared the wasteful management characteristics of single party rule. Public wealth was poorly spent and unevenly reallocated. (1998, 135)

Indeed, since independence from France in 1960, Gabon, first with President Léon M'ba, and later with Omar Bongo, seemed to have been on the right track mainly because of its economy and its financial backers (Barnes 1992, 71). Although ethnic tension has always been present, comfortable living standards mitigated its effects. A careful distribution of ministerial positions also diffused dissent (Messone and Gros 1998, 134). But, when the economic structure started falling apart, resentment set in and ethnic issues reappeared. And Bongo's search for absolute power (Barnes 1992, 47-55) did not help his case. The one party state came about in 1968 when Bongo declared in a speech:

> Gabonese Women, Gabonese Men...I have made the great decision to create a political party, which hereafter will be called the *Parti Démocratique Gabonais* [PDG]. From now on, there will be one

and single party, the *Parti Démocratique Gabonais*. (Messone and Gros 1998, 134-135)

Shortly thereafter, an ordinance established indeed the *Parti Démocratique Gabonais* as the sole legal party in the country. The single-party provided Gabon with a new stability. But not surprisingly, it also allowed Bongo and his associates to perpetuate themselves in power with little regard to the wishes of the people (Gardinier 1997b, 147).

Of course, the rationale behind this change resembled that behind other single-party political systems in Africa: to fight underdevelopment "in giant steps"; to create a stable environment for attracting foreign investment, which required that old social cleavages be tamed; to rally all active forces in the country, especially the youth, in mobilization efforts; and to achieve national unity, with the party acting as the crucible. In Barnes' views, "[Bongo's] major innovation was the dissolution of all parties and their replacement by a single party...Echoing Mba, Bongo argued that multipartyism was inimical to the development of Gabonese nationalism" (1992, 48). Unfortunately, Bongo's record on these promises was poor in the eyes of most Gabonese (Messone and Gros 1998, 134-135). When, on July 4, 1990, Bongo delivered what is known as the *Bitam Declaration*, clearly stating that "there will not be multipartyism, neither today or tomorrow" (Messone and Gros 1998, 135), it became obvious that Bongo's agenda did not include political reforms.

The northern Fang ethnic group became tired of the prominence of Bongo's own Batéké group in positions of power (Bratton and van de Walle 1992, 50). Their demands for fairer shares of the political cake, and subsequent open defiance of the regime, strengthened other members of society.

In January 1990, students at the *Université Omar Bongo* boycotted classes, denouncing inadequate facilities and a shortage of academic staff. Secondary school pupils followed suit, and the unrest spread to businesses. It took a great deal of repression and brutality to silence this dissent (Barnes 1992, 59). The government decided to close all educational establishments and imposed an overnight ban on public gatherings. However, these measures failed to deter the students and their supporters (Clarke 1995, 238). Continued unrest forced a meeting between Bongo and the representatives of the students. Faced with the seriousness of the movement, Bongo established a commission to look into the students' grievances (Messone and Gros 1998, 136).

To Bongo's surprise, workers joined the social unrest, protesting economic austerity. In his attempt to "highjack" or topple any fundamental political demand, he set up a "special commission for democracy," to provide recommendations for liberalizing the Gabonese political system (Clarke 1995, 238). The results of the commission conveyed clearly to Bongo and his acolytes that the single-party political system was no longer acceptable in Gabon. He, therefore, introduced some political reforms and changed the name of the old party, to make it all- inclusive (Barnes 1992, 66). These steps did very little to appease the workers. Still hoping to control the discontent, Bongo formed a leaner government, with new "neutral" members. Civil society was hardly moved by these reforms. In early March 1990, it became clear that some form of a national gathering was unavoidable (Barnes 1992, 67-68).

During a joint session of the single party's central committee, and the national assembly, multi-party democracy was formally introduced in Gabon, but not before a five-year transitional period (*Jeune Afrique* April 23, 1990). The session also called for a conference to determine the program for the transfer to pluralism. On March 27, 1990, Bongo opened what he dubbed the "national conference on the political future of Gabon" (Barnes 1992, 63). In Bongo's own words, "the acts of the national conference are not injunctions, but recommendations" (Messone and Gros 1998, 138). In order to avoid chaos, the conference outlawed all strikes and demonstrations during the course of its meeting. Because of good timing and control of state resources, Bongo managed to turn the gathering to his advantage. He skillfully transformed the event into a "domesticated and tamed conference which had become a structure of national concord and thus lost the aggressiveness that characterized conferences in other countries" (Messone and Gros 1998, 138).

Under the leadership of Monsignor Basile Mve, President of the Apostolic Conference of Gabon, the delegates embarked on their daunting task (Messone and Gros 1998, 138). But, on April 2, the gathering was suspended when the delegates demanded that the conference be given the status of a constituent assembly (*Africa Confidential* April 6, 1990). It was only reopened after that request was dropped. However, in a loud message the representatives rejected Bongo's proposal of a transitional term. Rather, they voted for immediate creation of a truly multi-party system, and the formation of a new transitional government (Clarke 1995, 239). Despite careful planning and control extraordinary skills of pre-emption and co-optation, Bongo failed to convince delegates. Opposition parties were legalized, and the decisions of the gathering were imposed on Bongo. A broad-based government was formed under the leadership of Casimir Oyé M'ba, with several opposition members (Gardinier 1997b, 153). Unfortunately, these far-reaching changes still seemed insufficient to some labor union and student representatives who continue to press for deeper political reforms: the departure of Bongo (Barnes 1992; Azevedo 1995, 272; Gardinier 1997b; Messone and Gros 1998, 140-142). If indeed, Barnes (1992, 139) is right in stating that "Gabon's authoritarian political culture may not be conducive to the development of democracy and pluralism without turmoil," Gabon still has a long way to go to become a genuine democracy. Through a combination of fraud, force, and external assistance, Bongo continues to maintain a somehow shaky grip on state power, and to block further reforms (Gardinier 1997, 145).

The Republic of Congo

The Congo Republic became independent in 1960 within the French Community, under the leadership of Abbé Fulbert Youlou. Youlou's administration was "notable for its corruption, autocracy, and neo-colonial political and economic stances" (Decalo 1990, 53). Because his ill-conceived development projects failed to address basic economic issues of ordinary Congolese, a three-day street riots in August 1963, known as *les trois glorieuses*, led to the demise of his regime. After Youlou's resignation, Alphonse Massamba-Débat took over. Known as an austere and honest man, Massamba-Débat seemed the best choice to lead the country out of its political and economic doldrums. However, if Youlou has leaned too far to the political right to suit his country, Massamba first leaned too far to the left, and then to the right after he too sought to create a single-party dictatorship (LeVine 1987, 123). Despite Massamba's references to "scientific socialism," and his adoption of some radical measures, his economic policies still deferential to French interests generated internal dissatisfaction. Consequently, six years later, in 1969, the country experienced a military coup that brought to power a socialist soldier, Major Marien Ngouabi, who, himself was assassinated in 1977

(Decalo, Thompson, and Adloff 1996, 14). In Clark's words, "Ngouabi was widely respected by many ordinary Congolese for his intelligence, incorruptibility, and hard work, and his murder left an indelible mark on the nation's political consciousness" (1997b, 64).

Colonel Joachim Yhombi-Opango became the new leader. However, Yhombi-Opango's term in office was rather short. Besides proclaiming himself general, he displayed extravagance, excessive tastes for the honors and luxuries of high office, not in the military's taste. He also showed a clear desire to reestablish goo relations with the West that contributes to his downfall. On February 5, 1979, the military committee of the single party divested Yhombi-Opango of all his powers and put him under house arrest (LeVine 1987, 125). The Army Chief of Staff, Colonel Denis Sassou-Nguesso, the Chairman of the single political party, who was designated to replace Yhombi-Opango, was confirmed, in March 1979, as the new president (Englebert 1999b, 371; LeVine 1987, 125).

Upon assuming power, Colonel Sassou-Nguesso confirmed the socialist path of development the Congo pursued under Ngouabi. In his attempt to ease the political atmosphere since Ngouabi's death, he agreed to release political prisoners, including those involved in the assassination of Ngouabi. He also urged Congolese abroad to return home without fear of repression (Decalo, Thompson, and Adloff 1996, 15). He clearly seemed to be embracing a pro-Western foreign policy and a liberal economic policy. Isolated and marginalized, the left-wing factions of the single party, the *Parti Congolais du Travail*—PCT, made their feelings known to the leadership (Decalo, Thompson, and Adloff 1996, 17; Legum 1998, B209).

Despite the holding of several congresses to iron out differences between the two main radical and liberal factions, serious diverging opinions prevailed (Decalo, Thompson, and Adloff 1996, 15). While the President himself was consolidating his power, economic rationale imposed the reduction of ministerial posts, alienating some members of the radical movement within the PCT. That reshuffling of the government generated more ethnic rivalries (Legum 1998, B209-B210).

While the political scene degenerated, disappointment in the country's worsening economic situation led to an increase in the opposition to Sassou-Nguesso. During the 1980s, given the open resentment to his power, the President ordered the arrest of any opponent (Decalo, Thompson, and Adloff 1996, 17). Consequently,

several army officers were sent to jail on suspicion of undermining
state security. The fact that most of these officers happened to be of a
different and rival ethnic group rekindled the ethnic division within the
army (Englebert 1999b, 376). As a matter of fact, when a commission
of inquiry, set up in 1987 to look into a failed coup, implicated and
sentenced officers of a rival ethnic group, tension rose within the army
(Legum 1998, B213). Decalo puts it aptly when he said:

> Congolese politics had historically been characterized by sharp
> ethnic cleavages that had formed the building blocs of power. The
> Marxist upheaval did little to change this. If anything, the
> ideological polarization, superimposed on existing ethnic rivalries,
> and the civil-military tug-of-war vastly complicated efforts to form
> a coalition of support for the new order. (1986a, 128-129)

Re-elected in 1989 as Chairman of the PCT, and President of the
Republic for a further five-year term, Sassou-Nguesso tried to take
steps to relax the political and economic situation in Congo (Englebert
1999b, 375). He reformed the political system, allowing non-members
of the PCT to run for legislative elections. A whole series of economic
transformations became effective hoped to redress economic
imbalances with a sound option for private enterprises, (Decalo,
Thompson, and Adloff 1996, 16). But, his efforts failed to prevent
further social unrest. Sassou-Nguesso realized that the Congolese
population required profound changes rather than mere alterations
(Englebert 1999b, 376). Congo faced typical structural impediments to
economic growth in developing countries: heavy reliance on a single
commodity for income, declining terms of trade, and a neomercantilist
relationship with its former colonizer (Clark 1997b, 66).

By the end of the 1980s, François Gaulme's 1983 evaluation of
the Congolese situation was still relevant:

> Twenty years after its revolution, the Congo is thus in a state of
> equilibrium: faithful to its revolutionary politics and alliances,
> overtly Francophile and on good terms with the United States;
> prosperous, thanks to its oil, but in a delicate financial situation
> itself engendered by the increase in petroleum revenues; faced with
> difficulties in a number of sectors in its economy, but with a history
> of industrialization and its social consequences much broader than
> that experienced by the average African state. (Quoted in LeVine
> 1987, 138)

Under very difficult economic and political conditions, an *ad hoc* committee was set up by the single party in February 1990, to examine the possible repercussions of democratization for the Congo, and for Africa in general. The committee was specifically asked to "analyze with intelligence and perception the on-going changes in Eastern Europe" (*Jeune Afrique*, January 15, 1990). That committee established an extraordinary congress to be held in 1991 that would design a multi-party system in Congo. In the meantime, the PCT announced its intention to keep its "executive role," while relinquishing its "leadership role" (*Jeune Afrique*, August 8-21, 1990). Sassou-Nguesso was hoping for a "long and painful" democratization process, to buy some time. But, events would betray his expectation (Decalo, Thompson, and Adloff 1996, 17).

Besides the street protests and a steady economic decline, the disaffiliation of the single labor union, the Confederation of the Congolese Trade Union, proved very damaging. A clear divorce between the trade union and the PCT, stimulated more social turbulence, this time, not only on the streets, but also in the factories and in the parishes. Worse, the rural areas demanded more open government and better living standards (*Le Monde*, October 2, 1990). It became obvious that the democratic debate no longer remained confined within the single party. After a general strike in response to the refusal of immediate political reforms, the government began to soften its position. A new "government of national union" was formed to calm the rumblings for political reform. However, the strategy failed and all emerging political parties were called on to register in preparation for a national conference (Legum 1998, B209).

On February 25, 1991, the Congolese national conference opened and was immediately deadlocked by the government last minute effort to dictate the quota of representations (Clarke 1995, 242). The next challenge of the conference was a debate on whether its decisions would be "sovereign." After some heavy negotiations, the opposition managed to gain seven out of the eleven seats at the conference, and also to gain its "sovereignty." Presided over by the Roman Catholic bishop of Owando, Monsignor Ernest N'kombo, the gathering voted itself a sovereign body whose decisions were going to be biding on the government. After several months of discussion, Ngouabi was presented as the scapegoat for Congo's past, present and future problems. On June 10, the conference ended with its decisions adopted "by acclamation" (Englebert 1999b, 376).

The conference suspended the old constitution, replacing it with a *Conseil Supérieur de la République* (Superior Council of the Republic). Sassou-Nguesso was forced to transfer power to a new transitional government under the leadership of André Milongo, a former African Development Bank official (Legum 1998, B211). After several months of hesitation and confusion, the Congo reconnected with democracy through multi-party legislative and presidential elections in 1993. Unfortunately, continued ethnic tensions, coupled with strategic and tactical errors by President Pascal Lissouba, gave Sassou-Nguesso an excuse to retake power through force in 1997 (Englebert 1999b, 377).

The Republic of Mali

Subjugated by France by the end of the 19th century, the territory known today as Mali became a colony in 1904 and took the name "French Sudan" (Soudan Français) in 1920 before joining the French Union in 1946. Independent in 1960 under the name of Sudanese Republic, it was federated in 1959 with the Republic of Senegal in the Mali Federation (Imperato 1996, 1). However, Senegal withdrew from the federation in August 1960, forcing the Sudanese Republic to take the name of the republic of Mali under President Modibo Keita (Englebert 1999d, 675).

Keita's regime was able to sustain itself with a strong support from the urban areas. Government workers and students, who received a variety of benefits including life-long employment, scholarships, and stipends, gave their full support to Keita (Vengroff and Kone 1995, 46). Emulating the Chinese Cultural Revolution, Keita began to build a party-controlled militia as an alternative to the Army, which he never trusted. Although he managed to eliminate potential opposition and take control of most associational groups, the army remained a formidable threat to his regime (Europa 1999, 2346). And, indeed, a potential menace to its corporate interests forced the army to move in.

On November 19, 1968, the armed forces, led by Colonel Moussa Traoré, overthrew Keita's government, putting an end to several years of personal power and leftist tendencies (Imperato 1996, 228). Although the new *Comité Militaire pour la Libération Nationale* (CMLN) committed itself to Keita's economic programs, some elements within the army sought to reinstate the old regime. The wave of arrests and imprisonment that followed did not bode well for the country. Besides the dissension within the army, there was a widespread unrest among the civil servants and students who displayed their loyalty to Keita. (Englebert 1999d, 675). The CMLN suspended the national trade union body in 1970 and arrested union leaders. Severe economic difficulties, and the consequences of a harsh drought (1968-1974) compounded these political problems (Europa 1999, 2347).

Aware of the rocky road ahead, the CMLN held a referendum on a new constitution in 1974, making good on its promise to return to civilian rule. With ninety-nine percent in favor, the new constitution allowed the military to remain in power for five years (Imperato 1996, xxx). To become more legitimate, the military leaders announced the formation of a more inclusive party, to be called the *Union Démocratique du Peuple Malien*—UDPM (Democratic Union of the Malian People). This decision was viewed with a great deal of skepticism. Many within the army and civil society saw rather delaying tactics (Europa 1999, 2346).

Despite the actual constitution of the UDPM, hostilities toward the government grew, and Keita's death in 1977 while in custody, worsened the political ambiance in Mali (Imperato 1996, 136). Even the composition of a "national government," to demonstrate Traoré's desire to open up the political system failed to deceive those opposed to his reign. He then resorted to imprisonment of political and student leaders (Legum 1998, B81). The academic year 1980-1981 was declared *année blanche* (nullified), due to primary school teachers' strike and university students' unrest. A bleaker economic situation, and the IMF/World Bank structural adjustment program, forced living standards to decline at a more rapid pace (Imperato 1996, 12).

In the meantime, cracks grew even within the ruling élites. Some officers pressed for immediate political reforms, but faced the obstinacy of Traoré and his close associates. In December 1989, the UDPM reiterated its opposition to a multi-party system in Mali (Englebert 1996, 242). But, by late 1990, President Moussa Traoré took notice of the wind of change blowing over the continent. Hoping to take the bull by the horns, he imposed a series of conferences throughout the country to consider the exercise of democracy within the UDPM (Press 1999, 56-57).

While rural areas were inconclusive, the conference in Bamako, the Capital, revealed a clear desire for political reforms. But, Traoré insisted that any political opinion be expressed within the framework of the single party (Nzouankeu 1993, 45). In mid-August, an 'open letter,' published in an independent newspaper, *Les Échos*, called for the gathering of a national conference to draft a new constitution and to determine the modalities of the transition to multi-party politics (Legum 1998, B81).

Before Traoré's persistence, opposition movements began to emerge. Three solid parties were formed, the *Comité National d'Initiative Démocratique* (CNID), the *Alliance pour la Démocratie au Mali* (ADEMA), and the *Rassemblement pour la Démocratie et le Progrès* (RDP). These new, but unregistered, parties were willing to take any opportunity to make their points and the eviction of the street-vendors in Bamako triggered violent demonstrations. In early January 1991, the single labor union, the *Union Nationale des Travailleurs du Mali*, dissociated itself from the UDPM and called also for multi-party democracy (Legum 1998, B82). Although the union and students officially went on strike for better living conditions, it gradually became obvious that, under the guidance of the new parties, workers and students wanted to topple Traoré's regime (Englebert 1999d, 676).

Pushed to the wall, the government reacted with violent repression against protest rallies and demonstrations, which generated more widespread unrest. In March 1991, the military was asked to bomb the UNTM headquarters, where opposition groups had gathered to launch a general strike. From harsh repression ensued an extraordinary death toll and number of injuries and arrests (Legum 1998, B82). Before Traoré's refusal to accede to demands for his resignation, the military deemed the time ripe to set in. On March 26, Traoré was arrested in a bloodless coup and all state bodies were suspended (Nzouankeu 1993, 46).

The new military leader, Lieutenant Colonel Amadou Toumani Touré (affectionately known as ATT), promised a return to civilian rule within a year. The transitional council (*Comité de Transition pour le Salut du Peuple*), composed of both civilian and military leaders, was to oversee the democratic transition (Imperato 1996, 224). A national conference was organized to seek views on constitutional, electoral and political reforms. After a new constitution, a new electoral code, and a new legal framework for establishing political parties, Mali experienced a smooth democratic transition that allowed Alpha Oumar Konaré of the ADEMA, to become the President of the third Republic (Europa 1999, 2347; Legum 1998, B83). Although, the current political situation remains uncertain, Mali seems to have resumed a democratic path.

The Republic of Niger

Formerly a part of French West Africa, Niger became a self-governing republic within the French Community in 1958. At independence in 1960, Diori Hamani, who favored closer economic ties with France, became the President (Decalo 1997b, 7). However, soon, authoritarianism allowed the Diori regime to maintain itself in power and to control the functions of appropriation and distribution of state revenues to the profit of the political class. Although multipartyism laws remained on the book, Diori ruled over a *de facto* single-party regime (Gervais 1997, 88-89). By the 1970s, Diori's regime started experiencing social turbulence due to economic difficulties. The fall of export revenues, the loss of pastureland and serious food shortages, created a widespread civil disorder (Europa 1999, 2653). Diori's inability to deal effectively with the new situation invited the Army Chief of staff, Lieutenant Colonel Seyni Kountché to stage a successful military coup in 1974.

Thanks to the uranium boom, Kountché increased his regime's margin for maneuver. Through a redistribution of national resources, he insured the stability of his power. But, soon, a deepening financial and economic crisis and its corollary, the structural adjustment program, threatened the privileges of the political class, and the very stability of Kountché's regime. Through clientelism, economic mismanagement and a lack of transparency in public sector, Niger plunged into recession. Kountché's pledge to restore public morality did not materialize until his death in 1987 (Decalo 1997b, 9).

After Kountché's term, Colonel Ali Saïbou, another Army Chief of staff, who has been acting as interim president during Kountché's illness, was confirmed as the president of the second republic, on November 14, 1987. However, he still had to deal with rivals who enjoyed the backing of some military factions, and Gervais maintains that

> Because he lacked sufficient support from either the military or civilian elements to maintain himself in office over the longer term, Saïbou adopted a strategy that might increase his personal power and consolidate his regime. To these ends he undertook a number of conciliatory measures toward critics and rivals of the Kountché regime. (1997, 90)

Through a wave of major government changes, Saïbou showed, however, his commitment to the continuing role of the military in Niger's political system (Englebert 1999e, 776). The diminishing number of civilian officials in his administration was a clear signal. As a matter of fact, the new constitution, adopted by the council of ministers in January 1989 and approved by more than ninety-nine percent in a national referendum in September, provided for a distinct role for the armed forces in national politics (Europa 1999, 2653). It became obvious that *décrispation* (political thaw) in Niger was going to be on Saïbou's terms.

Although the fourteen-year ban on political parties was lifted, Saïbou refused to permit multi-party democracy, and announced instead the formation of a new ruling party, the *Mouvement National pour une Société de Développement* (MNSD). Saïbou's opposition to an immediate establishment of a multi-party system was justified by his view that a single party and political pluralism were not necessarily incompatible (Legum 1998, B107). Like several other African political leaders who wanted to maintain their grip on power, Saïbou urged the expression of different views within a single political entity (Press 2000, 57). He went on with his program and was confirmed in a presidential election, in which he was the only candidate, for a seven-year term in 1989. Thus began a rocky adventure, because of the determination of the opposition to challenge his legitimacy (Decalo 1997b, 10).

In February 1990, students at the University of Niamey boycotted classes to denounce new educational reforms and the reduction in the level of graduate recruitment into the civil service. Security forces used unprecedented brutality to repress the opposition (Legum 1998, B107). Saïbou, who was out of the country, deplored the tragic events upon his return and appointed a commission to examine students' grievances. In hopes of appeasing students, he took other actions, like dismissing the ministers of higher education and interior for inefficiency. But, these measures brought only temporary relief, because the students wanted more than academic and social satisfaction (Europa 1999, 2653).

Students have joined with workers in seeking to replace Saïbou's one party government with a democratically elected regime. An increasingly resentful civil society exploited the government's failure to satisfy students' demands (Englebert 1999e, 776). Through active inducement by the opposition, student unrest continued unabated. In April 1990, a heavy deployment of security forces descended on several educational facilities to curb social disturbance. The government decreed a ban on all student gatherings and demonstrations. Following several arrests, the trade union federation, the *Union des Syndicats des Travailleurs du Niger* (USTN) broke its silence and joined the students in their demands for political reforms (Decalo 1997b, 10).

With a 48-hour general strike in protest against new austerity measures, which included a two-year salary "freeze" in the public sector, the USTN made its intentions known to the government. In response, the government announced the amendment of the constitution, to facilitate the transition to political pluralism (Europa 1999, 2654). However, the workers felt that the change of heart was merely an aesthetic suggestion and continued pressing for effective reforms (Decalo 1997b, 10). The USTN stuck to its demands for the cancellation of unpopular austerity measures, while requesting access to the state-owned media. In November, a five-day general strike, widely observed, halted the economy of the country and sent a louder message to the authorities (Englebert 1999e, 776).

On the eve of another strike, Saïbou finally announced, based on the findings of a constitutional review commission, the establishment of a multi-party political system in Niger. In consultation with donor countries and international financial institutions, less stringent austerity measures were taken (Decalo 1997b, 11). Pending a new constitution, provisions were made for the registration of political parties. For the first time, it became clear that Saïbou had no choice but to reform. However, the opposition demanded and got the convening of a national conference to determine the political future of the country (Legum 1998, B107).

On July 29, 1991, the conference opened with representatives of the government and civil society. After some intense negotiations over the legal status of the gathering, delegates declared the conference "sovereign" (Europa 1999, 2654). In early August, the constitution was suspended, and all state organs dissolved. Saïbou was stripped of his powers and remained a mere symbolic head of state (Decalo 1997b, 11). State officials were forbidden to leave the country. The government was deprived of its authority to engage in any official financial transactions. A special commission was set up to look into alleged abuses of economic and political power (Englebert 1999e, 776).

At the conclusion of the conference, a transitional government led by Amadou Cheiffou, a regional official of the International Civil

Aviation Organization, was charged with preparing an effective democratic transition (Legum 1998, B108). An interim legislature, the *Haut Conseil de la République* (HCR), guided by the Chairman of the conference, André Salifou, a university professor, ensured that the transitional government implemented the conference resolutions, supervised the activities of the head of state, and oversaw the drafting of a new constitution (Legum 1998, B109; Englebert 1999e, 777).

An atmosphere of national consensus emerged out of the conference and political reforms brought to Mahamane Ousmane power in 1993. His administration swiftly ended several months of industrial unrest and disbursed civil servants' back salaries (Englebert 1999e, 777). But, while relations between the government and workers seemed to be back on track, the government and the presidency remained locked into procedural disputes over prerogatives and competencies (Decalo 1997b, 13). When these difficulties of "cohabitation" reached their climax in 1996, the military moved in. Colonel Ibrahim Baré Maïnassara derailed democracy, seizing power to "avoid Niger's descent into political chaos" (Europa 1999, 2655).

Although it proclaimed its wish not "to cling to power," the military gradually started exhibiting its renewed taste for political power. By May, Maïnassara confirmed his intentions to run for presidential elections as a non-partisan candidate (Englebert 1999e, 779). In July, he became the President of the fourth republic. But, ethnic and political divisions made his term extremely difficult. While getting ready to make an internal trip, President Maïnassara was assassinated on the tarmac of Niamey's airport, on April 9, 1999 by members of his own guard. Although the new leader, Major Daouda Mallam Wanké, once again, promised democratic elections as soon as possible, past behavior of the military instilled doubt in the population (*Jeune Afrique*, April 20-26, 1999). However, Wanké honored his engagement, organizing presidential elections that saw Mahmadou Tandja as the new president of Niger. The hope is that this new chapter in Niger's history would last forever, with democracy solidly entrenched in the mores of *Nigériens*.

Endnote

[1] The 1974 Revolution put an end to Portugal's desire to maintain colonies overseas.

CHAPTER FIVE

THE MILITARY AND DEMOCRATIZATION IN AFRICA

> Until its recent decline, praetorianism since independence has constituted, with few exceptions, the standard model of accession and exercise of power in Sub-Saharan African countries.
>
> Martin 1997, 82

First viewed as symbols of national sovereignty through the early years of de-colonization (Schraeder 1997, 73), the African military increasingly became a part of the ruling group's enforcement apparatus. Although the actual size of the military and its relationship to the rulers varied in each country, the armed forces in most countries became politically powerful entities (Chazan et al. 1988, 55-57). As a result of their organization and control of weaponry, the armed forces were uniquely positioned to overthrow civilian regimes (Gordon 1996, 73).

Following the end of formal colonialism, several African civilian leaders naively expected the armed forces to remain loyal to civil administrations. In a speech to the cadets of the Ghanaian Military Academy in 1961, President Kwame Nkrumah conveyed his vision of the Ghanaian armed forces' subordination to his audience:

> You must have confidence that the government is doing what is best
> for the country, and support it without question or criticism. It is not
> the duty of a soldier to criticise or endeavour to interfere in any way
> with the political affairs of the country; he must leave that to the
> politicians, whose business it is. The government expects you, under
> all circumstances, to serve it and the people of Ghana loyally. (1961)

Nkrumah's myopic view failed to take into account the history of
African military. Very little in that history leads one to expect
professionalism from the armed forces. The transition from "Armies of
Africans" to "African armies" (Welch, Jr. 1986, 16) after independence
did not erase the political objectives these armies were called upon to
serve under colonialism. The concept of military disengagement from
politics, eagerly desired by new civilian leaders, simply never
materialized (Welch, Jr. 1993, 71). On the contrary, the "men on
horseback" toppled several civilian regimes, pledging in vain to do
better (Austin 1963). Between 1951 and 1985, Africa witnessed 131
attempted military coups, of which sixty percent succeeded (Schraeder
2000, 245).

   Although there has been an extensive politico-sociological
literature on the relationship between the armed forces and society in
the emerging nations, dealing mainly with the military as a potential
agent of economic modernization (Shils 1962; Pye 1962; Johnson
1962; Janowitz 1964), nobody expected the military to take a positive
stance on democratization. Indeed, the military's record in Africa
makes that prediction very unlikely. When Welch and Smith (1974, 6)
observed that "the military political role [in Africa] is a question not of
whether but of how much and of what kind," they did not envision the
military helping democracy to take root. The military became such a
threat to Africa's political systems that most scholars describe at length
its exploits. According to Corbett:

> In all the African States, the military is in a unique position of
> strength in relation to the other national institution. In contrast to
> most of those in civilian administration, the training both the armed
> forces and the police have received has given them a bent for action
> as well as a dedication to order and a sense of service. Their faith in
> team work and their confidence in their ability to cope with
> problems tend to make them impatient of civilian indecisiveness,
> and the lack of counterweights to their use of force makes it
> possible for them to act at will...The success of coups in those
> states now under military leadership is an implicit threat to the

civilian requires in neighboring states. Because so many of the Black African army leaders served together in the French forces, or at least underwent similar indoctrination, they are probably sympathetic to the objectives of their former comrades in arms, and may even be tempered to emulate them. (1972, 159)

In the late 1980s and early 1990s, the continent was marred by corrupt regimes, both civilian and military (Dabezies 1992, 21). But when the wind of change started blowing, the attitude of the military *vis-à-vis* the process of democratization varied from one country to another. Whether out of concern for corporate interests or because of the leaders' personal interests (Bebler 1973; Jackson 1978, 1986; Baynham 1986), the armed forces in most countries were reluctant to embrace democracy (Hutchful 1997). Only in a few countries was the military leadership willing to condone democratization. These two contrasting views are well illustrated by how events unfolded in Benin and Togo.

The Military and Politics in Benin

After independence, the African military assumed a new role. All over the continent, military interventions became endemic, and Benin followed the rule rather than the exception (Gutteridge 1969, 1975b; Luckham 1994). Contrary to expectations of the new civilian leaders, the military became a formidable political force to reckon with. As a political organization with its own agenda, the military played an important role in Africa in general and in Benin in particular (Welch, Jr. 1967; Norlinger 1970; Wells 1974; Decalo 1974, 1976). Political instability marked the first twelve years of Benin's independence, as the military intervened six times, "ostensibly to quell both incessant political bickering and the ethno-regional conflicts" (Ronen 1987, 93), and also to restore order.

As was the case in most former colonies, the army in Benin evolved out of the remnants of colonial armies in Africa. Until World War II, the training of African armies was rudimentary because of their limited role in quelling potential disputes on the continent (Martin 1986; Isichei 1977). But, with World War II and the wars of Indochina and Algeria where the French needed "qualified manpower" for their armies, Africans from the colonial armies were selected to join French forces and received a much superior training (Chaigneau 1984).

There was however, a common trait that would make a huge difference in the political development of most African countries. While southerners resented military recruitment, northerners seized the opportunity to become "évolués" (emancipated) (Decalo 1968, 1970a, 1970b, 1973a, 1973b; Eleazu 1973). Southerners counted on education and assimilation, while northerners sought military service to escape the domineering ethnic groups of the south (Bebler 1973; Chipman 1989).

Overall, French "Armies of Africans" were of considerable support and help to France. At the end of the conflicts in Europe, those soldiers were discharged and returned to their respective countries where they would confront some of the very problems they had tried to avoid by joining the military, including domination and imposition by Southerners (Carbett 1972; Andereggen 1994). Besides the regional or ethnic factor (Finer 1967), there was also a generational issue at stake. While older recruits praised France, younger ones displayed a clear disdain towards "*La Métropole*" (France) (Cornevin 1981).

Upon their return to Benin, these officers waited for the opportunity to strike. Before being sent back to their countries, the servicemen enjoyed higher standards of living in Europe. When they returned home, a change in their lifestyle became inevitable, and it would not take too long before signs of frustration appeared (Decalo 1996, 100). Yet, they resisted any outright display of anger and dissatisfaction. In the meantime, civilian leaders struggled to start the post-independence rebuilding process. Between 1960 and 1972, six military coups due to several factors, including ethnic rivalries, economic mismanagement, and political "rectifications."

The Military Coup of 1963

When the first military takeover occurred in Benin in 1963, several observers saw the coup as either the result of personal ambition or ethnic rivalry (Decalo 1976; Bebler 1973; Terray 1964)). In reality, that intervention reflected both, as well as the incapacity of the new civilian leadership, which had failed to engage the country on an adequate development path.

In contrast to other African countries, Benin did not have a single charismatic nationalist leader (Cornevin 1981). On the eve of independence, three main leaders with backing from their respective regions: Hubert C. Maga from the North, Justin T. Ahomadégbé from the Center (Abomey) (Decalo 1990, 94-99), and Sourou M. Apithy from the South (Porto-Novo). Although Dahomeans had voted "Yes" to remain within the French Community, local pressures and events in Anglophone countries forced Dahomean élites to declare their intention to leave the "framework of the Community" (Decalo 1968).

Since all three political leaders had a solid control over the votes of their regions, any coalition or partnership required negotiations. In what seemed to be a "two-against-the-third" scenario, Maga and Apithy emerged as winners of the December 1960 elections (Decalo 1990, 96-97). That coalition of the North and the South obviously annoyed the Center, which expected the common root of Abomey and Porto-Novo to come into play. However, the rivalry between the two sister kingdoms overshadowed their common heritage (Glèlè 1969).

In that political atmosphere, Ahomadégbé was arrested in May 1961 for allegedly plotting against the government. Although he was released in November 1962 for "good behavior," his very arrest was seen as a humiliation for the *Fon* (royal blood) of Abomey. That feeling was even shared by the army officers, creating a perfect opportunity for the army hierarchy made up with mainly *Fon* officers (Cornevin 1981; Martin 1986).

In the wake of widespread urban unrest against the excesses and corruption of the Maga-Apithy regime, two specific incidents triggered a great deal of resentment: the overspending on the presidential palace in Cotonou at a time of fiscal austerity (Finer 1967, 493), and the Bohiki affair (Glèlè 1969; Decalo 1990, 1995). While the first issue, exorbitant spending over the office of the president, generated anger given the sacrifices and sufferings the austerity program subjected the populations to, the Bohiki problem took the insensitivity of the regime in place to a higher level (Decalo 1973).

Although Christophe Bohiki, a parliament member of Maga's ruling party was accused of the murder of Daniel Dossou (an activist of Apithy's party), the National Assembly refused, under Maga's order, to lift Bohiki's immunity so that he could stand trial (Decalo 1995, 92). Because the victim was from Porto-Novo, ethnic strife burst out in that city and even the belated decision to bring Bohiki to trial could not appease the crowds. During those events, Apithy, the partner and Vice-President of Maga, felt obliged to support his base, further straining the relationship between himself and the President (Glèlè 1969; Ronen 1975, 191-2). The whole affair, quite legalistic in nature, was exploited for political purposes with heavy ethno-regional overtures appropriate to the Dahomean political scene.

Taking advantage of the tense political situation, the *Union Générale des Travailleurs du Dahomey* (UGTD), the trade union, a staunch supporter of Ahomadégbé, demanded the abolition of the five percent austerity tax. Before Maga's obstinacy, the union demanded his resignation, and staged massive demonstrations as well as a general strike (Onwumechili 1998, 43). Since no action was being taken, the army, conveniently, moved in and dissolved Maga's regime on October 28, 1963. General Soglo's military coup opened the door to political instability in Benin (Cornevin 1981).

The Military Coups of 1965

After the "October Revolution," Soglo asked Apithy and Ahomadégbé to form a coalition government to address the urgent needs of Benin. The unanimous vote confirming this decision (Glèlè 1969; Decalo 1990, 1995), suggested that the population wanted some unity, between the two sister regions: the Center and the South. Unfortunately, that golden opportunity was lost when, the two rivals failed once again to reconcile their fundamental differences (Decalo 1973).

In the meantime, nothing seemed to be "calming the spirits" in the North. In retaliation for Maga's dismissal, several southerners residing in the north were harassed and killed. Those who were not killed found their houses looted. In the meantime, the overall economic situation did not and could not improve, simply because the two leaders were preoccupied with their petty squabbles (Glèlè 1974, 289-293). By June 1965, it became evident that something needed to be done if the government were to continue paying civil servants' salaries. In July, the government decided to increase the austerity tax from ten to twenty-five percent (Decalo 1990, 104). Under a different government, that decision would have been accompanied by a general strike. But, because of the amicable relationship between the union and the regime, the country swallowed that bitter pill without noticeable reaction (Godin 1986)).

Despite the favorable wind, President Apithy and his Vice-President Ahomadégbé remained on different wavelengths concerning the direction Benin should take to resolve its problems (Decalo 1990, 103). Their antagonism reached its peak when the Vice-President pushed a bill through the National Assembly while Apithy was on a state visit in France. His refusal to sign said bill on his return prompted a serious constitutional crisis (Ronen 1980, 120). In spite of their common party's intervention, Apithy maintained his position and invited the military leaders to "take their responsibilities" (Decalo 1990, 103; Cornevin 1981).

Once again, Soglo demanded and obtained the resignation of both Apithy and Ahomadégbé on November 29, 1965 (Ronen 1975, 199). Following the provisions of the constitution, National Assembly President, Tahirou Congacou, was asked to assume the presidency. That provisional government was supposed to supervise the writing of a new constitution, but it never materialized. The population, disappointed by Apithy and Ahomadégbé, simply called for a military intervention (Decalo 1973a).

On December 22, 1965, Soglo unilaterally withdrew Congacou's mandate and assumed full powers (Onwumechili 1998, 43). His government of "technocrats" included another *Fon* officer, Colonel Philippe Aho and a cohort of civilians (Decalo 1990, 104). Before the failure of the stated goal of the new regime—to improve the economy of Benin—another coup became unavoidable.

The Military Coup of 1967

Despite widespread belief that General Soglo's government would redress the economic ills of the country (Ronen 1975, 202), the "technocrats" showed their hands when, rather than abolish or suspend the austerity tax, the new regime extended it to the private sector. With Ahomadégbé no longer involved in politics, the trade union was free to take appropriate measures (Godin 1986). Widely observed strikes and massive demonstrations forced Soglo to end his experience with technocrats. Through shuffling and reshuffling, seasoned politicians entered Soglo's cabinet (Decalo 1990). To guarantee the execution of government decisions and to carry out periodic examination of state institutions, the military formed a committee: the *Comité Militaire de Vigilance* (Ronen 1980, 122). That committee was composed of restless younger officers, who were very unhappy with the handling of accusations of corruption within the Soglo government (Lemarchand 1968).

With the continued deterioration of the economy, Soglo flew to France for help. When, on his return, he declared that "[he] did not come back empty handed," and raised expectations (Decalo 1968), wage earners read into that message, the end of the austerity tax. Unfortunately, their sense of relief was short-lived. The Finance Minister soon declared France's aid insufficient to abrogate the austerity law (Heilbrunn 1994). That declaration generated a strike by the teachers' union, which was followed by other corporations (Ronen 1975, 204). The government's maladroit handling of the early movement, when it arrested labor leaders, led to general social unrest (Cornevin 1968, 1981). Forced to retreat, the government freed the union leaders and promised to discuss the austerity issue with the workers (Decalo 1995). That situation sowed the seed of termination of Soglo's era.

Young officers of the *Comité Militaire de Vigilance*, who had been following the government moves, realized the time was ripe for them to act (Lemarchand 1968). On December 17, 1967, "the young officers of the army" took over. Led by Major Maurice Kouandété, a group of officers attempted to arrest Soglo when he escaped through a back door of the U.S. embassy (Decalo 1970). A month after their takeover, "the young officers" announced their government and their plan. A cabinet headed by Colonel Alphonse Alley (Decalo 1990, 102), announced that the military would transfer power to civilians within five months after the adoption of a new Constitution (Cornevin 1981).

After those requirements were met, the military decided to ban the three rival veteran politicians—Maga, Ahomadégbé, and Apithy—and their associates from running for the scheduled presidential elections (Decalo 1995, 7). Outraged, the former presidents called for the boycott of the elections, which were later declared unconstitutional by the Supreme Court. The military overruled the high court and proceeded with the elections (Genné 1978). After an obscure candidate from Abomey, Dr. Basile Adjou Moumouni, won the elections. Surprisingly enough, the military annulled the results of the elections, as if their "candidate" did not win (Onwumechili 1998, 43). They subsequently entrusted the reins of power to Dr. Emile Derlin Zinsou, another southerner (Decalo 1995, 7). By that time, tensions were rising among the "young officers." Those clearly in favor of a new head of state from the north resented Alley's attempt to place another *Fon* at the helm of Benin (Godin 1986). The internal dynamic within the military leadership prompted another coup.

The Military Coup of 1969

Out of the disgruntled officers, Major Kouandété, a *Somba* from the north, was clearly the most frustrated. So, it was not really a surprise when he decided to take matters in his own hands by staging another military coup (Onwumechili 1998, 43). However, his actions were neither mere ethnic retaliation nor a simple corporate adventure. President Zinsou could not escape the problems his predecessors faced (Decalo 1990, 114).

The new constitution sponsored by the military allowed the army to participate in the social, economic and cultural progress of the country. The new fundamental document also denied parliament members a salary (Cornevin 1981; Glèlè 1969, 1974), remunerating them instead for time actually spent in the Assembly. Despite the sense of a new beginning Zinsou's regime introduced, grim economic realities remained difficult to overcome. As a matter of fact, Zinsou's attempts to tackle these very problems resulted in his downfall (Decalo 1973a).

Included among his economic and fiscal measures aimed at balancing the budget, were new taxes that presented additional burdens for workers. His "backdoor" ascent to power and the ensuing resentment predisposed workers to be less tolerant vis-à-vis his regime (Godin 1986). Because of lack of support, and also due to pressure from politicians, the unions called for strikes and demonstrations to display the workers' anger. Within the army, rumors of coups and assassinations gained currency. All the preconditions seemed to be in place for a military action (Adjovi 1993; Welch, Jr. 1993, 81).

On December 10, 1969, Kouandété, and a very small clique of his, decided to end Zinsou's adventure. After a commando kidnapped the President and took him to the north, Kouandété simply put the majority of Benin army officers before a *fait accompli* (Decalo 1995, 7). On Radio Dahomey, Major Kouandété declared that "the Dahomean army, conscious of its duties, carries out once more its responsibilities and decides that Dr. Zinsou, President of the Republic, is relieved of his powers." To further justify the army's action he stated that:

> The Army entrusted the government of Dr. Zinsou in July 1968, to reconcile all the people of Dahomey [*tous les fils du Dahomey*] and to maintain the unity achieved by the Army. An objective analysis of the situation shows not only that the regime of Dr. Zinsou created total insecurity, but that he also deliberately abandoned the

guidelines set out by the proclamation of June 17, 1968, the task for which Dr. Zinsou was designated by the Army...In light of this situation the Army has, once more, assumed its responsibilities. (*Le Monde*, December 11-17, 1969)

He set up a temporary Military Directorate (*Directoire Militaire*) to lead Benin. But the Directorate's actions failed to save Benin from yet another coup (Bebler 1973).

The Military Coup of 1972

The *Directoire* was composed of the heads of the army (Kouandété), the *Gendarmerie* (Colonel Benoît Sinzogan), and the department of national defense (Colonel Paul Emile de Souza) who, because of his seniority, became the Chairman (Decalo 1995, 8). In its attempt to restore some normalcy, the Directorate invited the "old guard," Maga, Ahomadégbé, and Apithy, to participate in presidential elections (Decalo 1990, 108). The hope was that, after their experience, former political leaders would bind together to nominate one of them to run. Instead, all three former leaders, plus Zinsou, who was bent on vindicating his presidency, ran in the 1970 presidential elections (Decalo 1995, 8).

After passionate campaigns, the elections, marred by corruption, intimidation, and fraud, were stopped before any final result was given. That interruption of the electoral process provoked a serious crisis, since Maga, the apparent winner, threatened to lead the north to secede. Apithy also replied by suggesting the formation of a federation with Nigeria if Maga were to be declared the winner of rigged elections (Cornevin 1981; Decalo 1995, 8-9).

Faced with an extremely difficult situation, the Directorate urged the three main leaders to agree on a resolution of the crisis. But because personal ego and ambitions were at stake, the military suggested a rotational body to take over from the military. A first in Africa, a Presidential Council (*Conseil Présidentiel*) was formed as a compromise (Heilbrunn 1993, 1994). The two-year term started with President Maga on May 7, 1970. While the early part of his term was without major incidents, the last days were quite tense. By the time President Ahomadégbé took over on May 1972, the country was experiencing both economic and political difficulties. Within both civilian and military circles, a great deal of anxiety prevailed (Decalo 1973a).

By early 1972, two important mutinies had taken place within the army. While one revolved around several non-commissioned officers' demand that their commander be replaced, the other involved an attempt on de Souza's life (Godin 1986). As one of the main perpetrators of the second mutiny, Kouandété was sentenced to death. That judgment not only enraged the northerners in general, and *Somba* in particular, but also heightened tension within the army (Ronen 1975, 229). At the same time, civilians continued to display their inability to lead the country (Dossou 1993).

That and other reasons motivated the "young Turks" of the army to topple Ahomadégbé's regime. Led by a *Somba*, Major Mathieu Kérékou, the military ended the experimentation with a triumvirate on October 26, 1972 (Decalo 1990, 116-117). Allen describes perfectly the power struggle prevailing in Benin before the 1972 coup:

> As the instability induced by factional conflict within civil and military authorities prolonged itself, the bulk of the rural population, the urban workers and intelligentsia, and the rank-and-file in the army became alienated not simply from a given regime but from 'spoils politics' itself. The 1972 coup may be seen as an attempt to bring an end to spoils politics, and united the more radical among the junior officers in the army with union leaderships and the student groups based in the main towns. These groups saw the main defects of the former system as its elitism, its dependence upon and its subordination to France, and its elimination of political participation. (1989, 65)

That intervention, unlike previous ones, proved durable. If not for an economic downfall, the revolution might still be in progress (Laloupo 1992-1993). Besides injustice, torture, detentions without trials, flagrant human rights violations, declining living conditions made Kérékou's regime less and less bearable, making the military more amendable to the idea of a national conference (Adjovi 1993).

The Military and the National Conference in Benin

Contrary to expectations, Benin's second "October Revolution" came to stay. This coup turned out to be of a praetorian kind in that it marked the emergence of the armed forces as an autonomous political force, acting on its own and according to its own political vision. In the words of one *junta* member, Major Pierre Koffi, "this time the armed forces have assumed their responsibilities. We do not intend to give up power to anyone...we must have to show our abilities" (quoted in Martin 1986, 65).

Though one or two of the plotters were known to be favorably disposed to some members of the previous civilian triumvirate, and a few had acquired reputations as "conservatives" or "radicals," there was initially no indication that the coup of 1972 was any different from others (Decalo 1990, 117). However, an ideological militancy and a quest for a radical socio-economic change emerged very soon. It became gradually clear that this team, given the personalities of its leaders, and the nature of its early orientations, represented a radical branch of the army. The ideological stance of the new regime took Benin to the brink of economic and political bankruptcy (Decalo 1990, 119), and, ironically, brought it back to some sense of renewed hope. An understanding of the military's position towards the national conference can only be explained through the path of destruction taken by the leaders of the 1972 coup (Heilbrunn 1993, 1994, 1997; Adjaho 1992).

Although the main authors of the takeover were believed to be Major Michel Alladaye, Captains Janvier Assogba, Hilaire Badjogoumê, and Michel Aïkpé, Major Kérékou emerged as the leader. Besides his known stubbornness, nothing in Kérékou's past prepared him for a political career (Decalo 1990, 118). But the speech on political framework—*Discours Programme*—of November 1972 had a clear tone of radicalism that only the true coup leaders could have initiated (Martin 1986, 66). The new leaders intended to fight corruption, disorder, and inter-tribal rivalry. While they embraced a "new national independence," they denounced "foreign domination," and pledged to take Benin's economy to new heights (Heilbrunn 1994, 43).

The new military leaders seem, initially at least, to be motivated by the promotion of economic and social development of Benin, and Westebbe is accurate in stating that:

> After 1975, the process of transforming Benin into a mini Marxist state on the eastern bloc model began. The rationale was to use the state to promote the welfare of the people by preventing their exploitation by domestic and foreign capitalist interests. The objective was to accelerate economic growth and development by the state dominance of the means of production. Most formal sector activity was brought under state control, including distribution,

secondary-sector enterprises, and financial institutions. Public enterprises were created throughout the economy, with large industrial investments financed with foreign borrowing. (1994, 82)

Because they believe that economic planning would best achieve internally-oriented economic growth, Kérékou and his colleagues allowed the Beninese state an indispensable role in the promotion of entrepreneurs with policies. Unfortunately, their radicalism would blind their vision for a better society in Benin.

In the first two years of the *Révolution*, some hope remained that the radical rhetoric was just a façade that would be progressively reduced by economic realities. The decisive radical turn occurred in 1974 when Marxism-Leninism became the fundamental tenet of the new regime (Heilbrunn 1999, 47). In an eight-point speech delivered on November 1974 at Goho (Abomey), President Kérékou announced that Dahomey would follow a socialist path of development, with Marxism-Leninism as the guiding philosophy (Banégas 1997, 39). The country also got a new name, *la République Populaire du Bénin* (People's Republic of Benin), with a single political party, the newly-created *Parti de la Révolution Populaire du Bénin* (Benin People's Revolutionary party) (Cornevin 1981; Laloupo 1992-1993; Decalo 1995). In retrospect, that day tolled the death knell of Benin as a country with a viable economy.

As a socialist society, several fundamental changes became inevitable. The country experienced a huge wave of nationalization. The state monopolized of the means of informing and educating the citizens. A new school system, *l'École Nouvelle*, was to ensure an appropriate education to younger generations (Banégas 1997, 39). The renamed national radio, *la Voix de la Révolution*, and the national newspaper, *Ehuzu* (Change, in *Fon*), contributed to the drastic alterations within Benin's society. Even administrative and economic spheres were profoundly affected. Steps were taken to control the agricultural sector, primary industrial and commercial businesses, and the banking, trade, insurance and entertainment sectors (Martin 1986, 67).

Overall, the vanguard party and its leftist members reached its goal: a *Perestroika à la Béninoise*. There was an obvious concentration of power, with an organic fusion between the party and the government, and a high degree of militarization (Banégas 1997, 38). But, all along, very few military leaders were really involved in the restructuring of Benin society. Faithful to their leaders, who themselves trusted the "enlightened" civilian *idéologues* of the party, the armed forces simply supported the revolution (Cornevin 1981; Dossou 1993; Adjovi 1993). As an institution supposed to guarantee national integrity and order, the military was often called in to restore order. Despite the imposition of a single party a few pockets of resistance and resentment could be noticed within society.

One such rebel group was the National University of Benin, which battled the Marxist regime consistently to its very end (Decalo 1997, 51). In fact, a student movement prompted the massive demonstrations and strikes that took the country to a standstill in 1988. After several years of lonely challenge to Kérékou's power, the students started searching for means to widen their actions (Dossou 1993; Nwajiaku 1994). Ultimately, the decline of Benin's economic situation would help the students' case, allowing the whole country to demand fundamental changes.

After several months without pay, workers started paying some heed to the students' message: rise up to get rid of Kérékou and his cliques. The anger and resentment of the population increased both within civilian and military milieus. Sections of the military leadership blamed the civilians for taking the country to an economic dead-end (Decalo 1990, 122-123). The time was for decisions, rather than finger pointing. Consequently, both civilian and military *apparatchiki* embarked on the search for solutions to the drastic economic problems Benin was facing (Adjaho 1992). Clearly, the mood within the army ranks was one of frustration. The time was indeed ripe for a military coup, yet, the dynamics within the armed forces was not conducive to such an outcome. So, when Kérékou decided to convene a national conference, the military leadership jumped on the opportunity to rescue the country (Heilbrunn 1994; Nwajiaku 1994).

Although the decision to open up the political system came out of a meeting of the ruling party, the intention was rather to institute a merely cosmetic change. The military as an institution was feeling however embarrassed in light of Major Koffi's statement (Martin 1986, 65). Judging by the state of the economy, it is difficult to praise the "abilities" of the military. Everything seemed to have fallen apart around the armed forces, and resistance to democratization would have been illogical (Dossou 1993).

Despite the open and obstinate desire to remain in power displayed by civilian politicians, it is safe to speculate that the military leadership, beginning with Kérékou himself, was looking for a way out.

It became crystal clear that this time, no foreign aid would be forthcoming until some reforms were undertaken (Clark 1997, 23-34). Consequently, although the national conference stripped him of his powers, Kérékou, along with the majority of the army top brass, accepted the resolutions of the gathering (Laloupo 1992-1993). With that bold move, both the army in general, and Kérékou in particular, redeemed themselves, while at the same time allowing Benin to enjoy the peaceful democratic transition, neighboring Togo still seeks.

The Military and Politics in Togo

Until 1963, Togo had no formal army. As a mandate under the League of Nations, and then a United Nations trust territory, Togo possessed only a small force of *gendarmes* to maintain civil order, a police and a colonial army (Cornevin 1988; Heilbrunn 1994, 454). Although these forces were open to all, mostly northerners sought to join them to finally get an edge over the southerners. Besides escaping poverty, the colonial army gave northerners a perfect opportunity to level up socially with southerners (Decalo 1990, 217-218).

By 1963, what became the Togolese army included an asymmetrical regional representation, with eighty percent of northerners, giving a different twist to the traditional north-south cleavage (Decalo 1996, 48). That imbalance was increased by an influx of former soldiers, mostly northerners, of the French colonial army. At the end of the Algerian war, France demobilized several hundreds of Togolese enlisted men who came home, to seek employment (Decalo 1973a, 73).

Dispatched to Lomé by the French government, the unskilled former soldiers, unemployable and uneasy in the south, petitioned the Olympio regime for their integration into the national army. But Olympio rejected their request and harshly branded them as mercenaries for their activities in Algeria (Heilbrunn 1994, 456). His contempt not only for the establishment for regular armed forces, but also for *petits nordistes* (little northerners) became apparent.

He opposed enlarging the army for economic reasons,[1] and would rather entertain the idea of enlisting the mostly *Ewe* unemployed of Lomé. His anti-northern and anti-military attitudes reached their peak when he still rejected a counterproposal, requesting now for only sixty highly qualified men to be integrated into the army (Decalo 1996, 6). In the meantime, the Army commander, Major Kleber Dadjo, a *Kabiyè*, favored the expansion of the armed forces (Decalo 1973b; Decalo 1990, 218; Heilbrunn 1994, 458). Left with no choice, the veterans staged a mutiny that turned into a tragic coup d'état.

The Military Coup of 1963

While Olympio disliked the army, probably because of its ethnic configuration, the largely *Kabiyè* army also despised him. Besides the army, the general population, including *Ewe*, resented his social policies. With a background as the financial officer of the United Africa Company (UAC) in Togo, Olympio imposed a program of fiscal austerity on the population, in order to become economically as well as politically independent from France (Heilbrunn 1994, 398).

At an early stage of his presidency, he also alienated himself from former advisers and friends by relying exclusively on his own opinions. His authoritarian tactics (Finer 1967, 504) also created a great deal of animosity not only within his close circle, but also within the army (Press 1999, 86). Against the suggestions of several advisers, he persisted in his position and denied the veterans' petitions, becoming consequently the roadblock that needed to be removed (Decalo 1973b, Heilbrunn 1994, 457).

When the rumor of a coup, or at least a mutiny, started circulating, Olympio refused to lend it any credibility. As a strong believer of a docile army, under the control of civilians, it did not occur to him that the ex-soldiers had no choice but to get rid of him (Onwumechili 1998, 53). What began as a mutiny quickly became a military coup. The coup began with fake telephone calls to Olympio's ministers, convening them to an urgent cabinet meeting that January 13, 1963 (Decalo 1990, 213).

All but the ministers of Information and Interior responded and found themselves kidnapped by the ex-servicemen who had secured weapons through their contacts with the standing army (Heilbrunn 1994, 458-459). The plotters were a group of six men, none in active military service, operated under the leadership of Sergeants Emmanuel Bodjolle and Étienne (later Gnassingbé) Éyadéma, who assaulted Olympio's residence. Confronted by the plotters, Olympio tried to escape to the U.S. embassy. During Olympio's flight, Éyadéma shot him in cold blood (Decalo 1990).

Following that tragic shooting, all former political exiles were invited back to Togo. Power was handed over to Nicolas Grunitzky, a southerner, who returned from Cotonou, Benin, as President and Antoine Meatchi, a northerner, who returned from Accra, Ghana, as Vice-President. Although the plotters wanted Meatchi to be President, French opposition to his nomination allowed Grunitzky to take the higher position. Most of the coup ringleaders, were not only integrated, but also received an immediate promotion to officer rank (Heilbrunn 1994, 459; Onwumechili 1998, 53).

The new regime, very similar to Olympio's, raised some eyebrows, since the northerners thought that their time has come to be in control of Togo. The military did however tolerate the new cabinet, probably knowing that it was too diverse ideologically to withstand the test of time. Despite the rhetoric of "national reconciliation" (Agblemangnon 1966, 76), Grunitzky's indecisiveness exacerbated obvious factional and personal infighting. Without any significant power base on his own he failed to fulfill his mission as a conciliator. Ethnic, regional, ideological and personal tugs-of-war, resulted more often than not in stalemates (Cornevin 1988; Decalo 1990, 207).

But, the army was not immune from ethnic cleavage either. A long-standing disagreement between Bodjolle and Éyadéma resurfaced. The rumor of Bodjolle's attempt to tip off Olympio during the coup, was finally resolved by Bodjolle's ouster from the army (Decalo 1990, 218), which left Éyadéma as the *de facto* military leader. The army commander, Dadjo, although the highest-ranking officer in the army, had no real control over the forces (Decalo 1973b, 77).

Grunitzky's difficulties also stemmed from the fact that he had to placate his "sponsor," the military, by accommodating their demands. With increased financial difficulties, the civil service that had suffered from a major compression of wages under Olympio's regime, began to grow restless. Despite an across-the-board increase in wages, followed by a ten percent cut in government officials' salaries, union leaders demanded better living conditions. Union grievances rapidly built up in 1965, and were aggravated by the army's brutal dispersal of an authorized church service commemorating Olympio's death in Lomé (Heilbrunn 1994, Decalo 1973b).

This act radicalized the opposition movement. More demands had already been sent to the government when, in December 1965, the executive body decided to restructure and reclassify the entire civil service for greater efficiency and a more operating economy (Europa 1999, 3461). Such a move turned out to be a mistake. Because of strained relations between the government and workers, the latter assumed that the government decision was simply a punishment for their actions (Heilbrunn 1993, Nwajiaku 1994).

In retaliation, they called for a general strike that was averted through a combination of mutual compromises. But, these compromises only postponed the showdown, for the workers were determined to reach their goals. The government resisted any unilateral move by the unions, although Grunitzky and Meatchi disagreed on the strategies (Agblemangnon 1966, 121; Decalo 1990, 216; Heilbrunn 1994, 403-404).

By 1966, frustrations grew, while the friction at the helm of the government was increasing. An obvious fight within the government to win the favor of either Grunitzky or Meatchi was raging. Both the cabinet and the top echelons of civil service were polarized behind one or the other, with each group trying to embarrass and undermine the position of the other (Decalo 1973b, 80). As long as Grunitzky remained faithful to the army, he enjoyed the military support. Even after reductions of defense allocations and continued pro-south developmental policies, he was still supported by the armed forces (Decalo 1990, 219). His *faux pas* occurred with his demotion of the Vice-President Meatchi. After that act, his usefulness to the army came to an end and a military move became inevitable.

The Military Coup of 1967

Although a 1965 referendum had confirmed the Grunitzky-Meatchi coalition, and there were preparations underway for the merger of all political parties into a one-party system, political ambitions between both leaders sharpened (Onwumechili 1998, 53). Even the army was becoming polarized to the point where Meatchi's friends were trying to gain more support within the army. The latent crisis erupted in November 1966, while Grunitzky was in France for a medical check-up visit (Cornevin 1988, Heilbrunn 1994, 404). At a cabinet meeting presided over by Acting President Meatchi, Grunitzky's loyal Minister of Interior, Fousséni Mama, informed the cabinet that his forces had discovered that the anti-Grunitzky leaflets being distributed in Lomé were Meatchi's handiwork (Decalo 1973b; Decalo 1990, 216).

In an outrageous move, Meatchi denied the charges and dismissed Mama, precipitating a serious cabinet crisis. Upon his rushed return to Lomé, Grunitzky reinstated his friend, Mama, to a less important post as the minister of education. Given Meatchi's support within the army, and Grunitzky's own vulnerability, he could not purge his rival although it fell within his constitutional prerogatives (Onwumechili 1998, 53). That situation triggered massive demonstrations and open appeals by southern political leaders to march on the presidential palace. The *Ewe*, unhappy with Grunitzky's handling of the Mama-Meatchi crisis, called for the resignation of President Grunitzky, who had failed to remove his rival from his cabinet (Decalo 1990, 219).

On November 20, 1966, the situation reached its climax when elements of the armed forces took the national radio and assumed strategic positions around the capital, Lomé. But, a widely expected military coup never materialized. To the surprise of many, Éyadéma, instead, summoned the military to disperse the mobs and arrest their leaders. Through frenzied consultations with other ranking officers, Éyadéma gave Grunitzky more time to resolve the social unrest (Decalo 1973b; Heilbrunn 1994, 405). Unfortunately, the additional time did not improve relations between Grunitzky and the largely *Ewe* mobs. Adding insult to injury, Grunitzky made several belated moves, including repudiation of the moderates of his cabinet, and the removal of Meatchi's powers, which Éyadéma interpreted as an invitation to take over (Cornevin 1988; Decalo 1990, 220; Heilbrunn 1994, 405).

On January 13, 1967, a national holiday and the fourth anniversary of Olympio's murder, Éyadéma ordered Grunitzky's resignation and abolished all political parties and structures. He justified his acts by the high risks of civil war (Decalo 1973, 82). In Decalo's views,

> The 1967 overthrow of Grunitzky in Togo [cannot] be viewed as stemming solely from the very real failings of civilian rule. Grunitzky was very much a front man for General Éyadéma who had led the veteran's coup of 1963 that resulted in the death of President Sylvannus [sic] Olympio. With the rapid erosion of the few sources of support that Grunitzky did possess, Éyadéma had little choice but personally to seize power. The alternative – allowing the formation of a government by the only cohesive ethnic force in the country, the Ewes – was foreclosed all along since a prominent plank in their platform was the arrest and trial of Éyadéma for the murder of Olympio. (1973, 82)

An eight-man *Comité de Réconciliation Nationale* (Committee of National Reconciliation) was set up under the Chairmanship of Colonel

Dadjo. Despite promises of speedy elections and a new constitution, Éyadéma dissolved the new body, gathered all executive powers into his hands, and formed a government that lasted until 1990, when massive demonstrations forced political reforms through a national conference (Toulabor 1986; Nwajiaku 1994; Heilbrunn 1997).

The Military and National Conference in Togo

Actions of the military in Togo, an integral part of the old order, have disrupted the democratic process. The military found democratic reforms threatening and intervened several times in favor of Éyadéma's regime. The transitional government must manage a large, disgruntled army, which appears to be exclusively loyal to the *ancien régime* and its head of state (Conteh-Morgan 1997, 84). The institutional connections between the state, the army and the single party, conflict clearly with the requirements of the democratic process.

During his early years in office, Éyadéma surrounded himself with innovative technocrats and intellectuals, and gave them relative autonomy in their spheres of influence. Most of these technocrats were southerners who resented Éyadéma, but took some credit for Togo's the booming economy. Through an aggressive export-led economy and the nationalization of the phosphate industry, government revenues increased (Decalo 1990, 229). Éyadéma's regime found no difficulties meeting both civilian and military needs of Togo. As long as the population enjoyed a tranquil and happy life, the brutality with which Olympio was killed, and the identity of the person who pulled the trigger, were temporarily in oblivion. But all too quickly the good times waned when the late 1970s augured ill for Togo (Hodgkinson 1999c, 1096).

The early days of technocrats and intellectuals gave way to the appointment of relatives and political cronies. Mismanagement, embezzlement, and corruption marred the economy. And, since perpetrators of these economic crimes remained unpunished because of their political connections, they continued to damage Togo's economy bringing the country to its knees as public finances plunged and debts piled up (Decalo 1990, 229). While Togo hit bankruptcy and most citizens restricted their lifestyles, relatives and cronies continued to live beyond their means as long as they remained loyal to the system (Toulabor 1986; Cornevin 1988).

By the late 1980s, the southerners, frustrated by their replacement with northerners at the helm of most state enterprises, started displaying their anger. Southerners had never fully granted legitimacy to the Éyadéma's regime (Englebert 1999f, 1092), but only worked with him because it suited their interests at the time. Southerners started looking for ways to let Éyadéma know their feelings. Beginning with subtle requests to return to their previous position, the southerners' demands for political and economic reforms became louder (Heilbrunn 1993; Decalo 1990, 220). All of a sudden, Olympio's ghost started haunting the *Ewe* leadership. New momentum for a change in Togo's political scene coincided with the wave of democratization and events in neighboring Benin. After several years of economic mistakes and ideological myopia, civil society forced Togo to embark on a path of renewal (Dossou 1993; Adjovi 1993; Nwajiaku 1994; Robinson 1994).

Taking their cues from Benin, the political opposition of Togo, composed mainly of disgruntled southerners, organized a pro-democracy movement determined to change the political system within the country. Obviously, Éyadéma opposed any fundamental change. After several months of pressure, he became open to the idea of a national conference (Heilbrunn 1997, 230). Unfortunately, the military leadership as a whole was against any political gathering intended to alter Togo's political scene. The history of the relations between the army and civil society in Togo, and the mistrust and hatred between northerners and southerners, largely explained the reluctance of the military to convene a national conference (Clarke 1995; Decalo 1997).

From the birth of Togo's armed forces to its enlargement by force, the mainly northern components of the military have always been concerned about giving too much power to the southerners. They rightly perceived the democratic call as the *Ewe*'s way of getting even with the *Kabiyè*. Another serious concern of the military was the brutality with which it had been responding to massive demonstrations (Decalo 1990, 228). Almost as a private army, dedicated to the interests of Éyadéma and the *Kabiyè*, agents were constantly dispatched to severely repress any "subversive" actions, very common in the early 1990s in Togo, or Lomé specifically (Toulabor 1986; Englebert 1999f, 1090).

While the military never hesitated to use imprisonment, torture, and intimidation to reach its goals, the violence openly displayed by the armed forces in Togo had become outrageous (Decalo 1990, 229). Repressing the opposition only escalates the demands made by the southerners (Onwumechili 1998, 53). By 1991, the social unrest in Lomé exposed a clash between the army and civil society instead of an argument between a government and an opposition (Decalo 1996, 8). As a matter of fact, several high ranking elements of the army who happened to be from the south, have been conveniently replaced. They either died in the hospital of suspicious illnesses, or were sent into retirement. When Lomé erupted in turmoil in 1990, the military hierarchy saw the potential downfall of its "protector." Consequently, corporate interests demanded that all actions be taken to deter any opposition movement (Heilbrunn 1997, 228).

In the end, Éyadéma's yielded to the opposition's request for a national gathering to look into the economic and political problems of Togo against his inclination. Pressures, both endogenous and exogenous, required him to agree to the national conference. But, when the compromise between the government and the opposition broke down, due to the opposition's eagerness to reach its goals with or without Éyadéma's cooperation, the real intentions of the army and the government surfaced (Nwajiaku 1994; Heilbrunn 1993, 1994).

The military, following cues from the government and Éyadéma himself, simply threatened to shut down the proceedings, and did take actions to intimidate the Prime Minister elected by the conference. It became crystal clear that the military had never wanted a democratic transition in Togo, since it might have to answer some tough questions dealing with its past behavior (Heilbrunn 1997).

Endnote

[1] Olympio cited the wasteful nature of military allocations and Togo's severe budgetary constraints for his refusal of the ex-servicemen' request. See Decalo, Samuel, "The Politics of Military in Togo," *Geneva-Africa* 12 (1973), p. 73.

CHAPTER SIX

FRANCE AND DEMOCRATIZATION IN AFRICA

After so many decades of economic and political nightmares in Africa, democratization seems to have generated a great deal of hope for that continent's renewal (Ihonvbere 1998, 10). Western countries appear to have embraced political reforms conducive to economic transformation in Africa. This realization reflects itself a new orthodoxy in aid policy circles, which asserts a positive and complementary relationship between democracy and development. In an attempt to summarize the new links between aid and democratization, Robinson maintains that:

> The [North's] policy agenda emerged in the late 1980s in response to a changed global political context characterized by the ending of the Cold War and the diminished significance of superpower politics, and a series of political transition in Latin American, Sub-Saharan Africa and Eastern Europe. This was underpinned by a growing realisation that problems encountered in the implementation of structural adjustment policies were attributable to weak and unaccountable states, especially in Africa. Top-down development models were acknowledged to be successful development programmes, as well as an essential facet of democratic politics. Hence, there was a perception among Western donors that development assistance could be used to facilitate democratic political change, enhance civil and political liberties, and improve the functioning of government. Such concerns coalesced around three distinct sets of policies – democracy, human

rights and good governance – which constitute the core components of participatory development and good government. (1999, 410)

Unfortunately, a reading of the "fine prints" does not tell such a straightforward story.

While Africans were fighting for the "second liberation" of their continent (Somerville 1991), some Western countries continued to pursue their own agenda. For example, although France finally joined the unstoppable wind of change in Africa, her initial actions and cues did not always convey a message of support for democratic renewal to the continent (Cumming 1995). In the era of democratization in Africa, France clearly faces a dilemma in its relations with neo-colonial Francophone states. Until recently, French policy on the continent revolved around various autocrats, displaying a "better the devil you know" attitude (Messone and Gros 1998, 143). Culturally, economically, militarily, and thus politically, the newly independent Francophone states remained bound to the metropolis, and successive French Presidents since de Gaulle have cultivated and even nurtured this sphere of influence. However, these corrupt autocratic regimes now face pressure from a civil society that France is unfamiliar with, or in some cases, very suspicious of. Under such circumstances, inconsistencies are bound to appear (Raynal 1991; Clark 1997; Messone and Gros 1998)

Depending on economic and political interests at stake, France wanted some countries to democratize while others could just "reform" or, put bluntly, pretend to alter their political systems. While Benin faced pressure to open up its political system, Togo's government seems to have enjoyed (and might still be enjoying) France's full backing to resist any democratic move. Despite her apparent elation at democracy on the continent, France, given her relations with, and her objectives in Africa, wanted and got democratization at two different speeds (Schraeder 1997, 149). Like in George Orwell's *Animal Farm*, although all countries must democratize, some must be more democratic than others.

France's Historical Ties to Africa

In the wake of industrial revolution, mercantilism, and rivalries in Europe, several European countries began the search for new markets outside their boundaries. Although there were earlier contacts between

Europe and Africa, the 15th century ushered a new era. With Portugal's first settlement in Ceuta, Northern Africa, in 1415, Europe's intention to create a commercial zone in Africa became unveiled (Ellis 1996; Fage 1995, 215). France joined the "feast," by establishing some trading posts through her "explorers." Gradually, these posts also became important centers for imperial objectives. During the early genuine trade, France's contacts with Africa remained limited. However, when the Americas were "discovered," France changed her strategies (Baba 1977; Conklin 1997, 1).

Beginning with the 17th century, circumstances encouraged substantial and sustained interactions with the Black continent. The need for slaves to work the farm fields in the "New World" gave a new momentum to French interests in Africa (Freund 1998, 40-41). Former trading posts rapidly turned into slave collection stations. Along the West Coast of Africa, several collection and embarkation points emerged: Gorée in Senegal, El-Mina in Ghana, and Whydah in Danhomê (Fage 1995, 265). Besides strategic Gorée, European powers fought commercial and other interests in West Africa. These positions also became important as staging points on the voyage around Africa to the Indian Ocean (Boggio 1992, 25, 27).

In 1638, the *Compagnie Normande*, a French charter company created under policies laid down by Richelieu, King Louis XIII's Prime Minister, established a small trading post (*comptoir*) on an island off the coast of Senegal. Although that first French settlement did not pose a threat, it did serve as a springboard for French colonization in Africa (Griffiths 1995, 27). In 1656, the settlement moved to the present site of Saint-Louis and became the first permanent European installation on the continent (Biarnes 1987, 33-44). Through a remarkable and crafty policy of assimilation, France aimed at transmitting her culture to Africans without their consent (White 1979, 12).

The philosophy of enlightenment (*Siècle des Lumières*) was an efficient tool of domination and acculturation. By the early 1830s, Saint-Louis looked more like a French city than an African town, due to a deliberate French migratory policy (Lewis 1965; White 1979). The residents of the city adopted a French way of life, described themselves as French (Andereggen 1994, 1). Up to then, French interests in Africa were still primarily limited to trade through *comptoirs* located along the banks of the Senegal River (Conklin 1997, 33).

In 1837, a French trader named Jaubert living in Gorée introduced the peanut as a viable cash crop. Although the original intent was simply to supply the soap-making industries in Marseilles (France), peanut became a secure source of income for Jaubert and other French traders. Jaubert's innovation brought more French to that part of Africa. But, France's control or formal colonization started only with the nomination of Faidherbe as a French administrator in West Africa (Cohen 1971; White 1979, 26).

During the Second Empire, France was concerned about the competition among European powers in Africa, and appointed General Louis Faidherbe as "Governor" of Senegal. With that energetic and imaginative young officer, France's stakes in Africa increased dramatically (Carbett 1972). He established a French protectorate over a third of Senegal, reorganized the administration in Saint-Louis more efficiently and founded a bank. More importantly, he recruited and formed a small unit of armed forces, the *Tirailleurs Sénégalais* (Senegalese Riflemen), who played an important role in the attainment of France's colonial policies in West Africa (Lewis 1965; Quantin 1982; Gaillart 1995).

Beyond simple conquest or imperial expansion, Faidherbe wanted to detour the traditional Trans-Saharan caravan trade in such a way that France could benefit from it. He also strove to take trade from British ports established on that same Senegalese coast (Freund 1998, 80). In his efforts, Faidherbe managed to reinforce the original French enclave known as the Four Communes: Saint-Louis, Gorée, Dakar, and Rufisque (Andereggen 1994, 2). In 1848, the inhabitants of these cities were granted full French citizenship. If not for a tenacious Al-Hadj Omar of the Toucouleur Empire of Ségou (Fage 1995, 338), Faidherbe would have reached his goal of monopolizing West Africa. He did succeed in establishing a few important *comptoirs* in other parts of West Africa, and is considered, arguably, the father of French West Africa (Cohen 1971; Freund 1998, 65).

By the Berlin Conference in 1884, France possessed several trading posts and strategic positions in Africa in general, and in West Africa in particular. At that gathering, European powers were asked to "pacify" their conquered territories (Griffiths 1995, 38). That "pacification," triggered several wars among European powers on the one hand, and between European forces and Africans on the other (Martin 1985). France's colonial "armies" set up by Faidherbe enhanced her ability to quell revolts and rebellions.

With an "effective occupation" of her claimed territories, France felt justified in her ownership of colonies (Fage 1995, 339). Convinced of the implicit superiority of their own civilization, the French considered the imposition of their culture on other ethnic groups as part of their responsibility towards humankind (Andereggen 1994, 2). *La mission civilisatrice*, or *la France d'Outre-Mer*, intended to absorb the colonies into the French system (Carbett 1972; Conklin 1997).

By the early 1890s, France's conquest renewed under the stewardship of Captain (later General) Joseph Gallieni. But France's methods closely matched Britain's (Fage 1995, 339). In a very tough competition, France and Britain divided up the continent. While France occupied large parts of commercially useless lands, Britain conquered much smaller but commercially more valuable lands (Coquery-Vidrovitch 1976). Through a very effective "divide and rule" policy, France controlled a vast area in West Africa—Senegal in 1890, Soudan (now Mali) in 1893, Dahomey in 1894, Guinea in 1898, Niger in 1906, Mauritania in 1910, and Côte d'Ivoire in 1914 (Lewis 1965; Conklin 1997, 23).

These colonies were organized as an administrative unit divided into subdivisions known as *Cercles* under a General Governor (*Gouverneur-Général*), whose office was first in Saint-Louis, before being moved to Dakar in 1904 (Conklin 1997, 23). Contrary to British entities, local legislative councils could not propose legislation to the French authorities. Through "direct rule," France controlled life entirely within her possessions (Fage 1995, 336-337). The General Governor oversaw the appointments of senior executives and controlled the defense forces, postal and telegraph services, public works, and sanitary services. Tax and other excise collection also fell under his sole jurisdiction (McNamara 1989; Tordoff 1997, 31-32).

With a potency that allowed him to ignore the decisions of the Federal Advisory Council—*Le Conseil du Gouvernement*—the General Governor stood at the apex of a highly centralized administrative pyramid (Andereggen 1994, 5). Politically, France took all necessary measures to impose and assure her influence and power over her colonies without, however, discarding the economic advantages of her imperialist acquisitions (Isichei 1977; Martin 1985; Conklin 1997, 23-37).

Economics drove the initial search for new markets and the main preoccupation of the French administration in *Afrique Occidentale Française*, during the colonial era was the development and exploitation of economic resources (Tordoff 1997, 30-31). Several railroads and roads were built to have access to mining areas and agricultural centers. France tried to make each one of her colonies specialized in one cash crop, probably in the name of comparative advantage, and the importance of that crop dictated whether and how fast a colony received transportation and communications facilities (Lewis 1965; Fage 1995; Freund 1998).

While peanut-growing Senegal received modern facilities very early, it took a few years before Soudan, a producer of cotton, saw any improvement in her facilities. As a matter of fact, given the considerable investments in irrigation before getting cotton in Soudan, France shifted her strategy, by making Soudan provide foodstuff for Senegal (Andereggen 1994, 8). Niger and Upper Volta were given the "duty" to produce cotton. Guinea became the haven of bananas, while Dahomey and Togo were assigned the "comparative advantage" of specializing in palm oil products. The only colony allowed to produce a variety of crops was Côte d'Ivoire, which developed coffee, cocoa, bananas and lumber (Conklin 1997, 30-31).

The relationship between France and her colonies was governed by a "colonial pact" (Thompson and Adloff 1958, 249). According to that pact, the "Mother Country" comes before anything else. The colonies were forced to finance the development projects through their own resources. Africans had to abandon their traditional economy and embarked on cash crop production. The welfare of the colonies and their peoples had never been high on France's agenda (Coquery-Vidrovitch 1976; Conklin 1997; Freund 1998). The colonies' interests were rather subordinated to the enrichment of French companies that linked African economies to the metropolis. France even stimulated the economic activity of these companies through governmental subsidies intended for the purchase of African crops (Carbett 1972, 85-86).

The companies took advantage of government restrictions on the importation of goods manufactured outside France into French West Africa by sending the major share of their profits back to France. Overall, the market between France and her colonies was strictly protected by tariffs, quotas, and exchange controls, which only benefited France and her companies (Cohen 1971; Carbett 1972). France's commercial interest in Africa centered mainly around Côte d'Ivoire, Senegal, Gabon, and Cameroon, whose level of economic development offered attractive markets and investment opportunities. These countries provided the major share of French imports, while absorbing most of French exports to Africa (Staniland 1987).

As early as 1944, French colonial policy became unimaginative, illogical, and inconsistent. De Gaulle realized that the status of colonized countries would have to be greatly altered. After several years of hesitation, the *Loi-Cadre* was passed in 1956 to give semi-autonomous status to African territories, "balkanizing" and dividing up West and Equatorial Africa (de Lusignan 1969, 17). Faced with Africans' dissatisfaction with this political scheme, France proposed a new structure of a "fraternal and egalitarian Franco-African Community." According to the new proposal, "the right of states to some self-government was solemnly declared, but only in relation to internal matters such as administration and the management of the country. All matters of external policy, such as foreign affairs, defense, trade and finance, were to remain the responsibility of France (de Lusignan 1969, 19).

Even these reforms did not extend far enough for some. Because of the "Independence Now" movement, the Community lasted only eighteen months. No sooner was it established than it needed "renovating," then disappeared. Even more vague forms of Franco-African cooperation agreements, lacking any precise legal basis, replaced the Community, maintaining on Africa, a French cultural dominance that lingers through today's *Francophonie*.

Besides cultural ties that still linked African countries to France, the currency in use in Francophone Africa provided the best tool for controlling the continent. Through the Franc Zone, a monetary cooperation arrangement, Francophone African countries agreed to hold their reserves mainly in the form of French Francs, and to execute their exchange on the Paris market (Martin 1985). In this essential unequal relationship, France simply continued to control the economies of these countries as it had before independence (Chazan et al. 1999, 422-23). Under colonialism, all French West Africa shared the franc of the *Colonies Françaises d'Afrique*—**CFA**—(French Colonies of Africa) (Tordoff 1997, 212).

After independence, France's persistent desire to maintain a colonial mentality towards her former territories became evident when the acronym **CFA** was maintained even if it now stood for *Communauté Financière Africaine*. Pegged to the French franc, the CFA was equal to 1 metropolitan franc by World War I (Martin 1986). But, gradually, the CFA's value became a multiple of the French franc. From the 50 CFA francs to 1 French franc up to January 1994, the devalued CFA is now changed to 100 CFA to 1 franc since then

(Griffiths 1995, 75). The fixed parity between the CFA and French franc gave the French government a great deal of control, and African countries seemed to be unaware of the importance of that currency, and its leverage within their economies (Cumming 1995; Marchal 1998). Along with bilateral aid to the former African colonies, France used the franc zone to impose order on the otherwise unpredictable economies. The newly independent colonies purchased this order at the price of economic and political dependence (Chipman 1989, 190).

Contrary to expectations, independence did not really alter the lopsided relations France established with her former colonies (Clapham 1996, 89-98). Through a web of connections and links, France granted a "dependent freedom" to her territories. A host of agreements and pacts (Luckham 1982; Tordoff 1997, 68, 184-185) simply prevented African countries from finding *Uhuru*.[1] Like children who refused to grow up, African nations continued to be controlled by their former master (Gardinier 1997, 9-20). Clapham describes well the specificity of the relationship between France and her former colonies:

> The complex of relationships between the Francophone African states and France formed by far the most comprehensive set of mechanisms for maintaining African states and their rulers, and had no equivalent either among the other colonial powers, or in the clientele networks established by the United States and the Soviet Union. These relationships, moreover, extended over a substantial part of the continent, including a continuous block of states from Mauritania to Zaire; taken together, the Francophones (including the three former Belgian colonies) accounted for eighteen of continental Sub-Saharan Africa's forty-two states, and for just over a quarter of its estimated half a billion people. They provided the clearest example of the external ramifications of African state security, and their implications not only for foreign policy but for the domestic structure of power. (1996, 88)

Although formally independent, African countries can hardly make any decision without consulting with the French government, a position that suits France's domination very well (Conklin 1997). In the early days of democratization in Africa, France joined the wind of change, "championing" democracy, while in reality, her position has always been dubious since colonization, to say the least (Dabezies 1992).

La Baule Conference on Democratization in Africa

A thorough understanding of the meaning of *La Baule*, requires a review of France's policies towards Africa from de Gaulle to Mitterand. With his concept of *La Grandeur de la France*, de Gaulle wanted France to maintain a close association with African countries (Lewis 1965; Freund 1998, 176). That association not only allowed a reliable source of crucial raw materials, but also offered markets for goods and investments. Thanks to his charisma and skills, the General managed to create personal relationships with most Francophone African leaders. His father or godfather image portrayed him as caring and dependable (Andereggen 1994; Tordoff 1997, 262).

Not only was de Gaulle "helping" with the economies of these countries, but he was also directly involved in their internal politics by "suggesting" candidates for cabinet and other high level political positions to African Presidents (Freund 1998, 195-198). At times French civil servants were filled positions normally reserved for Africans. In the views of Chazan and her colleagues:

> De Gaulle's cult of national dignity and presidential authority appealed to many of the leaders of fragile newly independent states. Gaullist France cultivated this affinity by supplying the technical advisers and teachers that these new governments needed to build a stable apparatus and provide basic services. The French astutely named this dependent relationship "*la coopération*;" it assumed the flow of French goods into these markets and protected the environment for French capital investment. (1999, 423-4)

To maintain secrecy, several African leaders had European secretaries to assure the loyalty of Francophone African leaders (Bach and Kirk-Greene 1993). De Gaulle even created the *Ministère de la Coopération et du Développement* (Ministry of cooperation and Development) to oversee relations between France and Africa.

This policy extended beyond de Gaulle's regime as his successors, Georges Pompidou and Valéry Giscard d'Estaing, brought no structural change in France's policy toward Africa. Within the Gaullist tradition, they simply expanded the French sphere in Africa. Pompidou even kept an influential de Gaulle aide, Jacques Foccart, to ensure continuity of de Gaulle's aims in Africa (Gardinier 1997, 18). He also gave France an additional important control mechanism, known as the Franco-African summit, which proved crucial to setting up the French agenda on the continent (Chaigneau 1984; Bayart 1995).

Giscard's policies, while not off de Gaulle's track, took a still more personal touch. Given his new web of friends on the continent, Giscard was quicker to intervene in internal conflicts in Africa (Tordoff 1997, 184-185; Gardinier 1997, 18). His involvement in former Zaire and Central African Republic to repel a rebel invasion in Katanga in Zaire, and to help remove Bokassa from power, initiated a new French attitude in Africa. Giscard enlarged the Franco-African family and revived proposals for an Afro-European solidarity pact and a pan-African intervention force (Andereggen 1994, 80). Clearly, France's policies *vis-à-vis* Africa from de Gaulle to Giscard were never been concerned with democracy or democratization until François Mitterand became President in 1981.

Faithful to the election manifesto of the French Socialist party, which called for a new and closer rapport with Africa, Mitterand intended to establish relationships between France and Africa on a more integrated, egalitarian basis, devoid of nationalist and racist distinctions or elements of metropolitan exploitation (Clark 1997, 34). The Socialists clearly wanted to revolutionize Franco-African dealings. In 1990, Mitterand enthused about democratization in Africa when he said: "the wind blowing from Europe has begun to sweep Africa." (*Business Day*, February 14, 1996). However, Mitterand and the Socialists realized that a core to the Franco-African relationships must remain unaltered. According to a 1983 observation of the editor of *West Africa*, it quickly became evident that Mitterand's government shared "the idea that France's high profile in Africa should be maintained" (quoted in Chazan et al. 1999, 426). With a great deal of maneuvering, *La Baule* Franco-African Summit made democracy a new item on France's political agenda in Africa (Chafer 1992; Clark 1997, 34). However, France's position on the continent remained unchanged. In fact, Mitterand's *status quo* position is well expressed by Chazan and her colleagues:

> In practice, little changed under Mitterand, who himself had long been involved in the Franco-African network. Indeed, he had served as Minister of Overseas colonies during the Fourth Republic and had been instrumental in forging an important parliamentary alliance with Houphouet-Boigny in those days of shifting governmental coalitions. Although Mitterand talked of innovation,

he took care to reassure France's longstanding African partners. (1999, 427)

Mitterand's personal relations with African leaders and his involvement in African affairs dated back his tenure as Minister of Overseas colonies. In 1951, he convinced Houphouët-Boigny of Côte d'Ivoire to break with the French Communist party and join his *Union Démocratique et Socialiste de la Résistance* (UDSR) in the French Assembly (Mundt 1997, 184; de Lusignan 1969, 62). He also had a close friendship with Léopold Sédar Senghor. But, Mitterand was closely associated with the Franco-Algerian war. As the Minister of Interior during that infamous war, Mitterand made painful and memorable decisions (Andereggen 1994, 107; de Lusignan 1969, 63).

After the end of the Algerian conflict, Mitterand searched for redemption, and becoming the President of the French Republic was going to give him the long-awaited opportunity. With the help of his first Minister of Cooperation and Development, Jean-Pierre Cot, himself an anti-colonialist and strong advocate of human equality, Mitterand's rhetoric of radical change in Franco-African relations became crystallized (Gardinier 1997, 18). Cot, a self-portrayed *tiers-mondiste* (Third-Worldist), wanted a "moralization" of aid programs to African countries. Despite his determination, Cot was still aware of the importance of Franco-African relationships, and had to be tempered by political realities in France (Marchal 1998).

In the meantime, the Socialists' ascent to power in France generated great expectations within the opposition movement on the continent. Mistakenly, many opposition leaders saw in Mitterand the end of paternalist Gaullist policies of intervention in Africa (Gardinier 1997, 20). What they failed to take into account is that there have been, and remain traditionally "loyal" countries in Francophone Africa that France is not willing or ready to sacrifice on the altar of democracy. Because of this and other political and economic realities, it took Mitterand ten years (1981-1991) to finally demand some accountability from African leaders (Martin 1983, 1985).

As the thawing of the Cold War brought new issues to the development debate, topics such as human rights and democracy gained unusual importance on donors' agendas (Hyden and Mukandala 1999, 14). In the wake of events in Europe in the late 1980s, the World Bank, the IMF, and donor countries made clear that future aid would depend on "good governance" and respect for human rights (Tordoff 1997, 137). According to Westebbe:

> *Governance*, in the Bank's parlance, meant (1) improving public sector management in order to raise returns to investment, reduce poverty, and achieve growth, (2) increasing economic and financial accountability, (3) enhancing predictability and the rule of law, particularly as they effect business and redress of the public sector abuses, and (4) developing information and transparency to promote private sector efficiency and as safeguards against corruption. (1994, 90)

In his attempt to describe the new attitude in foreign aid policy, Robinson states that:

> Donor policies on democracy and good governance are relatively recent in origin and are still undergoing a process of evolution. Despite attempts to formulate a common interpretation, participatory development and good governance (PDGG) embraces a wide variety of policies and programmes, and official donors vary considerably in the emphasis they give to PDGG policies in their overall aid strategies and country programmes. Aid donors employ a number of different mechanisms to implement such policies, which range from punitive approaches based on aid conditionality through the more positive forms of assistance designed to strengthen political institution and groups in civil society. Moreover, since PDGG policies focus on domestic policy issues which are politically sensitive, there is potential for conflict between competing aid objectives on the part of individual donors and between recipient governments and donors. (1999, 408)

Alluding to the "field" of governance, Hyden maintains that:

> The connection between governance and development is relatively recent. It has taken analysts quite some time to accept that development involves more than choice of technique or even policy and is explicitly political. Development became an internationally recognized concept in the 1950s when economic analysts, spurred by the success of Keynesian interventions in the economies of postwar Western Europe – the Marshall Plan being the single most important such measure – began generating a new field within their discipline called "development economics." In the perspective of these economists, development in the emerging states of Africa – as in other parts of what subsequently became known as the "third

world" – would be best achieved through transfer of capital and expertise. This philosophy prevailed in the last days of colonial rule and the early years of independence in Africa. Because analysts perceived development as largely a replication of Western experience in compressed time, they treated is as relatively easy and non-controversial. (1999, 180)

In early June 1990, British Foreign Minister, Douglas Hurd gave a speech in which he linked economic development to "good governance" (Olsen 1998, 343). According to Hurd, "economic success depends extensively on the existence of an efficient and honest government, on political pluralism, and ...respect for the law and free and more open economies" (Olsen 1998, 343). During that same month, the traditional Franco-African Summit held at *La Baule* in France, gave Mitterand a golden opportunity to imply that, in the future, France would be less liberal in granting assistance to authoritarian regimes unwilling to make progress toward democratization (Olsen 1998, 344).

Although nervous about the new wind of political change in Africa, Mitterand joined the universal call for democracy on the continent. Unfortunately, at the same time, several senior French politicians continued to reminisce about the Africa that France had always envisioned (Gardinier 1997, 17). Mitterand's successor did very little to change France's relations with Africa, as described by Chazan and her colleagues:

In 1995 the Gaullists returned to power with the election of Jacques Chirac as president. Over his many years in government, Chirac has cultivated plenty of ties with Francophone leaders, and he devoted his first major trip to Africa in order, as he put it, to "listen to" France's friends in Africa. Officially committed to the support of democratization across Africa, Chirac's France, like that of Mitterand, comfortably accommodated a wide range of regimes old and new in the post-Cold War environment. Despite speculation in the early 1990s about a declining French role in Africa – and despite occasional disagreements among the Ministry of Foreign Affairs, the Ministry of Cooperation, and the presidential African bureaucracy over specific policies. France has retained a broad political consensus that its role as a major power in world affairs is rooted in Africa. (1999, 429)

In February 1990, while Benin's national conference was in session, Jacques Chirac, current French President and former mayor of Paris, who was attending the conference of Francophone mayors in Abidjan, Côte d'Ivoire, conveyed a contradictory message to Africa (Clark 1997, 34). In remarks that sent shock waves through three continents, Chirac characterized multipartyism as a "political error" for developing countries. To him, poor countries could ill-afford the luxury of democracy, which distracted them from economic growth (Robinson 1994, 585). Obviously, he meant to support his "friend" Houphouët-Boigny, who suggested democracy within the one-party system. But in reality, Chirac's views also exposed the true nature of what Bayart (1984, 140-5) calls the "politics of Franco-African hegemony."

Regardless of how much rhetoric is uttered regarding democracy in Africa, the continent unfortunately remains subject to a set of complex relationships involving French and African leaders (Heilbrunn 1997, 229). Through circuits of information and the financing of electoral campaigns in France, African rulers play a crucial role in French politics. In return, key French political players influence many important decisions affecting Africa (Robinson 1994, 585).

In the early 1990s, democracy seemed to have gained momentum in international development, to the point where the Treaty of the European Union, the Maastricht Treaty explicitly calls attention to democracy as an important aim of development of the Union (Gardinier 1997, 17). This new concern was also displayed in the Lomé IV Conventions between Europe and ACP (African-Carribean-Pacific) countries. Article 5 of the new convention states:

> Respect for human rights, democratic principles and the rule of law, which underpins relations between the ACP States and the Community and all provisions of the Convention, and governs the domestic and international policies of the contracting parties, shall constitute an essential element of this Convention. (Olsen 1998, 344)

Assessed in the light of the rhetoric, there seems little doubt that European powers wanted change in Africa. They intended to promote democracy. But, at issue is the type of democracy they want to initiate (Clark 1997, 26-27). From the situation in Algeria to the dubious attitude vis-à-vis democratization in Sub-Saharan Africa, it is however difficult to credit Europe in general, and France in particular, with a genuine intent to see a democratic Africa. What seems to matter is not true democracy, but, rather, "stability" (Gaillart 1995; Schraeder 1997; Gardinier 1997).

As long as African leaders maintained "good and loyal" relationships with France, they remained in power, even if they were undemocratic. The contradictory position of France towards democratization in Benin and Togo, unfortunately confirms the arguments of realism and neo-realism within international relations theory that international behavior of states is still based on national interests, irrespective of international changes and/or rhetoric (Waltz 1979; Buzan, Jones, and Little 1993; Viotti and Kauppi 1990). While socialist or totalitarian Benin was made to democratize, authoritarian Togo could "reform."

Democratic Reforms as a "Requirement" in Benin

Traditionally, France has "made" and "unmade" governments in Africa. To defend her interests, France had staged several coups d'état on the continent. In the early 1980s, when it became apparent that Bokassa of the Central African Republic no longer helped France's case, President Giscard, a "hunting buddy" of Bokassa's, did not hesitate to send in a unit of French paratroopers to effect his removal (Gardinier 1997, 18). French authorities since de Gaulle have always been adamant about the privilege to install and remove leaders. They were, therefore, seriously frustrated when the "October 1972 Revolution" occurred with little input from France (Martin 1986, 65).

At first, the 1972 coup seemed to be as nothing more than the latest of Dahomey's periodic military interruptions (Decalo 1997, 46), and France accepted the *fait accompli*. But soon, it became clear that this military takeover was far from being ordinary. The new government set out to "revise" the *"Accords de Coopération"* between France and Benin. The military regime viewed the April 1961 *Accords de Coopération* as the fundamental expression of Benin's bondage to France and wanted to sever them (Ronen 1975, 164-5). The desire to loosen ties with France could not have been clearer.

The army in Africa was not known to have an ideological stance, or the capacity to stage a coup for purely political reasons. The literature on military coups in Africa always cited reasons other than political to justify military interventions on the continent (Luckham 1994). Consequently, France expected the new military in Dahomey to simply list their grievances against the civilian regimes, and to promise a return to "normalcy" within months (Decalo 1990, 100-101).

At the outset of the 1972 revolution, however, the new leaders showed their hands, with a *Discours-Programme* that gave a clear sense of things to come. In addition to law and order issues, the military emphasized radical change. (Martin 1986, 65). In their program, the military squarely put the blame for Benin's misfortunes on foreign domination, According to the new leaders:

> [T]he basic characteristic and the prime source of [their] country's backwardness is foreign domination. The history of that domination is that of political oppression, economic exploitation, cultural alienation, and the blossoming of inter-regional and inter-tribal contradictions. (Ronen 1980, 133)

Even after the new leaders' program became known, France still hoped to curb the military leadership's ideological trend. An interview given by Kérékou in June 1973 could have given false hope to French authorities. In that interview, the new President stated:

> Our earnest desire is that the Dahomean revolution be authentic. It should not burden itself by copying foreign ideology. You see, we do not want communism, or capitalism, or socialism. We have a Dahomean social and cultural system, which is our own. (Quoted in Ronen 1980, 133)

This statement did not, however, quell France's anxiety. The Marxist Republic of Congo remained too fresh in the French authorities' minds, making them determined to prevent another radical revolution in another former French colony (Decalo 1986a, 39-57). Unfortunately, their apprehensions were justified when, on November 30, 1974, the new leaders proclaimed socialism for Dahomey. In Kérékou's own words:

> Some of our fellow countrymen can say that Marxism-Leninism is not an authentic Dahomean doctrine. Such people are only deceiving themselves because Marxism-Leninism comprises universal laws...relating to the struggles of mankind and radical transformation of the world and its societies, in order to completely eradicate the exploitation of man by man. (Quoted in Ronen 1980, 135)

African military Marxism is essentially an indigenous mutation of community life, and conceptually, it may be characterized as the radical pole on the continuum of "African Socialism." In Decalo's words,

> Tempered by pragmatic, parochial and system-unique considerations, constrained by existential domestic or international realities, narrowly circumscribed by the imperatives of continuing dependency relationships with the metropolitan powers, the global market economy, producer prices and sources of international risk capital, and watered down with the passage of line, the *practice* of African Marxism –disencumbered of esoteric adornments– appears at times as a relatively uncontroversial blend of *etatism* and cultural nationalism, albeit couched in Marxist jargon. (1986a, 131-2)

To add insult to injury, the revolutionary government outlined an eight-point program that clearly intended tomeant to remove Dahomey from France's *pré-carré* or *domaine réservé* (Tordoff 1997, 68). The measures supposed to eradicate foreign domination completely from Dahomey included the revival of Dahomey's culture, languages, and traditions. When, in November 1975, Dahomey was re-christened the People's Republic of Benin, the military leadership had completed the process of radicalization (Martin 1984; Decalo 1990, 120).

By June 1975, the educational system had been profoundly altered to reach pre-established goals. New curricula were introduced to bring about a new society devoid of French influence (Decalo 1990, 117). Through the *École Nouvelle*, new authorities intended to create an educational environment conducive to deeper knowledge about Benin and her peoples. The mass media under government control served as propaganda instruments in calling for a truly independent Benin (Dossou 1993; Heilbrunn 1994, 550).

In its zeal to transform society, the government also enacted administrative and economic changes. The administrative reform broke with the old French-styled system and granted greater social, economic, and cultural autonomy to local units, which were run by elected bodies and revolutionary committees (Martin 1986b, 66). On the economic plan, several foreign—mainly French—companies were nationalized, destabilizing relations between France and Benin.

The last blow came when the new authorities openly denounced France as the "foreign domination" they had alluded to all along. On the foreign policy front, the junta described its new diplomacy as one of rupture and independence (Decalo 1990, 118). Despite the nonalignment rhetoric, the new foreign policy was deliberately oriented towards socialist countries such as the Soviet Union, Cuba, China, Vietnam, North Korea and East Germany (Cornevin 1981; Martin 1984, 1986a and b). Benin managed to antagonize France on several issues, from the Soviet *rapprochement* to denouncing France's paternal attitude *vis-à-vis* Guinea. While it proclaimed solidarity with "progressive states and peoples engaged in the struggle for liberation," Benin distanced itself from traditional allies of regional groups such as *OCAM*, the *CEAO*, and the *Conseil de l'Entente* (Dossou 1993). In fact, a commission was appointed to review the agreements of economic, cultural, and military cooperation "with certain friendly countries," specifically France (Ronen 1987, 117).

By displaying open antagonism towards France, Benin alienated itself from the mother country that had been waiting for the opportunity to settle a few scores. So when Kérékou's regime broke down and was forced to turn to "imperialistic" France, his request was welcomed (Decalo 1997, 46-47). The French authorities used all means necessary to assure his departure. The involvement of the French Ambassador in Cotonou, Guy Azaïs, in the democratic movement in Benin was common knowledge to Benin's authorities (Adjaho 1992; Dossou 1993; Laloupo 1992-1993; Banégas 1997, 29). On behalf of President Mitterand, Azaïs made it clear to Kérékou that any financial support France was willing to grant was conditional on fundamental political and economic reforms. He presented the Kérékou regime with concrete proposals and steps to transform Benin into a democracy (Marchal 1998; Banégas 1997, 29).

Obviously, Kérékou would have preferred to resolve his mostly economic problems without being asked to engage in political reforms. He consequently turned to his "friends" within the socialist camp for help. Having failed to secure any financial assistance from that end, he turned back to Paris, agreeing, albeit reluctantly, to the terms of France's assistance. Benin's request for assistance, which followed Kérékou's scathing criticism, presented an opportunity for France to demand democratic reforms, which would certainly dislodge Kérékou's regime (Nwajiaku 1994).

Having shown his anti-France positions, Kérékou could not be allowed to continue "abusing" France with impunity. After several heated debates within the Political Bureau of the single party, the only choice left for Benin was to swallow the bitter pill France was prescribing, although neither Kérékou nor his cronies, envisioned such a radical change (Dossou 1993, 24). Benin, the *enfant terrible* (stubborn child), was clearly forced by France to democratize. In the meantime, Togo, the reliable former French colony, continued to resist democratization, defying civil society with the implicit, but unwavering, support of France (Heilbrunn 1997).

Political Reforms as a "Recommendation" in Togo

Despite the vibrancy of civil society in Togo, democracy has yet to come to life. France, the only power capable of inducing reform, lacks incentive to do so, simply because of strong and sustained relationship between Togo and the mother country (Andereggen 1994, 58). While France is forcing democratization elsewhere, fear of the unknown motivates France to salvage a loyal "friend." The history of the relationship between France and Togo explains France's wishes to keep Éyadéma in power.

After World War II, the two Togos saw a political movement, which, unlike the times of illiterate chiefs, was led by intellectuals making use of youth movements, political parties, and the press to convey their views. Along with the movements for *Ewe* national unity (Decalo 1996, 125) emerged other movements for the unification of Togo's two sections. Among the activists for the unification was a certain Sylvanus Olympio, who strongly opposed French intervention in Togo (Coleman 1956; Decalo 1990, 212; Heilbrunn 1994, 400).

With Nkrumah's help, Olympio hoped for a unified Togo until British Togo removed that hope by joining the Gold Coast following a UN-supervised plebiscite in 1956. In the meantime, the territory known as French Togo also changed its status (Decalo 1996, 6). In 1955, the introduction of a new statute and subsequent transfer of nearly all powers to a new government gave French Togo a large measure of internal autonomy (Chafer 1992; Englebert 1999f, 1089). France maintained control of defense, foreign affairs, and monetary policy.

Although, France strove to accommodate the wishes of the population of Togo by relaxing her policies towards the country, Olympio and others still called for Togo's independence (Cornevin 1988). So when the April 1958 elections for a new legislative assembly, held under the UN supervision gave victory to Olympio's party, the CUT, France viewed the results with apprehension (Decalo 1990, 212). A new era had been ushered in, and independence or *Ablodé*,[2] became the new *leitmotiv*. Two years later, on April 27, 1960, Togo was granted her independence with Olympio as the new President, much to France's displeasure (Lewis 1965; Carbett 1972; Martin 1983). Once in power, Olympio did very little to hide his feelings towards France. One of his first official acts was to start paying back Togo's debts to France. Regardless of the short-term hardships for the populations, Olympio sought to earn a "true" independence for Togo by honoring the country's obligations (Heilbrunn 1994, 398). Very early on, it became obvious that Olympio's eagerness to pay back France was simply due to his animosity towards the "Mother Country" (Austin 1963; Gaillart 1995). Olympio became a challenge that France had to defy, by all means. On the other hand, Olympio, unwillingly assisted France by antagonizing his former allies in Togo, imposing an austerity program on his compatriots, and denying former French servicemen an opportunity to be reintegrated in the Togolese military (Decalo 1973b).

Olympio's presidential style clearly undermined his abilities to govern effectively, and his economic measures, while keeping the budget within its limits, made the population miss the mandate era. But the refusal to take in ex-soldiers discharged by France made Olympio a prime target if France were to keep her control over her ex-empire of Africa (Decalo 1990, 213). Indeed, having been forced to grant independence to her former colonies, and with clear desire to maintain close relationships with them, the last thing France wanted was a rebellious African leader openly displaying his dislike towards her (Chipman 1989, 56). Olympio's death in 1963 came then as a relief to France. His successor, Nicolas Grunitzky, while lukewarm in his relations with British authorities, revived Togo's links with European powers, especially Germany and France. But the advent of Gnassingbé Éyadéma clearly gave a new momentum to the Franco-Togolese relationships (Cumming 1995, 71).

Unlike Olympio, Éyadéma had joined the French army and fought in Indochina and Algeria. His loyalty to France never wavered, and France welcomed his coups. After the first coup in January 1963, France wanted him to take control of Togo (Decalo 1990, 212). But the conditions were not yet ripe for Éyadéma to become President. He will have to wait for his "coup" in January 1967 to fulfill France's wish. Until the suspicious plane crash of 1974, France and Togo maintained exceptional relationships, marked by mutual respect (Conac 1993, 43).

The Sara Kawa accident, a suspicious plane crash, coincided with on-going delicate negotiations about the phosphate trade between France and Togo, and almost turned the exceptional relationships upside down. Upset by that event, Éyadéma nationalized the phosphate company and embarked on the *authenticité* – return to roots – road taken by Mobutu (Decalo 1996, 58-59). Since France could not afford to lose Éyadéma and vice-versa, other "loyal" African leaders such as Bongo of Gabon and Houphouët-Boigny of Côte d'Ivoire intervened to settle the differences between the Togolese President and French officials (Gaillart 1995, 67).

The renewed friendship between the two countries has been strengthened since then, and France refused to allow the new wave of democratization to damage several years of solid links. Éyadéma's position *vis-à-vis* democracy was well known to French authorities. His plan, similar to that of many other African leaders, was to create pluralism within the one-party system, and France raised no objection to that (Koné 1990). But when democracy became the new buzzword in international politics, France did not want to be left behind. As a country where democratic revolution occurred in 1789, France wanted to be seen as a pro-democracy power. However, the real goal was rather to force rebellious countries to democratize while permitting loyal ones to simply "reform" (Clark 1997, 97-122).

According to Bayart (1984, 31-48), Mitterand's first Minister of Cooperation, Cot, was asked to resign over Cot's insistence on exposing Éyadéma's human rights violations. His departure sent a clear message to those who still ignored the "special" character of Franco-Togolese relationships. On the eve of the democratization process in Africa, and after *La Baule*, France could no longer remain silent *vis-à-vis* the political situation in Togo (Bayart 1991; Olsen 1998, 344). Taking their cue from *La Baule*, the opposition movement in Togo increased its pressure on the government, taking any opportunity to raise the stakes. In a very deceptive move, Mitterand recalled his ambassador to Togo, Mr. Georges-Marie Chenu, apparently because of his closeness to Éyadéma, and replaced him with a more neutral and energetic Bruno Delaye (Heilbrunn 1997, 229).

Many perceived that move as France's desire to force Togo to democratize. But, what most observers ignored was the influence of Mitterand's advisor on African affairs, who happened to be his own son, and, a very close friend of Éyadéma's (*La Parole*, May 29, 1991). Neither father nor son wanted a truly democratic Togo, given the uncertainty of who might emerge as a new leader through democratic means. Despite that underlying position, Mitterand officially asked Delaye, to undertake the transformation of the political scene in Togo.

However, "Paristroika"[3] never materialized in Togo. According to several informants, Delaye's role in Lomé, unlike that of Azaïs in Cotonou, was to help Éyadéma more effectively silence the opposition, in which he succeeded very well (Heilbrunn 1997, 229).

After intense negotiations, Ambassador Delaye managed to bring the government and the opposition to an agreement about reforms and how they should come about. On June 12, 1991, both parties agreed on a national forum, which could suggest new measures for Togo's political and economic renewal (Nwajiaku 1994). But there was a catch in the agreement that the opposition failed to detect. The gathering should proceed, according to Éyadéma's and France's wishes, through a "quiet" conference that should reconcile the entire nation rather than divide it by "digging up" old dirt. The hard-liners within the opposition called for a real national conference to redress Togo's misfortunes. The debate was on when Mitterand sent a clearer message about his new conception on democracy (Marchal 1998).

In June 1990, Mitterand praised democratic changes in Benin as a model for reform in Francophone Africa and tied French aid to "movement towards democracy" at *La Baule*. However, his views changed unexpectedly the following year at *Chaillot* Palace in Paris, when Mitterand declared that France would not interfere in the political affairs of African states. He further stated that each African country must find its own "rhythm" for reform and political change (Saga 1991, 4-9). By a bizarre coincidence, in Lomé, the dissolved former single party of Togo, the RPT, was holding its congress. Both the newly elected Prime Minister, Koffigoh, who was at the *Chaillot* conference, and the Chairman of the national conference in Togo, Monsignor Fanoko Kpodzro, were shocked. As a matter of fact, the latter felt compelled to reiterate the dissolution of the RPT (Heilbrunn 1997, 238).

Outraged by that second "death" of the RPT, young members of the party and some security forces took over the offices of national television and radio. In every corner of Lomé, they harassed the opposition and their supporters (Legum 1998, B914). Using Mitterand's fresh declarations, Éyadéma's activists obviously created a chaotic situation that would require strong intervention by the army. Informed about his country's internal state, Koffigoh returned to see what could still be salvaged (Decalo 1996, 179).

Upon his return, he was taken hostage by a group of soldiers, who claimed to be acting on behalf of Éyadéma, and demanded both the "end of the transition," and Koffigoh's resignation (*Le Monde*, November 29, 1991). Confused and angry, Koffigoh, with Delaye's assistance, called on Mitterand to send troops in the framework of the defense agreement between France and Togo. However, Koffigoh's request was denied on the basis that only Éyadéma, as President, could make it. That position, also taken by French Ministers of Defense, Foreign Affairs, Cooperation, and Ambassador Delaye, allowed the "mutineers" to capture Koffigoh and take him to Éyadéma for "consultation" (Decalo 1996, 10).

Lomé erupted in violence and terror, forcing the French President to send French paratroopers to protect French citizens in Lomé. But once again, France's strategy became evident, if not awkward, when the troops supposed to be safeguarding French citizens living in Lomé were deployed to Cotonou, in Benin (Tordoff 1997, 185). Although the official reason cited was the security of Lomé airport, it became difficult to convince anyone that the troops were ever meant to be sent to Lomé. The very fact that they never set foot in Togo until the end of hostilities in Lomé speaks volumes about the undisclosed agendas (Marchal 1998). After a terror campaign, Éyadéma reasserted his full control over Togo. By September 12, 1992, when Koffigoh announced his new cabinet, influential members of the "defunct" RPT re-emerged in prominent ministries, which confirmed the return of Éyadéma's stewardship (Heilbrunn 1997, 239).

Frustrated, vulnerable, betrayed, divided, and powerless, the opposition in Togo was left with the only choice: to negotiate with Éyadéma as though there had never been a national conference. Scheduled for February 5, 1993 in Strasbourg, France, the first attempt at resolving the political crisis in Togo finally happened on February 8 in Colmar, Germany, under the co-aegis of Germany and France (Heilbrunn 1997, 237). Right from the beginning, Éyadéma's representative, the Foreign Minister, Ouattara Natchaba, challenged the modalities of the meeting, and blocked any genuine discussion. The German envoy, Minister of Cooperation Carl-Dieter Spranger frustrated, blamed France for a lack of enthusiasm for a peaceful resolution of the crisis. What Spranger did not realize, or was not prepared to state, was that France never intended to see any progress on that front. But the failure of Colmar did not end France's pretence to halt political chaos in Togo (Ellis 1995, 44).

Mitterand solicited Benin's help and a high level delegation went to Lomé,[4] with the hope of making a difference. However, both parties to Togo's crisis held onto their position and foiled Benin's efforts. By that time, Mitterand faced more pressure to keep his *La Baule* promise from both within and outside Togo, In the meantime, legislative elections in France brought to power the right wing, which had traditionally been a stronger supporter of Éyadéma (Heilbrunn 1997). With his new Minister of Cooperation, Michel Roussin, Mitterand looked for ways to end the stalemate in Togo. Mitterand approached the President of Burkina Faso, Blaise Compaoré, to serve as an intermediary, and the latter was pleased to be given an opportunity to alter his status on both regional and international planes. After his victory despite controversial elections in his country, Compaoré has been looking for ways to remake his image, and could not ask for a better occasion. Ouagadougou, the capital of Burkina, was therefore chosen for the next round of dialogue between Éyadéma's cronies and the opposition. For reasons still unknown, but easily imagined, Germany and the U.S. were given the observer status, and did not participate in negotiations. (Hicks 1992; Marchal 1998).

After several days of discussions, France made it known to the opposition that its only option was to cooperate with Éyadéma, and the "agreements" reached at Ouagadougou set up presidential elections for August 1993. But besides France's desire to force Éyadéma's "victory" through the ballots, nothing has been resolved in Burkina (Heilbrunn 1997, 240; Europa 1999, 3461).

Despite the Ouagadougou gathering, harassment of the opposition and human rights violations continued unabated and tension within Togo rose. Several opposition leaders remained at bay. Under these circumstances the Éyadéma regime proceeded with the presidential elections despite the opposition's boycott (Englebert 1999f, 1092). Two token candidates, Adani Ifé and Jacques Amouzou, served as opposition for Éyadéma's "competitive" re-election. With more than ninety-six percent of the votes, Éyadéma was easily confirmed. Several observers, including former U.S. President Jimmy Carter and the European Union's representatives, expressed shock that the results of the elections were even proclaimed, given the alleged irregularities (Englebert 1999f, 1093).

Despite these objections, Éyadéma took office, in defiance of the opposition and foreign observers. Worse, he continued to use the divided opposition to his advantage. After several feeble attempts at resolving Togo's political dilemma, France gave up, placing, interestingly, blame on the opposition for its intransigence. Guaranteed by France's position, Éyadéma now has no incentive to see the crisis resolved (Heilbrunn 1997, 240-241). In fact, he became so comfortable with the situation that he organized another presidential election following his controversial 1993 election. He managed to "win" again the June 1998 election, though the opposition claimed that candidate Gilchrist Olympio, one of Sylvanus' sons, was the real winner (Europa 1999, 3462). Once again, France's support made a huge difference. By endorsing the results of the election, France demonstrated that *La Baule* was more an empty preaching than a genuine intention to place Africa on a democratic path (Rijnierse 1993, 660). In addition to French political backing, Éyadéma continues to enjoy the support of international lenders. For example, in May 1998, the World Bank made a $17 million loan to the government of Togo, and the IMF announced plans for further financial assistance (Press 1999, 95).

Endnotes

[1] *Uhuru* means Freedom in Kiswahili.

[2] *Ablodé* means independence in the *Ewe* language of Togo.

[3] In allusion to Gorbachev's *Perestroika* (restructuration), several observers saw *la Baule*'s conference as *Paristroika*, a desire by Paris to impose a genuine political restructuration on African leaders.

[4] On December 14, 1991, Monsignor de Souza, former President Maga, and Foreign Minister, Theodore Holo were in Togo, attempting to resolve the political crisis between Éyadéma and the opposition.

CHAPTER SEVEN

INTERPRETATION OF FINDINGS

The inquiry into the military's role in democratization in Africa has revealed an inescapable problem: the relationship between law and norms on the one hand, and power and interests on the other (Glickman 1995). There are those who might argue that the current wave of democratization indicates an evolving global democratic culture and that great powers are helping to spread that culture (Conteh-Morgan 1997, 25). But at the same time, the process of democratization, its speed and outcome also depend on the interest and goals of the same great powers. While it is undeniable that some great powers want some Third World countries to democratize, others are not willing to let democracy supersede economic and political vital interests (Schraeder 1997, 146).

In an ideal world, one would expect that both Togo and Benin, given the rhetoric in *La Baule*, would embark on a truly democratic path. However, both political and economic realities dictate the pace at which France wants to see progress (Conteh-Morgan 1997, 26). However, external factors alone do not explain why Togo and Benin pursued two different routes to democracy (Nwajiaku 1994). Despite their similarities, these two countries possess different political cultures and their leaders have different stakes, explaining the divergent attitude held by their respective militaries (Conteh-Morgan 1997, 28).

The Culture of Politics in Benin and Togo

In examining the culture of politics, social science aims to link culture to causality. Pierre Bourdieu, in his *Outline of a Theory of Practice*, explained the connection by asserting that a society's political practices are molded by *habitus*, "a system of dispositions" which is "practiced, hired in and enacted" (Robinson 1994b, 52). While *habitus* cannot be viewed as immutable or timeless, it clearly impacts on the prospects for a democratic system. In fact, Diamond is right when he asserts that to "ignore the beliefs of the wider society is to fail to appreciate the considerable degree to which influence and pressure for action may flow from the bottom up, constraining élites and perhaps vitiating or undermining even their sincerely democratic inclinations" (quoted in Yoder 1998, 487). Democratic values and orientations necessary to a stable democracy reside in *habitus*, and divergent democratic outcomes in Benin and Togo suggest two different cultural systems (Yoder 1998, 487).

Without denying the impact of *Perestroika* or *Glasnost* on democratization in Africa in general, and in Benin and Togo in particular, the ability to capitalize on the wind of democracy that came from Eastern Europe requires a certain political culture (Eckert 1991; Conteh-Morgan 1997, 25; Mbaku and Ihonvbere 1998). Without a receptive environment, the mere blowing of a democratic wind might not alter the political conditions within a country. Just as democratic institutions rest on a healthy civil society, civil society in turn has precursors and preconditions at the level of culture. Phenomena such as family structure, religion, moral values, ethnic consciousness, civism and particularistic historical traditions all play an important role in whether or not democracy can succeed (Fukuyama 1995, 8).

Democratic societies obviously cannot survive for long if citizens do not view democracy as a legitimate form of government. As a link between the individual and society, "culture is the configuration of learned behaviour and results of behaviour whose component elements are shared and transmitted by the members of a particular society" (Linton 1945, 21). Although in basic agreement with Linton, Goodenough (1971) adds a nuance to the significance of culture to the individual. He states that "culture is a set of beliefs or standards, shared by a group of people, which helps the individual decide what is, what can be, how to feel, what to do and how to go about doing it." On the basis of Goodenough's definition, culture cannot be equated with the whole of one particular society.

As "incomplete or unfinished animals who complete or finish [themselves] through culture" (Geertz, 1973), the populations of Benin and Togo, evolved on different wavelengths due to their different historical and colonial experiences. From Robinson's emphasis on the cultural dynamics of democratization or the relationship between the culture of politics and regime change, culture of politics is defined as the "political practice that is culturally legitimated and societally validated by local knowledge," should lead us to understand "the changing meaning of politics and the cultural and social patterns that shape and reshape the basic character of political life" (Robinson 1994, 39). In terms of attitude vis-à-vis colonialism, the political culture of Benin diverges sharply from that of Togo (Cornevin 1981, 1988; Heilbrunn 1993, 1994; Nwajiaku 1994). As a set of rights and duties, culture engaged both countries on two different paths. Viewed as the tolerance for opposition, political culture means different thing to both peoples.

Resistance to European colonialism in Africa depended on the power of organized society to confront the colonizers (Fage 1995, 83-107). Conquering the *Malinke* of the Empire of Mali by the French had nothing to do, in terms of difficulties, with "pacifying" the various ethnic groups of Côte d'Ivoire (Lewis 1965; Freund 1998). Similarly, the British met more resistance from the Asante than they did from the Benin peoples. While Togo had various traditional chiefs and kings, the resistance of these monarchs did not equate with that offered by the much more powerful kings of Danhomê (Argyle 1966; Akinjogbin 1967; Glèlè 1969). The potency of the kingdom of Danhomê was actually demonstrated by Danhomê's control over most of Togo until a rivalry and competition developed between Dahomean and Asante kings over the territory (Baba 1977; Fage 1995, 350; Freund 1998, 45).

From its very inception, the kingdom of Danhomê asserted its authority over the "stateless" *Fon*. As the head of a centralized state, the king of Danhomê, "the ultimate owner of the land," introduced direct taxation on the produce of the land, which was only "lent" to its occupants (Boahen 1986, 83). Against their resentment, traditional village chiefs endured Danhomê's humiliation and imposition. Gradually, the resentment grew deeper and only compromises could allow Danhomê to continue its domination over other smaller chiefdoms (Cornevin 1981; Boahen 1986, 86).

Despite their inferiority in size and military power, these chiefdoms were willing to, and did, confront Danhomê, on the basis that no society should be under the control of any other group. The confrontation between Danhomê and its neighbors, incidentally, inculcated in Danhomêans a culture of resistance that colonialists did not expect (Coquery-Vidrovitch 1976; Fage 1995, 284). By the time the French ventured into Africa, Danhomê had developed a political culture of opposing higher authorities at various levels. The indigenous populations drew limitations on how far a monarch could go before encroaching upon their rights. It is therefore not surprising that colonization met fierce resistance from the very first day of its imposition (Lewis 965; Boahen 1986; Fage 1995). While neighboring populations always resented Danhomê's imperialism, they willingly joined hands with their eternal foe to repulse the French. In an unusual display of nationalism, Danhomê and its traditional vassal states confronted colonialism in a variety of ways. From the formation of secret societies to open clubs and *amicales*, all means were explored to counter Europeans (Corbett 1972; Boahen 1986, 87).

Although sheer military superiority played a role in "taming" the population of Danhomê, it did not stop the population from fighting for what they believed was right. Their opposition to French reform of the traditional chieftancy forced a new order, *arrêté* of 1929, allowing chiefs a greater voice in local affairs. The purpose of that *arrêté* was specifically "to hasten the political, economic, and social evolution of the country, and to give to the indigenous population a solid framework of command" (Heilbrunn 1994, 212). At various levels of social organization, the desire to confront or, at least to warn against mistreatment and abuses exhibit itself.

But while the early days of resistance took the form of direct and sometimes physical encounter with French soldiers, the resentment later took other forms. Political organizations translated heir message into the press. Newspapers played an important role in the nationalist movement (Boahen 1986, 134). As part of a propaganda machine, they helped the nationalist leaders reach and convey their message to a very receptive audience. In 1933, several newspapers circulated in Dahomey: *La Voix du Dahomey, Le Phare du Dahomey, la Presse Porto-Novienne, L'Éveil Togo-Dahoméen, Le Courrier du Golfe du Bénin, L'Étoile du Dahomey, and L'Écho des Cercles du Dahomey* (Heilbrunn 1994, 218).

As voices of dissent, these newspapers endured all kinds of obstacles from Europeans. First, only French nationals, as *citoyens* (citizens), were allowed to publish newspapers. A French merchant in Porto-Novo owned the very first newspaper, the *Écho du Dahomey*. Obviously a French-owned newspaper had a different objective than a Dahomean-owned publication that was more virulent and accusatory (Cornevin 1981, 56).

The role of the newspapers in generating political ferment in Dahomey became evident, and the French took note of that. As a matter of fact, Mr. Dubois, the chief of colonial security in Dahomey, was very adamant:

> There exists in Dahomey a secret association that includes several hundred members so cleverly organized as to allow them until now to escape the vigilance of local authorities, extend their influence throughout Dahomey and Togo, and even to France, Dakar, Niger and other foreign countries. This association is a Dahomean nationalist movement, clearly anti-French, and has infiltrated all administrative services to commit sabotage of the administration. The political objectives of this association have been at the origins of a systematic anti-French campaign led for many years in Dahomey and Togo... (Glèlè 1969, 62-63)

With their influence, the newspapers monitored the behavior of the colonial state. They also contributed to the birth of several unions that enabled territory-wide strikes, which paralyzed Dahomey (Lewis 1965; Heilbrunn 1994, 220).

In Togo, resistance to colonialism took a milder form for at least three reasons. First, the lack of a "hegemonic" group to impose its will on other smaller ethnic groups, seems to have created a culture of passivity. Although most chiefs resented both British and French powers, the kind of animosity against a domineering kingdom that existed in Dahomey, and fermented a rebellious attitude vis-à-vis the French, was simply not present in Togo (Boahen 1986, 140). Second, the transition from German colonialism to those of the British and the French did not help the Togolese populations focus on a single "enemy." Third, the political union suggested by French colonialism made some populations in Togo, identify with the struggle in Dahomey (Coquery-Vidrovitch 1976).

Unlike in Dahomey, Togo's newspapers abstained from the fight against occupation. The most vehement newspaper denouncing French colonialism in Togo was actually printed in Dahomey: *L'Éveil Togo-Dahoméen*. Dahomey's assistance also played a key role in the 1933 riots that sent a serious warning to the French. With the backing of Dahomean opposition Togo's *évolués* (intellectuals), organized a demonstration most massive than the French ever expected in Lomé (Heilbrunn 1994, 229-230).

In terms of tolerance of opposition, political culture in Benin and Togo got two different expressions. From Danhomê to Benin, through Dahomey, the concept had always existed, even if it has not always been admitted. In the days of the kingdom of Danhomê, the very nature of Danhomêan power made opposition inconceivable because of (Boahen 1986, 83-84). It did not, however, prevent neighboring chiefdoms from challenging the powerful *Abomey*, and the numerous wars between the kingdom of Danhomê and its vassals showed the resilience of these smaller entities (Glèlè 1969, 1974).

That period sent a clear message that any authority should expect and allow opposition both from within and from outside. The culture of opposition grew during colonialism, and, by the time Dahomey became independent, it had become practically impossible to curb political opposition (Decalo 1990, 92). On the eve of independence, several political groupings (parties, clubs and *amicales*) actively vied for control of power in Dahomey (Lewis 1965; Carbett 1972).

In Togo, political opposition never became an important issue. Since most chiefdoms had control over their subjects and any opposition was more internal dissent than a serious opposition to a leadership (Decalo 1996, 5). On the eve of its independence, French Togo had fewer parties than Benin: the *Comité de l'Unité Togolaise* and the *Parti Togolais du Progrès*, led by Olympio and his brother-in-law. These two political groups possessed few ideological differences, narrowing the political spectrum relative to Dahomey (Coquery-Vidrovitch 1976).

In terms of a set of liberties to act as they pleased, Danhomêans used political culture in a variety of ways. Before newspapers, unhappy populations used dance, songs, and popular spectacles to send their message to the monarch of Danhomê. Through their version of *baraza*[1] (Haugerud 1995), Danhomêans demanded political changes. The cultural belief in a right to open political expression continued through independence.

No post-independence leader has successfully banned newspapers, dance, songs, and spectacles in either Dahomey or Benin.

Any attempt by early leaders to restrict free press and speech was doomed to failure because both leaders and followers recognized the importance of these freedoms in their political culture (Lewis 1965; Boulaga 1993). Even under the totalitarian regime of Kérékou, which forbade independent voices, both Kérékou and his opposition faced leaflets and pamphlets. Other blatant displays of freedom of speech were the strong student demonstrations Kérékou's regime experienced from the late 1970s through the advent of a national conference (Heilbrunn 1994; Decalo 1997, 51). In Togo, the new leaders more easily controlled these freedoms. Olympio, bent on building "his" Togo, and with no real history of free press and speech, feared nothing by shutting down newspapers or pamphlets. And it is not surprising that Éyadéma displayed a clear abhorrence of independent newspapers, considering his performance. It took a great deal of courage and emulation for the opposition in Togo to start challenging Éyadéma's regime through what is known in most African countries as "seditious literature" (Nwajiaku 1994, Heilbrunn 1994; Englebert 1999f). As a matter of fact, the role of the leaflets in forcing Éyadéma to open up the political system cannot be overstated. Both students and opposition leaders finally understood the critical importance of forced "free press," and the result, though still imperfect, can testify to that (Clarke 1995, 251-252).

Different Stakes and Strategies

Although explaining the different outcomes of the national conferences in Benin and Togo is complex, there are at least two reasons why Benin was successful in turning its political situation around while Togo is still experiencing a political deadlock (Conteh-Morgan 1997, 26). Although both leaders dealt ruthlessly with the opposition, Éyadéma's role in Olympio's death makes leaving power very dangerous. On the other hand, Kérékou's handling of Aïkpé's death generated less hatred and a minimal desire for revenge (Decalo 1990, 216; Decalo 1997, 47). The other potential issue of the parallel outcomes of the two national gatherings is the strategy used by the opposition. In Benin, the opposition emphasized on getting rid of the defunct political system, and incidentally Kérékou himself, through a well-crafted strategy In Togo, the opposition was rather bent on liquidating Éyadéma, regardless of the means (Toulabor 1986).

Given the importance of the army in politics in both Benin and Togo, its composition and control have always been a concern to any leader. In both countries, northern ethnic groups dominate the army, which remained loyal to Éyadéma and Kérékou (Decalo 1990; Heilbrunn 1993). While the birth of the Togolese army might explain such a phenomenon, the army in Benin was not initially in the hands of northerners. Kérékou's coming to power, probably by design, ensured greater enlistment from northern ethnic groups (Cornevin 1981; Decalo 1990, 100-101).

By forcing the formation of an army in Togo, Éyadéma realized that he had to set up a military that could take his orders without question. That blind trust could only be guaranteed in a predominantly *Kabiyè* army. He did not take the risk of "filling" the army with just northerners. He made sure these northerners were from his own ethnic group (Decalo 1990, 220; Heilbrunn 1997, 228). The outcome of his "mutiny," Olympio's death, made the *Ewe* almost unwelcome in top positions within the army, and most southerners in high level in the military were "taken care of" during Éyadéma's tenure. By a bizarre coincidence, most southern officers of the army were either accused of involvement in "fictitious" coups, declared incompetent, or simply demoted (Cornevin 1988; Decalo 1990, 228).

With the army literally in his hands, Éyadéma retains control over both the armed forces and the security apparatus. His appetite for unshared power has only grown stronger because of effective harassment and deterrence of the opposition. Most of the numerous political crimes committed under the Éyadéma regime remain unaccounted for. Torture and other human rights abuses mar the political system in Togo (Heilbrunn 1997, 229). Very often, opposition leaders were sent to jail with no regard for due process. It is clear that the lack of checks and balances within the system, and also, the solid grip on the army, did not create an environment conducive to a genuine political pluralism (Toulabor 1986; Heilbrunn 1993).

In Benin, Kérékou also managed to create a northern majority within the army through a carefully designed plan. If not at the rank and file level, at least among the officers, the majority has clearly tilted towards northerners since Kérékou's taking over (Decalo 1990, 114). Although there was, initially, no reason to bring northerners in the army to match the southerners' supremacy, it became evident that to remain in power, as indicated by the military leadership in 1972, the army would have to take a shape and composition of unquestioned loyalty (Martin 1986, 65).

According to the new military leaders,[2] recruitment in the northern region remains the ideal scenario. In an extraordinary effort, high salaries and other benefits were used to attract northern intellectuals in the army. After a few years of training outside Benin, most of them returned with the rank of officer and took comfortable positions within the army hierarchy, serving as the bedrock of Kérékou's power (Decalo 1995; Decalo 1997, 57).

As in Togo, a firm grip on the army and state security organs only strengthened Kérékou's will to maintain himself in power by all possible means. The creation of a single party system signaled to those still in doubt that Kérékou intended to crush any dissent (Martin 1986, 67). Obviously, those who dared to challenge his power were treated "appropriately." Until the national conference, anyone opposed to Kérékou's regime was subjected to abuses of all kinds (Dossou 1993). There were several "special" detention camps all over the country to deal with dissenters. Students, teachers, and other citizens, associated or not with the *PCD*—Parti Communiste du Dahomey—(Communist Party of Dahomey), were sent to *Segbana, Parakou, Natitingou*, and other torture centers where political opponents were "brought in line" (Adjovi 1993; Decalo 1997, 51).

Another explanation for the different results in democratization in Benin and in Togo lies in the significance of Olympio's death in Togo, as opposed to that of Aïkpé's in Benin. While both of these events shook their respective countries, they never had the same meaning and importance (Decalo 1990, 1997). According to several accounts, Éyadéma is the one who shot Olympio during the fatal mutiny. The fact remains engraved in the southerners' minds in general, and in Olympio's children in particular. Either from Europe or from Ghana where they reside, Olympio's children threaten retaliation (Decalo 1973b; Europa 1999, 3461). Their resolve to make the "murderer" of their father pay back is a well-known refrain in Togo. As a matter of fact, there were several attempts (both genuine and staged) on Éyadéma's life and regime. Aware of this threat, Éyadéma has no incentive to relinquish power (Cornevin 1988; Heilbrunn 1997, 240).

Constrained by the wind of political renewal in Africa, and upon France's insistence, Éyadéma agreed to the principle of a national conference, knowing that he would not accept its conclusions should he be asked to step down. By pretending to favor a democratic change in

Togo, Éyadéma simply trapped the opposition that rose to the bait (Heilbrunn 1997, 241-242). Any excuse would justify the government's walking out of the conference room, and the declaration of sovereignty, against the June agreement, provided the best opportunity for Éyadéma and his cronies to retreat to their initial position: to keep the *status quo* (Tordoff 1997, 186; Heilbrunn 1997, 237).

In Benin, Kérékou's regime was confronted with the death of one of the initial instigators of the October 26, 1972 *Révolution*, the Minister of Interior, Captain Michel Aïkpé (Eades and Allen 1996, xxxviii). Since 1967, Aïkpé's influence within the army was well known. As a member and later Vice-President of the *Comité Militaire Révolutionnaire* that tried to supervise the policies of the government of General Soglo in 1967, Aïkpé held firm control over the *Comité* to prevent the northerners from monopolizing it (Martin 1986, 70). Already on bad terms with some officers from the north, his denying Major Kouandété total powers by supporting a three-man Military Directorate in 1969 did not improve his relations with the northern officers in the army. Against that background, he helped engineer the October Revolution and was put in charge of security (Cornevin 1981; Decalo 1990, 117).

His rising popularity created concern that his ascension might generate some fear and anxiety among the northern officers. But, nobody expected what happened on June 25, 1975. Out of the blue, a radio announcement conveyed the news of Aïkpé's death (Martin 1986, 70; Decalo 1995, 46). According to the official version of events, he was shot while having an affair with the estranged wife of the President (Eades and Allen 1996, xxxviii). Because the southerners refused to believe that justification of Aïkpé's death, massive demonstrations ensued. Trade unions and students took to the streets to demand a better explanation (Godin 1986; Decalo 1997, 51).

Unlike Éyadéma in Olympio's death, Kérékou was not directly involved in the murder of his Minister of Interior and Security. It was obvious that the assassins acted on his orders, and the social unrest was severe enough to reach the army. But Kérékou managed to bring the situation under control and has never been seriously threatened by supporters of Aïkpé. His regime was tarnished by that murder and to this date, no other explanation has been given to elucidate Aïkpé's death (Jouffrey 1983).

Another reason for Kérékou's willingness to sacrifice his cronies in accepting democratization Benin was his disappointment in his surroundings (Decalo 1997, 48). With an average education, he relied heavily on intellectuals, both within civilian and military leadership for advice. By the late 1970s, he started becoming uneasy with some of his close advisers, especially those from the south (Martin 1986, 74). His northern allies also failed him badly by the 1980s, and he could not convince them to change the course of events. According to witnesses and informants,[3] Kérékou made it clear to his ministers and members of the Political Bureau of the single party that he would have everyone pay for his failure (Adjovi 1993).

Consequently, when poor economic performance and other factors forced him to open up his political system, Kérékou seized the opportunity to redeem himself at the expense of his followers. In retrospect, his move to allow and accept the resolutions of the national conference was the best thing that could happen to someone whose catastrophic management took his country to an economic and political dead end (Adjaho 1992).

In terms of the different strategies explaining the different outcomes of the national conferences in Benin and Togo, the excitement to remove Éyadéma from power was overwhelming, as opposed to a strong but calculated desire to put an end to Kérékou's calamity in Benin. Unlike Togo, where the opposition managed to force the government to embark on a democratization path, Benin's government, under Kérékou's leadership called for the organization of a national gathering to discuss the serious problems facing the nation (Dossou 1993). There was never any agreement between the government and the opposition about the procedures and the conduct of the conference. It is once in place that the delegates realized what their best option at replacing Kérékou's regime was: to declare the sovereignty of their gathering in order to impose their conclusions on the incumbent government (Heilbrunn 1994; Decalo 1997).

The focus has never been on Kérékou as an individual, but rather on his political system. The representatives made a clear distinction between the man and his system, allowing them to attack the system without appearing to be attacking him. Although in the end the result seems the same, the strategy used in Benin camouflaged a direct attack and prevented both a potential war between the north and the south, and a serious conflict between civilian and military sections of the populations (Decalo 1990).

In Togo, on the contrary, the goal was clearly to put Éyadéma on trial. After several years of frustration, the opposition, made of mostly southerners, wanted to use the national conference as a forum to settle a few scores with Éyadéma. Not only did they want him to answer for Olympio's death, but they also deemed the time ripe to take their revenge on him for having belittled the southerners for so long (Toulabor 1986).

In that eagerness to reach their goal, they forgot an important compromise they made with him through the June 12 accord. That agreement stipulated how the conference should proceed, what should be covered during the gathering, and, more importantly, the form it should take. Having agreed in principle to the fundamentals of the framework agreement, the opposition failed to keep its part of the bargain by declaring the forum sovereign (Heilbrunn 1994).

According to several opposition members, they intended to put Éyadéma before the *fait accompli*, forcing him to step down. But, the opposition's blunder is that it failed to take into account the composition and the loyalty of the army. Although there was never a real and genuine intention to democratize, if the opposition had played its hands differently, maybe, things could have turned out differently. The opposition had been betrayed by its own zeal, and its myopia to realize not only the importance and loyalty of the army, but also France's double talks (Schraeder 1997).

France's Policy of Double Standards

After several decades of firm control of African politics, European powers discovered that only "good governance" and "democracy" could help the beleaguered African countries escape their misery (Hyden and Mukandala 1999, 14-15). With the focus on characteristic virtues of democratic governance – transparency, responsiveness, accountability, official propriety and tolerance (Luckham and White 1996, 3) – democratization became an important item on the agendas of Western nations. Donor approaches fall into two broad categories: those which use aid as a lever for pressuring governments to opt for reform, and policies founded on positive measures. The first generally takes the form of political conditionality, where donors suspend, reduce or terminate development assistance pending improved performance on a range of PDGG indicators. The second hinges on a more supportive approach in which aid donors seek to strengthen an ongoing reform process through carefully selected projects and programs. However, while the end of the Cold War permitted former colonial powers to sing the new tune of "democratization" (Baynham 1991a) and to proclaim a "new" aid policy, the sincerity of Western nations' intention to see democracy take hold in Africa has been called into question because of national interests (Conteh-Morgan 1997, 26; Whitehead 1996, 270-271).

And indeed, France's attitude *vis-à-vis* the political situation in Algeria, and her position in the democratization process in both Benin and Togo, suggest a gap between the theory and practice of democratization in Africa (Allison 1994; Marchal 1998). Since the term of President de Gaulle, France acted as a provider of legitimacy to its former colonies, and both incumbents and their opponents in Francophone Africa factor this variable into their political calculus, as most take their cues from Paris (Messone and Gros 1998, 142).

Undoubtedly, the international community seems to be rejoicing at Africa's emerging democracies, in the hopes that democracy's new dawn on the continent could help change the course of Africa's recent history. The change from a bipolar international system to a multipolar one has opened the way for the introduction of issues such as human rights and democracy to the international aid rhetoric (Conteh-Morgan 1997, 161). However, there is hardly any coherence in foreign aid policy. While some view the lack of coherence over objectives, approaches and delivery mechanisms as a source of poor implementation (Robinson 1999, 425), the fact remains that policy incoherence could also be part of a deliberate strategy reflecting the stake or goals set up by donor countries.

Both bilateral and multilateral actions were ostensibly geared towards democratization. The promotion of democracy and observance of human rights became so important that even the European Union tied its aid to democratization efforts in Africa. In 1993, Hans Smida, the head of the Directorate General VIII in the European Commission, with responsibility for development aid to Africa emphasized that:

> the Community's support for the democratisation processes in Africa is a practical illustration of its determination to make the promotion of human rights and democracy one of the linchpins of its development. (Quoted in Olsen 1998, 345)

In the academic debate following the proclamation of the new political agenda of aid conditionalities, a number of motives emerged to explain the *raison d'être* of these new conditionalities. One argument suggested that introducing democracy and human rights as conditions for aid would ensure a continued minimum of popular support for aid in the donor country, since development assistance had lost most of its political rationale with the thawing of the Cold War (Lancaster 1993; Conteh-Morgan 1997). Another motive was allegedly to establish a set of politically acceptable arguments for cutting aid, now that aid no longer serves its former political and security purposes (Olsen 1998, 346). But, it could also simply be that the euphoria following the fall of the Berlin Wall led to a somewhat arrogant belief that Western political values were the "best" (Fukuyama 1992) and should be exported anywhere, anyhow and at anytime.

Another parallel debate in the literature on foreign aid relates to the motivations of state actions in the form of aid. For several years, one prominent trend in this debate has used a two-model explanation of the motives of bilateral donors: the "recipient needs" model and the "donor interest" one (McKinlay and White 1978; McKinlay and Little 1979). According to the second model, donors are motivated by economic interests such as trade and investment interests, security interests, political interests including stability and possibly democracy (Tordoff 1997, 136-137). On the other hand, the "recipient needs" model relates to the economic and social development of the poor countries measured by the level of real income, or alternatively measured by the growth rate per capita GDP in real terms or the ratio of current account deficit of the balance of payments to GDP and population size (Chalker 1994).

Although there are only a few studies on the aid motives of the European Community, Bowles (1989, 31) concluded in a study that donor interests have been far more important than recipients' needs. It has also been demonstrated that countries' behavior within the Community was different. The influence of the member-states is unequal, and France is by far the most influential member within the development aid system of European Union (Chipman 1989). Another study confirms this conclusion, which emphasizes the difference between the European countries as far as aid motivations are concerned. That study showed that French aid is almost exclusively donor interest driven whereas Dutch aid was almost totally determined by recipient country needs (Grilli and Riess 1992).

France's position as the most influential member of the European Union should be of little surprise, given France's openly stated desire to dominate both Europe and Africa. It is obvious that France has been forced to go along with the Union most of the time in order to avoid being seen as a dissenter (Gardinier 1997, 20). However, the reality is that the Union's agenda cannot supersede France's, and democratization is a good illustration. Despite the "positive" attributes of democracy, France is not ready to sacrifice her interests on the altar of democratization, and Algeria and Togo's current political situations demonstrate the shortcomings of France's policy (Schraeder 1997; Clark and Gardinier 1997).

While what happened in Algeria in 1992, exposed not only the insincerity of Western nations' rhetoric of democratization, but also France's obstinacy in seeing democratization move at France's chosen speed. In the new mood of political reforms, Algeria embarked on a democratization path. Given the recent past of the country, Algerians saw in the new move, a chance to turn things around. They went to the polls and voted for a new regime (Alam 1986; Riley 1992, 539).

Unfortunately, their choice shocked both Algerian and French authorities. The first round of parliamentary elections gave a clear majority to the "Islamic Fundamentalists," which both Algerian and French governments found unacceptable (Riley 1992, 540). Consequently, and with no apparent alternative, the second round was called off, and since then an open war has been going on between the government and the "Fundamentalists" (Stromberg 1996, 141). The strong belief in democracy simply vanished when it became apparent that the government might take an "Islamic" turn, the issue of "security" took precedence over considerations about the development of democracy (Conac 1993).

Referring to the misguided fundamentalist or extremist concern in the West, Falk shed some light on why countries such as Algeria are turning towards the "wrong" way:

> In North Africa…grassroots support for Islamic orientation toward political arose out of disenchantment with secular government, its corruption and indifference to the plight of the poor. Islamic groups often delivered social services in local communities of the poor, thereby winning support of many people and fulfilling, to some extent, the mandate to promote social and economic rights, especially the provision of the basic necessities of life. We [the West] cannot grasp the success of fundamentalist political if we do not also appreciate the failures of secular politics. (1995, 105)

Although, there were recent controversial presidential elections in which Abdel-Aziz Bouteflika became the new President of Algeria, nothing guarantees security in the country, and the defiance of the "Fundamentalists" is not a good omen. If the goal was to ensure security at the expense of democracy, France might have miscalculated her moves, since Algeria, like Togo, enjoys neither security nor democracy (Conteh-Morgan 1997).

The tide of democratization reached Africa's shores, and Togo was not spared. France seemed to require all African countries to reform their political systems if they were to continue maintaining good relations with France. However, the special relationship between France and Togo clearly put Togo on a different footing. As a member of the French *pré-carré* (closed circle) in Africa, France sacrificed democracy (Andereggen 1994, 137-138). Regardless of the rhetoric within the international community, powerful nations continue to be guided by their national interests (Schraeder 1996, 146).

There was a great deal of expectation that France, the country that had experienced an important revolution in 1789 should take advantage of the wind of change to help finally bring a new era in Africa. That belief was bolstered by France's declaration at *La Baule*, which was interpreted as a genuine intent to contribute to the restoration of democracy on the continent (Clark 1997, 34). But, unfortunately, a year later at *Chaillot*, African leaders received a reality check, when France brought a very important nuance to her position.

Having linked any further aid to democratization a year earlier, France, subsequently recommended that African countries follow their own pace of democratization. In other words, the first injunction to reform was replaced with a tremendous amount of flexibility, creating a great deal of confusion. On September 30, 1999, both the Togolese government and the opposition met in Lomé to end their tug-of-war. After several hours of discussions, both sides agreed on how future election results should be proclaimed. However, the absence of a representative of Gilchrist Olympio's *Union des Forces du Changement* does not bode well for the political future of Togo (*Pana News*, September 30, 1999).

The "Military" Society's Difference in Benin

By now, it should be apparent that the success of the national conference in Benin is primarily due to the cooperation of the military.

But, while that cooperation might appear mystical, a closer look at Benin's history and politics can explain why the leadership of the armed forces chose the path of conciliation (Heilbrunn 1994; Decalo 1997). While the traditional role of the military within the population in the kingdom of Danhomê could justify the military's posture (Glèlè 1969, 1974), the growing dissatisfaction within the modern Benin's army called for a different type of relationship between civil society and the armed forces (Cornevin 1981).

From its inception to its apogee, the kingdom of Danhomê has always counted on the military to achieve its goals: conquest and control of smaller chiefdoms. Even female regiments, the *Amazones*, were called upon to contribute to the rise of the kingdom. But the armed forces enjoyed a very peculiar status (Boahen 1986, 86; Fage 1995, 342). Without formal barracks, soldiers lived among the population as ordinary citizens in time of peace. With hardly any difference between the military and civilians, there was a strong bond between the two spheres of the populations. As a matter of fact, the military and the intelligence service relied heavily on the civilians to accomplish many of their duties (Smith 1976).

Out of pride and loyalty, many Danhomêans were willing to play the role of scouts in potential vassal chiefdoms. As traders in these entities, unsuspecting civilians could and did provide valuable information to the kingdom and its army (Potholm 1979, 13). Because of the recognized importance of the civilian contribution in conquering other territories, civil-military relations had a different character. The deliberate blend between military and civilian populations dictated friendlier and less adversarial relations (Coquery-Vidrovitch 1976).

Within the kingdom, a symbiotic rapport existed between the armed forces and intelligence community on the one hand, and the ordinary citizens on the other. While defending the kingdom and preventing any subversive activities, the military managed the crucial link between the ruler and his or her subjects, by maintaining cordial relations with the population (Hull 1980, 26).

The reign of a vicious king by the name of *Adandozan* (1797-1818) came to an end because of his deliberate attempt to alter the relations between civilians and the military (Glèlè 1969). Before his cruelty and authoritarianism, and especially his orders to bring the civilian populations to their knees if they refused to pay their taxes, his entourage staged the first "coup" in the kingdom of Danhomê (Decalo 1995, 23). In a clear display of resentment, a rival royal group, with the support of the military leadership, simply removed *Adandozan*, and replaced him with *Guézo* (Argyle 1966).

Whether it is in the kingdom of Danhomê, or in the Republic of Dahomey, the military chose to be by the civilians' side on several key occasions. Although it later on turned into a military chaos, the first coup of 1963 was more to support the civilian demands for a different type of regime (Ronen 1980, 117-119). To some extent, even Kérékou's regime was first viewed as a salvation, given the political confusion Benin was going through. But the military's participation in the national conference resulted from another important factor, the dissatisfaction within the army (Adjovi 1993; Dossou 1993; Clark 1997, 26).

By the 1980s, the configuration of Benin's armed forces had changed dramatically. From a mostly southerner-controlled army, the leadership of the military started taking a northern "pigmentation." Incentives of all kinds encouraged northerners to join the army, and that change of equilibrium created an initially contained, but later diffuse, disenchantment within the ranks of the armed forces (Decalo 1997, 57). With more northern intellectuals in the army, most scholarships for advancement based on exams and tests went to them, at the expense of the mostly illiterate southerners. Consequently, while the northerners rapidly climbed the appropriate ladders and joined the rank of officers, most southerners remained at the Non-Commissioned-Officers (NCOs) level (Cornevin 1981; Decalo 1990, 213).

In the meantime, Kérékou's revolutionary regime was using officers in key positions within the government. Consequently, northerners, either civilian or military, enjoyed a prominence clearly resented by southerners. Despite the pivotal role played by southerners in bringing down the *Conseil Présidentiel* in 1972, the government was literally taken over by northerners, according to most southerners (Dossou 1993). Some southern military officers contemplated a coup to rectify the northern bias of the regime, but ultimately, rejected that option because of its likely failure (Laloupo 1992-1993).

Nevertheless, the gap between the south and the north within the army continued to grow, generating obvious frustration among southerners. It was therefore a big relief when the idea of a national conference to redraw the political framework surfaced. According to some informants,[4] the national gathering was viewed by southerners as the best option to redress several years of control of the country by northerners (Adjaho 1992; Dossou 1993). A hidden agenda was set up, and a rare collaboration between military and civilian authorities from the south dictated that the national conference should be held. Whether at the Political Bureau of the single party, or within a section of the army, no stone remained unturned to guarantee the holding of the gathering (Gbado 1991).

Even during the conference, uncharacteristic tolerance was noticed on the part of the southerners. As though the event was their only salvation, political leaders from the south remained unmoved by obvious provocation from northern politicians. Aware that northerners might deliberately create havoc in order to give an excuse to the military to dispel the gathering, southern politicians refused to give in to insults and slanders (Fondation Friedrich Naumann 1994).

The north-south divide was flagrant during the conference when the northern officers resented the path that the gathering was taking: a public forum to criticize the Kérékou regime. While their position became evident, the southern military leadership's resolve to seek a peaceful changing of the guards exposed dissenting voices within the armed forces (Adjovi 1993; Heilbrunn 1994).

In the end, their strategy prevailed since the northerners did not want to be viewed as those who sabotaged the advent of a new era: a democratic dawn in Benin. The northerners' position was also helped by the "compromise" made by the conference by not prosecuting Kérékou (Heilbrunn 1997, 54). With Kérékou's own clear position, to support the national conference and its decisions, it was difficult for any northern military officer to stage a coup or try to derail the resolutions of the gathering (Nwajiaku 1994).

Since the national conference, the relationship between civilians and the armed forces has improved. Suspicion and cruel handling of political opponents have given way to a smoother rapport between civilians and the military (Glèlè 1969; Smith 1976; Hull 1980, 26). Without reaching the level of cooperation or collaboration of the days of the kingdom of Danhomê, the contribution of the population in preventing conflicts, crimes and other disorders has been praised by both the armed forces and the government. In their fight against criminal activities all over the territory, the police forces found the population's help and assistance crucial in arresting and detecting gangs of all sorts (Lewis 1965; Coquery-Vidrovitch 1976; Isichei 1977).

Endnotes

[1] A popular gathering in the form of spectacle in Kenya that serves as a forum for political rhetoric.

[2] Interview with Colonel Abdoulaye Moussa on 12/21/96 in Cotonou, Benin.

[3] Through a series of interviews in Cotonou, Parakou, and Natitingou (Benin) in December 1996, it appeared clearly that Kérékou was very upset with his lieutenants by the mid-1990s.

[4] Interviews with both Northerners and Southerners in Cotonou in December 1996 revealed that position.

CONCLUSION

At independence, several African states possessed some form of democratic government. However, the very circumstances, which dictated the event of the democratization process at that time greatly contributed to the subsequent failure of democracy (Finer 1967, 507; Sandbrook 1987, 25). Having destroyed any democratic structure on the continent, Europeans did not really intend for European-style democracy to bloom in Africa. During the colonial era, democracy was dualistic and selective, and was necessarily oppressive (Baba 1977; Diagne 1986, 74). For the élite white settler, democracy was seemed perfectly functional, while the colonized African saw it as an irrationality laced with contradictions (Onwumechili 1998, 2).

According to Europeans, democratic institutions such as multiparty and federal systems, written constitutions, Bills of Rights, and houses of parliament, constituted an appropriate response to a particular set of political circumstances, in which the colonial rulers abandoned power to be inherited by a new set of nationalist politicians (Berg-Schlosser 1984; Tordoff 1997, 82).

> For the colonialists it was a convenient mechanism for getting out, dignified with the title of the "transfer of power," which conveyed a comforting impression of successful disengagement. For the nationalists, conversely, it was a convenient mechanism for getting it. (*West Africa*, January 19-25, 1998)

In many cases, multiparty elections preceded independence to enable qualified citizens to choose their new post-colonial leaders through the ballot box. Whatever the circumstances at its inception, democracy managed to survive in Africa, for varying periods of time, at least in a small number of states, and in the aspirations of many Africans (Lewis 1965; Conteh-Morgan 1997, 35-36).

One of the major obstacles to sustainable democracy in Africa lay in the profound *statism* of African political systems. African leaders, at independence, inherited states rather than nations. As a consequence of this situation, the new leaders found themselves saddled with the Herculean task of forging nations (Conteh-Morgan 1997, 37). Thus, in the vast majority of African states, there was hardly any domestic value consensus capable of maintaining support for democracy (Cohen 1971).

Despite majority support for political independence as well as the prospect of economic growth, both internal and external factors made the expected economic gains difficult to materialize (Clark 1997; Tordoff 1997; Ayittey 1998; Ihonvbere 1998). In this context of disillusionment and growing antipathy towards both civilian and military incompetent regimes, demands for a democratic system re-ignited in the late 1980s and early 1990s, and the continent seems to have embarked on a new path (Berton 1992).

While "democracy" itself remains a concept that defies precise definition, Africans agree that they want democratic government. They no longer speak of democracy in general, but specifically refer to *pluralistic* democracy (Diagne 1986; Conteh-Morgan 1997), and the calls for multiparty systems voiced in many African countries symbolized the belief that a multiparty system is the most manifest criterion of a pluralistic democracy. Africa has certainly provided a remarkable package of experience in the revival of democracy (Buijtenhuis and Thiriot 1995).

Contrary to the opinions of scholars like Huntington, democracy reached the shores of the continent without the expected prerequisites. Nevertheless, the process of democratization, in its second wave in Africa, is still on track in some countries. However, its birth, consolidation and stability remain uneven. While in some countries political and economic reforms allowed a renewed sense of hope, other countries continued to wallow in misery, chaos and uncertainty (Chole and Ibrahim 1992). While civil society is a vital instrument for containing the power of the state, checking its potential abuses and violations of the law, and subjecting it to public scrutiny, a vibrant civil society is more essential for consolidating and maintaining democracy than for initiating it (Diamond 1994, 7).

In fact, Chazan's warning needs to be taken seriously, if the continent is to enjoy its "second liberation:"

> If democracy is everywhere under construction, in Africa it has assumed especially imaginative expressions and accumulated particularly strident setbacks. The need for imposed design is especially acute in light of the monumental human costs of continuous impoverishment. The problems of democracy in Africa focus on two main issues. First, at the national level, inherited state institutions still have to undergo a process of decolonization and local entrenchment; otherwise no regime stabilization, let alone democratic consolidation, is possible. Second, on the level of civil society, intermediary organization need to be fortified as a means to linking social groups with one another and with the state. In Africa in recent years, fragments of democracy have flourished. The challenge for Africa's political future rests in putting these segments together in workable ways. (1994, 89)

There have been serious attempts at reversing the democratization process in several countries. The Gambia, which had been a multiparty democracy since independence in 1965, became a military dictatorship in 1994 while the wave of democracy was sweeping the rest of the continent. In Sierra Leone, the "yo-yo" political situation, in which power seems to be swinging back and forth between the military and civilian authorities, continues to raise serious concerns about stability in the country (Onwumechili 1998, 51). The democratically-elected regime in the Congo (Brazzaville) has been overthrown by the armed forces. In former Zaire, now Democratic Republic of Congo, the "democratic forces" that managed to oust Mobutu regime, the most corrupt and dictatorial regime of Africa, find themselves facing serious challenges from rebels (Conteh-Morgan 1997; Clark and Gardinier 1997). In Niger, the military leader who toppled a democratically elected government in January 1996 perished in a countercoup.

As these unfortunate events demonstrate, democracy, despite all its elation, still depends to a great extent, on the whims of the military in Africa (Hanneman 1985; Luckham 1996; Hutchful 1997; Decalo 1998). The military remains a potent political actor, working behind the scenes to defend its own interests and those of its allies (Riley 1992, 54). Louis Martin posits well the conditions of democratic success in Africa:

Although the success of democratic transitions in Sub-Saharan will depend ultimately on institutionalization of civil control of the military (the prerequisite to the idea of the rule of law), it will depend in the short run on the manner in which former praetorians [military leaders] are dealt with...Establishing a stable relationship with the armed forces and ensuring their withdrawal from politics...will require "rewarding" means of subordination. (1997, 96)

In the same vein, Huntington (1957, 84-88) believes that to impose an "objective civilian control" over the military in order to render it "politically sterile and neutral," civilian leaders will have to work with the military at the initial stage of democratization. Advising on the strategies for democratization in the Third World, Diamond rightly states that "where the military remains firmly in control, openly or behind the scenes, negotiating with it a plan for gradual democratization of political institution may offer the best hope for committed democrats" (1989a, 147).

After many decades of mistrust, the military and civilian politicians will need to redesign their relationship for a smooth political transition of their country. In fact, Diamond and Plattner make a good case for a badly needed new civil-military relationship in Africa:

Sound civil-military relations are the product of longstanding national tradition and a complex set of formal and informal measures that affect the government, civil society, and the military itself. If civil-military relations are to be given an ideal framework, it is vital that the state clearly demarcate the limits of the military's role and that both the broad public and the military feel that a role is legitimate. This requires that civilian leaders take the lead in defining the military's overall strategy and defense planning, in laying out the armed forces' roles and missions, and in regulating the military's budget, recruiting and training practices, force structure, and level of armaments. (1996, xx-xxi)

Civil control of the military is managed and maintained through the sharing of control between civilian leaders and military officers. This theory of shared responsibility, suggested by Bland (1999), rests on two assumptions. First, the term "civil control" means that the sole legitimate source for the directions and actions of the military is derived from civilians outside the military/defense establishments. Second, civil control is a dynamic process susceptible to changing ideas, values, circumstances, issues, and personalities and to the stresses of crises and war (1999, 10).

Foreign influence in the democratization process in Africa, as elsewhere in the world, has played a quite ambiguous role, ranging from open pressure for democratization to defense of vested interests. In many cases, foreign patrons who had supported authoritarian regimes in the past, either actively assisted in their removal, or at least allowed their removal by benign inaction at the crucial moment (Schraeder 1996). However, depending on the importance of the relationship between the patrons and their puppets, foreign powers also chose to do everything in their power to openly derail the democratization process, and the two cases under study here demonstrate a clear ambiguity about France's position *vis-à-vis* the experiences both countries are going through (Decalo 1997; Heilbrunn 1997; Marchal 1998).

While two former French colonies, Benin and Togo, were forced to alter their political systems after several years of poor performance, they took different paths. Owing to the resilience of civil society and also to the critical role played by the army, democracy became a reality in Benin, while it is still marking time in Togo. This difference results in France's control over the process (Andereggen 1994, 139). The totalitarian regime of Kérékou was forced to give up power, while the authoritarian one of Éyadéma, a close ally of France, remained in power, raising a disturbing question, that is whether democracy can be promoted for democracy's sake (Gardinier 1997, 20; Tordoff 1997, 143)

Authoritarian rule has proven incapable of improving Africans' standard of living, contrary to the arguments of those who rationalized it, and that sad experience might increase the chance of democracy. However, if democracy is to play a significant role as a viable alternative (Wiseman 1990, 32) to authoritarianism in Africa, both leaders and followers have to endorse the rules of democratic theory. Enduring democracy, Rustow (1970) contends, is most often the result, not just of élite consensus or a mass civic culture, but more of the difficult negotiations between contending actors with widely divergent interests and the military in Africa is a political actor to be taken seriously.

A peaceful transition to democracy must also resolve the problem of institutionalization of uncertainty, without threatening the interests of those who can still reverse this process (Przeworski 1986, 60).

Constitutionalism, the legal limitations on the power of a government in its relationship to its citizens, will help remedy that concern by stipulating the fundamental rights and obligations of citizens and by defining the appropriate scope of governmental activity (Kimenyi 1997, 12)

The crisis of enduring poverty, though stemming from various sources, results primarily from the policy failures of African governments, and democracy could present a new opportunity for redemption. As stated by Adebayo Adedeji, who served as Executive Secretary of the UN Economic Commission for Africa from 1975 until 1991, Africa must rely on its own economic and political policies for a future with rising prosperity. In other words, only self-discovery and self-respect can help Africa to reshape its future (Legum 1999, 69).

An Afro-optimist argument might use Kérékou's return to power through the ballots in 1996, and Abdoulaye Wade's recent victory in Senegal, as signs of democracy taking roots on the continent. But at the same time, unfortunate events such as the December 1999 military coup in Côte d'Ivoire, continue to remind Africans of the complexity of civil-military relations on the continent, and to bolster the Afro-pessimist view of an epiphenomenal democracy that is destined to fail. Assessing the chances of the process of re-democratization in Africa, Diamond notes that:

> It is unrealistic to think that such [African] countries can suddenly reverse course and institutionalize stable democratic government simply by changing leaders, constitutions and/or public mentalities. If progress is to be made toward developing democratic government, it is likely to be gradual, messy, fitful and slow, with many imperfections along the way. (1989b, 24)

Although the international community seems to be rejoicing at Africa's emerging democracies, the genuineness of that attitude remains to be seen. Until the gap between some Western powers' vested interests and the desire for a democratic society narrows, the rhetoric of universal democratization might not match the reality on the ground, requiring Africans to take matters into their own hands. Instead of being thought of as a struggle for power between irreconcilable adversaries, civil-military relations should be conceived of as exchanges between "friendly adversaries" (Sarkesian 1981, 291), in order to avoid African democratization from ending up as a mere fleeting vogue.

While democracy has a new chance on the continent, African leaders, both political and military, need to reach the *modus vivendi* capable of expanding democracy's longevity in Africa. Human agency in democratization cannot be stressed enough, and Wiseman is quite wise in saying that:

> To all but the most obdurate structuralist, human agency is a crucial factor in shaping political life. The characteristics of individual leaders are extremely relevant in determining political outcomes and this holds as true in relation to democratisation as it does to any other political developments...Given the plasticity of the democratisation process in contemporary Africa, key decisions taken by key leaders at key points in the process have a great impact in enhancing or weakening the prospects for democracy. (1996, 165)

However, in spite of the centrality of the question of political leadership, outside influence on leaders could also be crucial, and Huntington (1991, 316) makes an excellent point when he writes that "democracy will spread in the world to the extent that those who exercise power in the world and in individual countries want it spread." While democracy seems to be generating excitement worldwide, the sincerity of outside powers in encouraging and promoting democracy continues to be a key factor in its global fate. Both African leaders and followers, civilian and military, will have to work hand in hand to allow democracy to take hold on the continent.

BIBLIOGRAPHY

BOOKS AND ARTICLES

Abrahamsen, Rita. 1997. "The Victory of Popular Forces or Passive Revolution? A Neo-Gramscian Perspective on Democratisation." *Journal of Modern African Studies* 35/1: 129-152.

Adjaho, Richard. 1992. *La Faillite du Contrôle des Finances Publiques au Bénin (1960-1990)*. Cotonou: Éditions du Flamboyant.

Adjovi, Séverin. 1993. *De la Dictature à la Démocratie sans les Armes*. Paris: Éditions CP 99.

Africa Demos. 1995. "The Promise of Democracy." 3/4 (March): 1, 4.

_____. 1996. "Phases of Transition to Democracy." 3/5 (May): 27-31.

Agblemangnon, Ferdinand N'Soungan. 1966. "Masses et Élites en AfriqueNoire: Le Cas du Togo." In *The New Elites in Tropical Africa*, ed. P.C. Lloyd. Oxford: Oxford University Press.

Agüero, Felipe. 1990. *Democratic Consolidation and the Military in Southern Europe and Latin America*. Paper presented at the Conference on Democratic Consolidation in Southern Europe, in Rome, December 14-15.

Agyeman-Duah, Baffour. 1990. "Military Coups, Regime Change and Interstate Conflicts in Africa." *Armed Forces and Society* 16/4: 547-570.

Ake, Claude. 1990. "The Case for Democracy." In *African Governance in the 1990s: Objectives, Resources, and Constraints*, ed. Richard Joseph. Atlanta: Carter Center.

_____. 1991. "Rethinking African Democracy." *Journal of Democracy* 2/1 (Winter): 33-44.

_____. 1993. "The Unique Case of African Democracy." *International Affairs* 69: 239-244.

_____. 1996. *Democracy and Development in Africa*. Washington, D.C.: The Brookings Institute.

Akinjogbin, I. A. 1967. *Dahomey and Its Neighbors*. New York: Cambridge University Press.

Alam, Mohammad B. 1986. "Democracy in the Third World: Some Problems and Dilemmas." *Indian Journal of Politics* 20/1-2: 53-68.

Albright, David E. 1980. "A Comparative Conceptualization of Civil-Military Relations." *World Politics* 32/4 (July): 553-576.

Allen, Chris. 1989. "'Goodbye to All That': The Short and Sad Story of Socialism in Benin." *Journal of Communist Studies* 8/2: 63-81.

Allen, Chris. 1992. "Restructuring an Authoritarian State: Democratic Renewal in Benin." *Review of African Political Economy* 54: 42-58.

Allen, Chris, et al. 1992. "Surviving Democracy?" *Review of African Political Economy* 54: 3-10.

Allen, Chris, Michael S. Radu and Keith Somerville. 1988. *Benin, the Congo, and Burkina Faso: Politics, Economics and Society*. London: Pinter Publishers.

Allison, Lincoln. 1994. "On the Gap between Theories of Democracy and Theories of Democratization." *Democratization* 1/1 (Spring): 8-26.

d'Almeida-Topor, Hélène. 1973. "Les Populations Dahoméennes et le Recrutement Militaire Pendant La Première Guerre Mondiale." *Revue Française d'Histoire d'Outre-Mer* 60/219: 197-241.

Almond, Gabriel and Sydney Verba. 1963. *The Civic Culture*. Princeton: Princeton University Press.

Andereggen, Anton. 1994. *France's Relationship with Subsaharan Africa*. Westport, CT: Praeger Publishers.

Anyang' Nyong'o, Peter, ed. 1987. *Popular Struggles for Democracy in Africa*. New Jersey: Zed Books Ltd.

_____. 1988. "Political Instability and the Prospects for Democracy in Africa." *Africa Development* 13/1: 71-86.

_____. 1991. "Democratization Processes in Africa." *CODESRIA Bulletin* 2/3: 13-17.

_____. 1992. "Africa: The Failure of One-Party Rule."
Journal of Democracy 3/1: 90-96.

Arato, Andrew. 1981. "Civil Society versus the State." *Telos* 47: 23-47.

Argyle, W.F. 1966. *The Fon of Dahomey: A History and Ethnography of
an Old Kingdom*. New York: Oxford University Press.

Austin, Dennis. 1963. "Coup d'État in the Republic of Togo." *World
Today* 19/1: 56-60.

_____. 1966. "The Underlying Problem of the Army Coup
d'État in Africa." *Optima* 16/2 (June): 65-72.

Ayittey, George B. N. 1990. "La Démocratie en Afrique Précoloniale."
Afrique 2000 2: 39-75.

Ayoade, John A. A. 1986. "The African Search for Democracy." In
Democracy and Pluralism in Africa, ed. Dov Ronen. Boulder, CO:
Lynne Rienner.

Azarya, Victor. 1988. "Reordering State-Society Relations: Incorporation
and Disengagement." In *The Precarious Balance: State and Society
in Africa*, eds. Donald Rothchild and Naomi Chazan. Boulder, CO:
Westview Press.

Azevedo, Mario. 1995. "Ethnicity and Democratization: Cameroon and
Gabon." In *Ethnic Conflict and Democratization in Africa*, ed.
Harvey Glickman. Atlanta, GA: ASA Press.

Baba, Kaké I. 1977. *L'Afrique Coloniale: De la Conférence de Berlin
(1885) aux Indépendances*. Paris: ABC.

Baker, Gideon. 1998. "Civil Society and Democracy: The Gap between
Theory and Possibility. *Politics* 18/2: 81-87.

Balandier, Georges. 1955. *Sociologie Actuelle de l'Afrique Noire:
Dynamique Sociale en Afrique Centrale*. Paris: Presses
Universitaires de France.

Banégas, Richard. 1995a. "Action Collective et Changement Politique en
Afrique: La Conférence Nationale du Bénin." *Cultures et Conflits*
17 (Printemps): 137-175.

_____. 1995b. "Mobilisations Sociales et Oppositions sous
Kérékou." *Politique Africaine* 59 (Octobre): 25-44.

_____. 1997. "Retour sur une Transition Modèle: Les
Dynamiques du Dedans et du Dehors de la Démocratisation
Béninoise." In *Transitions Démocratiques Africaines: Dynamiques
et Contraintes (1990-1994)*, eds. Jean-Pascal Daloz et Patrick
Quantin. Paris: Khartala.

Bangura, Abdul K. 1994. "Explaining and Predicting the Causes of
Military Coups d'État in Africa: A Meta-Analysis." In *Research*

Methodology and African Studies, Vol. 1, ed. Abdul K. Bangura. Lanham: University Press of America.

Barnes, James F. 1992. *Gabon: Beyond the Colonial Legacy*. Boulder, CO: Westview Press.

Barnes, Samuel H. 1994. "Politics and Culture." In *Research on Democracy and Society*, Vol. 2: Political Culture and Political Structure – Theoretical and Empirical Studies, ed. Frederick D. Weil. Greenwich, CT: JAI Press Inc.

Bates, Robert H. 1994. "The Impulse to Reform in Africa." In *Economic Change and Political Liberalization in Sub-Saharan Africa*, ed. Jennifer Widner. Baltimore: The John Hopkins University Press.

_____. 1995. *Democratic Transition in Africa: A First Report on an Empirical Project*. Development Discussion Paper, no. 514. Cambridge: Harvard Institute for International Development.

Bayart, Jean-François. 1983. "La Revanche des Sociétés Africaines." *Politique Africaine* 11 (September): 95-127.

_____. 1984. *La Politique Africaine de François Mitterand*. Paris: Khartala.

_____. 1986. "Civil Society in Africa." In *Political Domination in Africa*, ed. Patrick Chabal. Cambridge: Cambridge University Press.

_____. 1989. *L'État en Afrique: La Politique du Ventre.* Paris: Fayard.

_____. 1991. "La Problématique de la Démocratie en Afrique Noire: La Baule et puis après?" *Politique Africaine* 43 (Octobre): 5-20.

_____. 1993. *The State in Africa: The Politics of the Belly*. London: Longman.

_____. 1995. "Réflexions sur la Politique Africaine de la France." *Politique Africaine* 58 (Juin): 41-50

_____, Achille Mbembe, and Comi Toulabor, eds. 1990. *La Politique par le Bas en Afrique Noire: Contributions à une Problématique de la Démocratie*. Paris: Karthala.

Baynham, Simon, ed. 1986. *Military Power and Politics in Black Africa*. London: Croom Helm.

_____. 1991a. "Geopolitics, Glasnost and Africa's Second Liberation: Political and Security Implications for the Continent." *Africa Insight* 21/4: 263-268.

_____. 1991b. "Security Issues in Africa: The Imperial Legacy, Domestic Violence and the Military." *Africa Insight* 21/3: 180-189.

Bebler, Anton. 1973. *Military Rule in Africa: Dahomey, Ghana, Sierra Leone, and Mali.* New York: Praeger.

Beckman, Bjorn. 1989. "Whose democracy? Bourgeois versus Popular Democracy." *Review of African Political Economy* 45: 84-97.

_____. 1993. "The Liberation of Civil Society: Neoliberal Ideology and Political Theory." *Review of African Political Economy* 58: 20-33.

Beetham, David. 1994. "Conditions for Democratic Consolidation." *Review of African Political Economy* 60: 157-172.

Berg-Schlosser, Dirk. 1984. "African Political Systems: Typology and Performance." *Comparative Political Studies* 17/1: 121-151.

Bermeo, Nancy. 1990. "Rethinking Regime Change." *Comparative Politics* 22/3 (April): 359-77.

_____. 1993. "Democracy and the Lessons of Dictatorship." *Comparative Politics* 24/3 (April): 273-291.

Berton, Georges. 1992. "Afrique: L'État de la Démocratisation." *Croissance* (October): 25-28.

Biarnes, Pierre. 1987. *Les Français en Afrique Noire, de Richelieu à Mitterand.* Paris: Colin.

Bienen, Henry S. 1979. *Armies and Parties in Africa.* New York: Africana Publishing.

_____. 1984. "Military Rule and Military Order in Africa." In *Africa in the Post-Decolonization Era*, eds. Bissell, Richard E. and Michael S. Radu. New Brunswick, NJ: Transaction Books.

_____. 1985. "Populist Military Regimes in West Africa." *Armed Forces and Society* 11/3: 357-377.

_____. 1989. *Armed Forces, Conflict, and Change in Africa.* Boulder, CO: Westview Press.

_____. 1993. "Leaders, Violence, and the Absence of Change in Africa." *Political Science Quarterly* 108/2 (Summer): 271-282.

_____ and Jeffrey Herbst. 1991. "Authoritarianism and Democracy in Africa." In *Comparative Political Dynamics: Global Research Perspectives*, eds. Dankwart A. Rustow and Kenneth P. Erickson. New York: HarperCollins.

_____ and William J. Foltz. 1985. *Arms and the African: Military Influences' International Relations.* New Haven: Yale University Press

Bland, Douglas L. 1999. "A Unified Theory of Civil-Military Relations." *Armed Forces and Society* 26/1: 7-25.

Blaney, David L., and Mustapha K. Pasha. 1993. "Civil Society and democracy in the Third World: Ambiguities and Historical Possibilities." *Studies in Comparative International Development* 28/1 (Spring): 3-24.

Boahen, Adu. 1986. *Topics in West African History*, 2nd ed. London: Longman.

_____. 1991. "Military Rule and Multi-Party Democracy: The Case of Ghana." *Africa Demos* 1/2: 5-9.

Boggio, Philippe. 1992. "Soleil Noir sur Gorée." *Le Monde*, 21 March.

Boulaga, F. Eboussi. 1993. *Les Conférences Nationales: Une Affaire à Suivre*. Paris: Karthala.

Bourgi, Albert and Christian Castern. 1992. *Le Printemps de l'Afrique*. Paris: Hachette.

Bovy, Lambert. 1968. "Histoire du Mouvement Syndical Ouest-Africain d'Expression Française." *Revue Juridique et Politique* 1 (Janvier-Mars): 111-130.

Bowles, Paul. 1989. "Recipient Needs and Donor Interests in the Allocation of EEC Aid to Developing Countries." *Canadian Journal of Development Studies* 10/1: 27-45.

Bratton, Michael. 1989. "Beyond the State: Civil Society and Associational Life in Africa." *World Politics* 41/3: 407-30.

_____. 1995. "Are Competitive Elections Enough?" *Africa Demos* 3/4: 7-8.

_____ and Nicolas van de Walle. 1992. "Popular Protest and Political Transition in Africa." *Comparative Politics* 24/4 (July): 419-42.

_____. 1992. "Toward Governance in Africa: Popular Demands and State Response." In *Governance and Politics in Africa*, eds. Goran Hyden and Michael Bratton. Boulder, CO: Lynne Rienner.

_____. 1994. "Neopatrimonial Regimes and Political Transitions in Africa." *World Politics* 46/4 (July): 453-489.

_____. 1998. *Democratic Experiments in Africa*. Cambridge: Cambridge University Press.

Brinton, Crane. 1963. *A Decade of Revolution, 1789-1799*. New York: Harper and Row.

Bryant, Christopher G. A. 1993. "Social Self-Organization, Civility and Sociology: A Comment on Kumar's 'Civil Society'." *British Journal of Sociology* 44/3: 397-401.

Buijtenhuijs, Rob and Elly Rijnierse. 1993. *Democratisation in Sub-Saharan Africa, 1989-1992: An Overview of the Literature.* Leiden, The Netherlands: African Studies Center.

Buijtenhuijs, Rob and Céline Thiriot. 1995. *Democratization in Sub-Saharan Africa, 1992-1995: An Overview of the Literature.* Leiden, The Netherlands: African Studies Center.

Busia, Kofi A. 1967. *Africa in Search of Democracy.* London: Routledge & Kegan Paul.

Buzan, Barry, Charles Jones, and Richard Little. 1993. *The Logic of Anarchy: From Neorealism to Structural Realism.* New York: Columbia University Press.

Calhoun, Craig. 1993. "Civil Society and The Public Sphere." *Public Culture* 5: 267-280.

Callaghy, Thomas M. 1994. "Africa: Back to the Future." *Journal of Democracy* 5/4: 133-145.

Carbett, Edward M. 1972. *The French Presence in Black Africa.* Washington, DC: Black Orpheus Press.

Carlton, Eric. 1997. *The State against the State: The Theory and Practice of the Coup d'État.* Hants, UK: Scolar Press

Carter Center. 1989. *Beyond Autocracy in Africa.* Atlanta: Emory University.

_____. 1990. "African Governance in the 1990s," Working Papers from the Second Annual Seminar of the African Governance Program. Atlanta: Emory University.

Cartwright, John R. 1983. *Political Leadership in Africa.* Cambridge: Cambridge University Press.

Catt, Helena. 1999. *Democracy in Practice.* London: Routledge.

Chabal, Patrick, ed. 1986. *Political Domination in Africa.* Cambridge: Cambridge University Press.

_____. 1991. "Pouvoir et Violence en Afrique Post-Coloniale." *Politique Africaine* 42 (Juin): 51-64.

_____. 1994a. *Power in Africa: An Essay in Political Interpretation.* New York: St. Martin's Press.

_____. 1994b. "Democracy and Daily Life in Black Africa." *International Affairs* 70/1: 83-91.

_____. 1998. "A Few Considerations on Democracy in Africa." *International Affairs* 74/2: 289-303.

Chafer, Tony. 1992. "French African Policy: Towards Change." *African Affairs* 91/362: 37-51.

Chaigneau, Pascal. 1984. *La Politique Militaire de la France en Afrique.* Paris: Centre des Hautes Études sur l'Afrique et l'Asie Modernes.

Chalker, Linda. 1994. "Development and Democracy: What Should the West Be Doing?" *The Round Table* 329: 23-26.

Chan, Steve. 1994. "Mirror, Mirror on the Wall...Are the Freer Countries more Pacific?" *Journal of Conflict Resolution* 28/4: 617-648.

Chandhoke, Neera. 1995. *State and Civil Society: Explorations in Political Theory.* New Delhi: Sage Publications.

Charlick, Robert B. 1991. *Niger: Personal Rule and Survival in the Sahel.* Boulder, CO: Westview Press.

Charlton, Roger. 1983. "Dehomogenizing the Study of African Politics: The Case of Interstate Influence on Regime Formation and Change." *Plural Societies* 14/1-2: 32-48.

Chazan, Naomi. 1982. "The New Politics of Participation in Tropical Africa." *Comparative Politics* 14/2: 169-189.

_____. 1989. "Planning Democracy in Africa: A Comparative Perspective on Ghana and Nigeria." *Policy Sciences* 22/3-4: 325-357.

_____. 1992. "Africa's Democratic Challenge: Strengthening Civil Society and the State." *World Policy Journal* (Spring): 279-307.

_____. 1994. "Between Liberalism and Statism: African Political Cultures and Democracy." In *Political Culture and Democracy in Developing Countries,* ed. Larry Diamond. Boulder, CO: Lynne Rienner.

Chazan, Naomi, et al. 1992. *Politics and Society in Contemporary Africa.* Basingstoke: Macmillan.

_____. 1999. *Politics and Society in Contemporary Africa,* 3rd ed. Boulder, CO: Lynne Rienner.

Chege, Michael. 1995a. "Between Africa's Extremes." *Journal of Democracy* 6/1: 44-51.

_____. 1995b. "The Military in the Transition to Democracy in Africa: Some Preliminary Observations." *CODESRIA Bulletin* 3/13: 7-9.

Chenu, Georges-Marie. 1991. "Democracy in Africa." *Revue Juridique et Politique, Indépendance et Coopération* 45/1 (January): 6-9.

Chipman, John. 1989. *French Power in Africa.* Cambridge: Basil Blackwell.

Chole, Eshetu and Jibrin Ibrahim, eds. 1992. *Democratisation Processes in Africa: Problems and Prospects*. Dakar, Senegal: CODESRIA.

Clapham, Christopher. 1985. *Third World Politics: An Introduction*. Madison: University of Wisconsin Press.

_____. 1993. "Democratization in Africa: Obstacles and Prospects." *Third World Quarterly* 14/3: 423-38.

_____. 1996. *African and the International System: The Politics of State Survival*. Cambridge: Cambridge University Press.

_____ and George Philip, eds. 1985. *The Political Dilemmas of Military Regimes*. London: Croom Helm.

Clark, John F. 1993. "Theoretical Disarray and the Study of Democratisation in Africa." *Journal of Modern African Studies* 31/3: 529-534.

_____. 1997. "The Challenges of Political Reform in Sub-Saharan Africa: A Theoretical Overview." In *Political Reform in Francophone Africa*, eds. John F. Clark and David E. Gardinier. Boulder, CO: Westview Press.

_____. 1998. "National Conferences and Democratization in Francophone Africa." In *Multiparty Democracy and Political Change: Constraints to Democratization in Africa*, eds. Mbaku, J.M. and J.O. Ihonvbere. Bookfield, Vermont: Ashgate.

Clark, John C. and David Gardinier, eds. 1997. *Political Reform in Francophone Africa*. Boulder, CO: Westview Press.

Clarke, Walter S. 1995. "The National Conference Phenomenon and the Management of Political Conflict in Sub-Saharan Africa." In *Ethnic Conflict and Democratization in Africa*, ed. Harvey Glickman. Atlanta: ASA Press.

Cohen, Herman J. 1991. "African Political Changes and Economic Consequences." *Dispatch* 2/36: 675-676.

Cohen, Jean L. and Andrew Arato. 1992. *Civil Society and Political Theory*. Cambridge, MA: MIT Press.

Cohen, William B. 1971. *Rulers of Empire: The French Colonial Service in Africa*. Stanford: Hoover Institution Press.

Coleman, James S. 1956. "Togoland." *International Conciliation* 509: 3-91.

_____ and Belmont Brice, Jr. 1962. "The Role of the Military in Sub-Saharan Africa." In *The Role of the Military in Underdeveloped Countries*, ed. John J. Johnson. Princeton: Princeton University Press, 359-405.

Collier, Ruth B. 1978. "Parties, Coups, and Authoritarianism Rule: Patterns of Political Change in Tropical Africa." *Comparative Political Studies* 11/1: 62-93.

_____. 1982. *Regimes in Tropical Africa: Changing Forms of Supremacy, 1945-1975*. Berkeley: University of California Press.

Conac, Gérard. 1993. *L'Afrique en Transition vers le Pluralisme Politique*. Paris: Economica.

Conklin, Alice L. 1997. *A Mission to Civilize: The Republican Idea of Empire in France and West Africa, 1895-1930*. Stanford, CA: Stanford University Press.

Conteh-Morgan, Earl. 1997. *Democratization in Africa: The Theory and Dynamics of Political Transitions*. Westport, CT: Praeger.

Coquery-Vidrovitch, Catherine. 1976. "L'Afrique Coloniale Française et la Crise de 1930: Crise Structurelle et Genèse du Sous-Développement." *Revue Française d'Histoire d'Outre-Mer* 63, 232-233: 386-424.

_____. 1979. "Colonialisme ou Impérialisme: La Politique Africaine de la France Entre les Deux Guerres." *Mouvement Social* 107 (Avril-Juin): 51-76.

_____. 1992a. "History and Historiography of Politics in Africa: The Need for a Critical Re-reading regarding Democracy." *Politique Africaine* 46 (June): 31-40.

_____. 1992b. "Trente Années Perdues ou Étapes d'une Longue Évolution?" *Afrique Contemporaine* 164/4 (Numéro Spécial): 5-17.

Cornevin, Robert. 1959. *Histoire du Togo*. Paris: Berger Levrault.

_____. 1968. "Les Militaires au Dahomey et au Togo." *Revue Française d'Études Politiques Africaines* 36: 65-84.

_____. 1981. *La République Populaire du Bénin: Des Origines Dahoméennes à nos Jours*. Paris: Académie des Sciences d'Outre-Mer.

_____. 1988. *Le Togo: Des Origines à nos Jours*. Paris: Académie des Sciences d'Outre-Mer.

Cox, Robert W. 1999. "Civil Society at the Turn of the Millenium: Prospects for an Alternative World Order." *Review of International Studies* 25/1: 3-28.

Crocker, Chester A. 1974. "Military Dependence: The Colonial Legacy in Africa." *Journal of Modern African Studies* 12/2: 265-286.

Crowder, Michael. 1987. "Whose Dreams Was It Anyway? Twenty-Five Years of African Independence." *African Affairs* 86/342: 7-24.

Cumming, Gorden. 1995. "French Development Assistance to Africa: Towards a New Agenda?" *African Affairs* 94/376: 383-398.

Dabezies, Pierre. 1992. "Vers la Démocratisation de l'Afrique." *Défense Nationale* (Mai): 21-33.

Dahl, Robert A. 1970. *Polyarchy: Participation and Opposition.* New Haven: Yale University Press.

_____. 1989. *Democracy and Its Critics.* New Haven: Yale University Press.

_____. 1992. "The Problem of Civic Competence." *Journal of Democracy* 3/4: 45-59.

_____. 1998. *On Democracy.* New Haven: Yale University Press.

Daloz, Jean-Pascal et Patrick Quantin. 1997. *Transitions Démocratiques Africaines: Dynamiques et Contraintes (1990-1994).* Paris: Karthala.

Danopoulos, Constantine P., ed. 1992. *From Military to Civilian Rule.* London: Routledge.

_____, ed. 1992. *Civilian Rule in the Developing World: Democracy on the March?* Boulder, CO: Westview Press.

Dealy, Glen C. 1974. "The Tradition of Monistic Democracy in Latin America." *Journal of the History of Ideas* 35/4: 625-646.

Decalo, Samuel. 1968. "The Politics of Instability in Dahomey." *Geneva-Africa* 7/2 (Winter): 5-32.

_____. 1970a. "Dahomey 1968-1971: Return to Origins." *Geneva-Africa* (Winter): 456-491.

_____. 1970b. "Full Circle in Dahomey." *African Studies Review* 13/3: 445-458.

_____. 1973a. "Regionalism, Politics and the Military in Dahomey." *Journal of Developing Areas* 7/3 (April): 449-477.

_____. 1973b. "The Politics of Military Rule in Togo." *Geneva-Africa* 12/2: 62-96.

_____. 1974a. "The Colonel in Command Car: towards a Re-examination of Motives for Military Intervention in Politics." *Cultures et Développement* (January): 273-282.

_____. 1974b. "The Military Takeovers in Africa." *International Problems* (September): 80-90.

_____. 1985. "The Morphology of Radical Military Rule in Africa." *Journal of Communist Studies* (December): 23-35.

_____. 1986a. "Socio-Economic Constraints on Radical Action in the People's Republic of Congo." In *Military Marxist Regimes in*

Africa, eds. John Markakis and Michael Waller. London: Frank Cass.

_____. 1986b. "The Morphology of Radical Military Rule in Africa." In *Military Marxist Regimes in Africa*, eds. John markakis and Michael Waller. London: Frank Cass.

_____. 1989. "Modalities of Civil-Military Stability in Africa." *Journal of Modern African Studies* 27/4: 547-578.

_____. 1990. *Coups and Army Rule in Africa*, 2nd Edition. New Haven: Yale University Press.

_____. 1991a. "Towards Understanding the Sources of Stable Civilian Rule in Africa: 1960-1990." *Journal of Contemporary African Studies* 10/1: 66-83.

_____. 1991b. "Back to Square One: The Re-Democratization of Africa." *Africa Insight* 21/3: 153-161.

_____. 1992. "The Process, Prospects and Constraints of Democratization in Africa." *African Affairs* 91/362: 7-35.

_____. 1994. "The Future of Participatory Democracy in Africa." *Futures* 26/9: 987-992.

_____. 1995. *Historical Dictionary of Benin*, 3rd Edition. Lanham, MD: Scarecrow Press, Inc.

_____. 1996. *Historical Dictionary of Togo*, 3rd Edition. Lanham, MD: Scarecrow Press, Inc.

_____. 1997. "Benin: First of the New Democracies." In *Political Reform in Francophone Africa*, eds. John F. Clark and David E. Gardinier. Boulder, CO: Westview Press.

_____. 1998. *The Stable Minority: Civilian Rule in Africa, 1960-1990*. Gainesville: FAP Books.

_____, Virginia Thompson, and Richard Adloff. 1996. *Historical Dictionary of Congo*. Lanham, MD: Scarecrow Press.

Demirovic, Alex. 1991. "Civil Society, Public Sphere, Democracy." *Argument* 33/1: 41-55.

De Tocqueville, Alexis. 1990. *Democracy in America*. Trans. George Lawrence. Chicago: Encyclopedia Britannica, Inc.

De Lusignan, Guy. 1969. *French-Speaking Africa since Independence*. New York: Praeger.

Di Palma, Guiseppi. 1990. *To Craft Democracies*. Berkeley: University of California Press.

Diagne, Pathé. 1976. "De la DémocratieTraditionnelle." *Présence Africaine* 97: 18-42.

_____. 1981. *Le Concept de Pouvoir en Afrique*. Paris: UNESCO.

_____. 1986. "Pluralism and Plurality in Africa." In *Democracy and Pluralism in Africa*, ed. Dov Ronen. Boulder, CO: Lynne Rienner.

Diamond, Larry. 1989a. "Beyond Authoritarianism and Totalitarianism: Strategies for Democratization." *Washington Quarterly* 12/1 (December): 141-163.

_____. 1989b. "Beyond Autocracy: Prospects for Democracy in Africa." In *Beyond Autocracy in Africa*, ed. Carter Center. Atlanta: Emory University.

_____. 1992. "Economic Development and Democracy Reconsidered." *American Behavioral Scientist* 35: 450-499.

_____, ed. 1992. *The Democratic Revolution: Struggles for Freedom and Pluralism in the Developing World*. New York: Freedom House.

_____, ed. 1993. *Political Culture and Democracy in Developing Countries*. Boulder, CO: Lynne Rienner.

_____. 1994a. "Towards Democratic Consolidation." *Journal of Democracy* 5/3: 4-17.

_____. 1994b. "Introduction: Political Culture and Democracy." In *Political Culture and Democracy in Developing Countries*, ed. Larry Diamond. Boulder, CO: Lynne Rienner.

_____. 1996. "Is the Third Wave over?" *Journal of Democracy* 7/3: 20-37.

_____. 1997. *Prospects for Democratic Development in Africa*. Stanford: Hoover Institution, Stanford University.

_____. 1998. "Africa: The Second Wind of Change." In *Africa: Dilemmas of Development and Change*, ed. Peter Lewis. Boulder, CO: Westview Press.

_____ and Marc F. Plattner, eds. 1993. *The Global Resurgence of Democracy*. Baltimore: John Hopkins University Press.

_____, eds. 1996. *Civil-Military and Democracy*. Baltimore, MD: John Hopkins University Press.

_____, eds. 1999. *Democratization in Africa*. Baltimore, MD: Johns Hopkins University Press.

_____, Juan Linz, and Seymour M. Lipset. 1988. *Democracy in Developing Countries: Vol. 2: Africa*. Boulder, CO: Lynne Rienner Publishers.

Diop, Cheikh Anta. 1974. *The African Origin of Civilization*. Westport, CT: Lawrence Hill & Company.

_____. 1987. *Pre-Colonial Black Africa*. Westport, CT: Lawrence Hill & Company.

Dossou, Robert. 1993. "Le Bénin: Du Monolithisme à la Démocratie Pluraliste, Un Témoignage." In *L'Afrique en Transition vers Le Pluralisme Politique*, ed. Gérard Conac. Paris: Économica.

Dowden, Richard. 1993. "Reflections on Democracy in Africa." *African Affairs* 92: 607-613.

Downs, Anthony. 1957. *An Economic Theory of Democracy*. New York: Harper & Row.

_____. 1987. "The Evolution of Democracy: How its Axioms and Institutional Forms Have Been Adapted to Changing Social Forces." *Daedalus* 116/3: 119-148.

Doyle, Michael W. 1983. "Kant, Liberal Legacies and Foreign Affairs, Part I & II." *Philosophy and Public Affairs* 12: 205-235 & 323-353.

_____. 1986. "Liberalism and World Politics." *American Political Science Review* 80/4: 1151-1169.

Dunn, John, ed. 1978. *West African States: Failure and Promise*. Cambridge: Cambridge University.

_____, ed. 1992. *Democracy: The Unfinished Journey*. Oxford: Oxford University Press.

Eades, J.S. and Chris Allen. 1996. *Benin*. Oxford: Clio Press.

Eckert, Paul. 1991. ed. "Sub-Saharan Africa in the 1990s: Continent in Transition." Special Issue, *Fletcher Forum* 15 (Winter): 1-81.

Eckstein, Harry. 1988. "A Culturalist Theory of Political Change." *American Political Science Review* 82/3: 789-804.

Ekeh, Peter. 1992. "The Constitution of Civil Society in African History and Politics." In *Democratic Transition in Africa*, eds. B. Caron, A. Gboyega and E. Osaghae. Ibadan: CREDU.

Eleazu, Uma O. 1973. "The Role of the Army in African Politics: A Reconsideration of Existing Theories and Practices." *Journal of Developing Areas* 7/2 (April): 265-286.

Ellis, Stephen. 1993. "Rumour and Power in Togo." *Africa* 63: 462-476.

_____. 1995. *Democracy in Sub-Saharan Africa: Where Did It Come From? Can It Be Supported?* ECDPM Working Paper, no. 6. The Hague, The Netherlands: European Center for Development Policy Management, September 7.

_____. 1996. *Africa Now: People, Policies and Institutions*. London: James Currey.

Englebert, Pierre. 1999a. "Benin: Recent History." In *Africa: South of the Sahara 1999*, 28th ed. London: Europa Publications Ltd.

Emerson, Rupert. 1960. *From Empire to Nation*. Cambridge, MA: Harvard University Press.

_____. 1999b. "Republic of the Congo: Recent History." In *Africa: South of the Sahara 1999*. 28th ed. London: Europa Publications Ltd.

_____. 1999c. "Gabon: Recent History." In *Africa: South of the Sahara 1999*, 28th ed. London: Europa Publications Ltd.

_____. 1999d. "Mali: Recent History." In *Africa: South of the Sahara 1999*, 28th ed. London: Europa Publications Ltd.

_____. 1999e. "Niger: Recent History." In *Africa: South of the Sahara 1999*, 28th ed. London: Europa Publications Ltd.

_____. 1999f. "Togo: Recent History." In *Africa: South of the Sahara 1999*, 28th ed. London: Europa Publications Ltd.

Ergas, Zakis, ed. 1987. *The African State in Transition*. New York: St. Martin's Press.

Ethier, Diane, ed. 1990. *Democratic Transition and Consolidation in Southern Europe, Latin America and Southeast Asia*. London: Macmillan Press.

European Center for Development Policy. 1992. *Democratization in Sub-Saharan Africa: The Search for Institutional Renewal*. ECDPM Occasional Paper. Maastricht, The Netherlands: EDCPM, July 1992.

Fage, John D. 1995. *A History of Africa*, 3rd ed. New York: Routledge.

Falk, Richard. 1995. *On Humane Governance: Toward a New Global Politics*. University Park, PA: The Pennsylvania State University Press.

Fatton, Jr., Robert. 1990. "Liberal Democracy in Africa." *Political Science Quarterly* 105: 455-473.

_____. 1991. "Democracy and Civil Society in Africa." *Mediterranean Quarterly* 2/4: 83-95.

_____. 1992. *Predatory Rule: The State and Civil Society in Africa*. Boulder, CO: Lynne Rienner.

_____. 1995. "Africa in the Age of Democratization: the Civic Limitations of Civil Society." *African Studies Review* 38/2: 67-99.

Feit, Edward. 1968. "Military Coups and Political Development." *World Politics* 20/2 (January): 179-193.

Finer, Samuel E. 1962. *The Man on Horseback: The Role of the Military in Politics*. London: Penguin Books Ltd.

_____. 1967. "The One Party Regimes in Africa: Reconsiderations." *Government and Opposition* 2/4 (July-October): 491-509.

First, Ruth. 1970. *Power in Africa*. New York: Pantheon Books.

Fitzsimmons, Michael P. 1994. *The Remaking of France: The National Assembly and the Constitutions of 1791*. Cambridge: Cambridge University Press.

Foltz, William J. 1993. "Democracy: Officers and Politicians." *Africa Report* 38/3: 65-67.

_____. 1994. "Democracy, Development and the Military: Some Lessons from Africa." Paper presented at the annual meeting of the African Studies Association, Toronto, November 3-6, 1994.

Fondation Friedrich Naumann, ed. 1994. *Les Actes de la Conférence Nationale*. Cotonou: Éditions ONEPI.

Forde, Daryll C. and P.M. Kaberry, eds. 1967. *West African Kingdoms in the Nineteenth Century*. London: Oxford University Press.

Fortman, Bas de Gaay. 1994. "Conceptualizing Democracy in an African Context." *Quest* 8/1: 31-47.

Frazer, Jendayi. 1995. "Conceptualizing Civil-Military Relations during Democratic Transition." *Africa Today* 42/1-2: 39-48.

Freund, Bill. 1998. *The Making of Contemporary Africa: The Development of African Society since 1800*, 2nd ed. Boulder, CO: Lynne Rienner.

Fukuyama, Francis. 1992. *The End of History and the Last Man*. London: Penguin Books.

_____. 1995. *Trust: The Social Virtues and the Creation of Prosperity*. New York: Free Press.

Gaile, Charles M. 1970. "The Military in Developing System: A Brief Overview." In *The Human Factor in Political Development*, ed. Monte Palmer. Waltham, MA: Ginn and Co.

Gallie, W.B. 1956. "Essentially Contested Concepts." *Aristotelian Society* 56: 167-198.

Garcia, Luc. 1970. "Les Mouvements de Résistance au Dahomey." *Cahiers d'Études Africaines* 37: 144-178.

_____. 1988. *Le Royaume du Danhomè Face à la Pénétration Coloniale: Affrontements et Incompréhensions (1875-1894)*. Paris: Karthala.

Gardinier, David E. 1994. *Historical Dictionary of Gabon*, 2nd ed. Metuchen, NJ: Scarecrow Press.

_____. 1997. "The Historical Origins of Francophone Africa." In *Political Reform in Francophone Africa*, eds. John F. Clark and David E. Gardinier. Boulder, CO: Westview Press.

Gbado, Béatrice. 1991. *En Marche vers la Liberté: Préludes du Renouveau Démocratique au Bénin*. Cotonou: SYNES.

Geertz, Clifford. 1973. *The Interpretation of Cultures: Selected Essays*. New York: Basic Books.

Gellner, Ernest. 1991. "Civil Society in Historical Context." *International Social Science Journal* 129: 495-510.

Gendzel, Glen. 1997. "Political Culture: Genealogy of a Concept." *Journal of Interdisciplinary History* 28/2 (Autumn): 225-250.

Genné, Marcelle. 1978. "La Tentation du Socialisme au Bénin." *Études Internationales* 9/3: 383-403.

George, Alexander. 1982. "Case Studies and Theory Development: The Method of Structured Focused Comparison." In Paul G. Lauren ed. *Diplomacy: New Approaches in History, Theory, and Policy*. New York: The Free Press.

Geremek, Bronislaw. 1992. "Civil Society Then and Now." *Journal of Democracy* 3/2: 3-12.

_____, et al. 1992. *The Idea of Civil Society*. Research Triangle Park, NC: National Humanities Center.

Ghosh, A. 1989. "Civil Liberties and the Uncivil Society." In *Seminar*, special issue on *"New Social Movements"* 355: 34-37.

Glèlè, Maurice Ahanhanzo. 1969. *Naissance d'un État Noir (L'Évolution Politique et Constitutionnelle du Dahomey, de la Colonisation à nos Jours*. Paris: Librairie Générale de Droit et de la Jurisprudence.

_____. 1974. *Le Danxome: Du Pouvoir Aja à la Nation Fon*. Paris: Paillart.

Glickman, Harvey. 1988. "Frontiers of Liberal and Non-Liberal Democracy in Tropical Africa." *Journal of Asian and African Studies* 23/3-4: 234-254.

_____, ed. 1991. "Challenges to and Transitions from Authoritarianism in Africa: Issue on Political Liberalization." *Issue: A Journal of Opinion* 20/1: 5-53.

_____, ed. 1995. *Ethnic Conflict and democratization in Africa*. Atlanta: A.S.A. Press.

Godin, Francine. 1986. *Bénin 1972-1982: La Logique de l'État Africain*. Paris: L'Harmattan.

Goldsworthy, David. 1981. "Civilian Control of the Military in Black Africa." *African Affairs* 80/8: 49-74.

Good, Kenneth. 1997. "Development and Democracies: Liberal versus Popular." *Africa Insight* 27/4: 253-257.

Goodenough, Ward H. 1971. *Culture, language and Society.* Modular Publications 7. Reading, MA: Addison-Wesley.

Gorbachev, Mikhael. 1985. *Perestroika: New Thinking for our Country and the World.* London: Collins.

Gordon, Donald L. 1996. "African Politics." In *Understanding Contemporary Africa,* eds. April A. and Donald L. Gordon. Boulder, CO: Lynne Rienner.

Gramsci, Antonio. 1971. *Selections from the Prison Notebooks.* Edited and Translated by Quintin Hoare and Geoffrey N. Smith. London: Lawrence and Wishart.

Griffiths, Ieuan Ll. 1995. *The African Inheritance.* New York: Routledge.

Grilli, E. and M. Riess. 1992. "EC Aid to Associated Countries: Distributions and Determinants." *Weltwirtschaftliches Archiv* 128/2: 202-220.

Gros, Jean-Germain, ed. 1998. *Democratization in Late Twentieth-Century Africa: Coping with Uncertainty.* Westport, CT: Greenwood Press.

Guha, R. 1989. "The Problem." *Seminar,* special issue on "*New Social Movements*" 355: 12-15.

Gutteridge, William F. 1969. *The Military in African Politics.* London: Methuen

——————. 1975a. *Africa's Military Rulers.* London: Institute for the Study of Conflict.

——————. 1975b. *Military Regimes in Africa.* London: Methuen.

——————. 1985. "Undoing Military Coups in Africa." *Third World Quarterly* 7/1: 121-146.

Gyimah-Boadi, E. 1998. "The Rebirth of African Liberalism." *Journal of Democracy* 9/2: 18-31.

Habermas, Jurgen. 1989. *The Structural Transformation of the Public Sphere.* Cambridge: Polity.

Hadenius, Axel. 1992. *Democracy and Development.* Cambridge: Cambridge University Press.

——————— and Fredrik Uggla. 1996. "Making Civil Society Work, Promoting Democratic Development: What can States and Donors Do?" *World Development* 24/10: 1621-1639.

Hanneman, Robert A. 1985. "The Military's Role in Political Regimes." *Armed Forces and Society* 12/1: 29-51.

Harbeson, John, Donald Rothchild, and Naomi Chazan. 1994. eds. *Civil Society and the State in Africa*. Boulder, CO: Lynne Rienner.

Haugerud, Angelique. 1995. *The Culture of Politics in Modern Kenya*. Cambridge: Cambridge University Press.

Haynes, Jeff. 1991. "The State, Governance, and Democracy in Sub-Saharan Africa." *Journal of Modern African Studies* 31/3: 535-539.

Hayward, Fred. 1987. *Elections in Independent Africa*. Boulder, CO: Westview.

Hazoume, Guy landry, Jean-Suret-Canale, and A.I. Asiwaju, eds. 1977. *La Vie et l'Œuvre de Louis Hunkanrin*. Cotonou: Librairie Renaissance.

Hegel, George W. F. 1942. *Philosophy of Right*. Oxford: Oxford University Press.

Heilbrunn, John R. 1993. "Social Origins of National Conferences in Benin and Togo." *Journal of Modern African Studies* 31/2: 277- 99.

_____. 1997. "Togo: The National Conference and Stalled Reform." In *Political Reform in Francophone Africa*, eds. Clark, John F. and David E. Gardiner. Boulder, CO: Westview Press.

_____. 1999. "The Flea on Nigeria's Back: The Foreign Policy of Benin." In *African Foreign Policies*, ed. Stephen Wright. Boulder, CO: Westview Press.

Held, David. 1987. *Models of Democracy*. Stanford: Stanford University Press.

_____. 1991. "Democracy and Globalization." *Alternatives* 16: 201-208.

_____. 1993. *Prospects for Democracy*. Cambridge: Polity Press.

_____. 1995. *Democracy and the Global Order*. Cambridge: Polity Press

Herskovits, Melville J. 1967. *Dahomey: An Ancient West African Kingdom*, 2 Vols. Evanston: Northwestern University Press.

_____ and William Bascom, eds. 1959. *Continuity and Change in African Cultures*. Chicago: University of Chicago Press.

Hicks, John F. 1992. "Supporting Democracy in Africa." *TransAfrica Forum* 9/2: 69-77.

Higley, John and Michael G. Burton. 1989. "The Élite Variable in Democratic Transitions and Breakdowns." *American Sociological Review* 54: 17-32.

Hippolyte, Mirlande. 1968. "Coups d'État et Régimes Militaires d'Afrique." *Revue Française d'Études Politiques Africaines* 3 (Septembre): 35-53.

Hirschman, Albert O. 1994. "Social Conflicts as Pillars of Democratic Markets Society." *Political Theory* 22/2: 203-218.

Hirst, Paul Q. 1996. "Democracy and Civil Society." In *Reinventing Democracy*, eds. Paul Q. Hirst and Sunil Khilnani. London: Blackwell.

Hodges, Tony and Malyn Newitt. 1988. *Sao Tomé and Príncipe*. Boulder, CO: Westview Press.

Hodgkinson, Edith. 1999a. "Benin: Economy." In *Africa: South of the Sahara 1999* (Encyclopedia), 28th ed. London: Europa Publications Ltd.

_____. 1999b. "Republic of the Congo: Economy." In *Africa: South of the Sahara 1999* (Encyclopedia), 28th ed. London: Europa Publications Ltd.

_____. 1999c. "Togo: Economy." In *Africa: South of the Sahara 1999* (Encyclopedia), 28th ed. London: Europa Publications Ltd.

Holm, John D. and Patrick P. Molutsi. 1990. "Developing Democracy when Civil Society is Weak: The Case of Botswana." *African Affairs* 89: 323-340.

Holo, Théodore. 1990. "La Transition vers la Démocratie: Le Cas du Bénin." *Alternative Démocratique dans le Tiers-Monde* 2: 131-169.

Honneth, Axel. 1993. "Conceptions of 'Civil Society'." *Radical Philosophy* 64 (Summer): 19-22.

Horowitz, Donald L. 1993. "Democracy in Divided Societies." *Journal of Democracy* 4/4: 18-38.

Houngnikpo, Mathurin C. 1999. "Peaceful Democracies on Trial in Africa." *Peace Research: The Canadian Journal of Peace Studies* 31/4 (November): 33-43.

_____. 2000. "Stuck at the Runway; Africa's Distress Call." *Africa Insight* 30/1 (May): 5-12.

_____. 2000. "The Military and Democratization in Africa: A Comparative Study of Benin and Togo." *Journal of Political and Military Sociology* 29/2 (Winter): 210-229.

_____ and Henry Kyambalesa. 2001. *Contemporary Problems Facing Africa and Viable Strategies for Redress*. Lewiston, NY: Edwin Mellen Press.

Hull, Richard W. 1980. *Modern Africa: Change and Continuity*. Englewood Cliffs, NJ: Prentice-Hall, Inc.

Huntington, Samuel P. 1956. "Civilian Control of the Military: A Theoretical Statement." In *Political Behavior: A Reader in Theory and Research*, ed. Eldersveld S. Eulau and Morris Janowitz. Glencoe, IL: Free Press.

_____. 1957. *The Soldier and the State: The Theory and Politics of Civil-Military Relations*. Cambridge, MA: Belknap.

_____. 1968. *Political Order in Changing Societies*. New Haven: Yale University Press.

_____. 1984. "Will More Countries Become Democratic?" *Political Science Quarterly* 99/2 (Spring): 193-218.

_____. 1991. *The Third Wave: Democratization in the Late Twentieth Century*. Norman: University of Oklahoma Press.

_____. 1992. "How Countries Democratize." *Political Science Quarterly* 106: 4-17.

_____. 1995. "Reforming Civil-Military Relations." *Journal of Democracy* 6/4: 9-17.

_____. 1996. "Democracy for the Long Haul." *Journal of Democracy* 7/2: 3-13.

_____. 1997. "After Twenty Years: The Future of the Third Wave." *Journal of Democracy* 8/4: 3-12.

Hutchful, Eboe. 1997. "Militarism and Problems of Democratic Transition." In *Democracy in Africa: The Hard Road Ahead*, ed. Ottaway, Marina. Boulder, CO: Lynne Rienner.

Hyden, Goran. 1997. "Foreign Aid and Democratization in Africa." *Africa Insight* 27/4: 233-239.

_____. 1999. "Governance and the Reconstitution of Political Order." In *State, Conflict, and Democracy in Africa*, ed. Richard Joseph. Boulder, CO: Lynne Rienner.

_____ and Michael Bratton, eds. 1992. *Governance and Politics in Africa*. Boulder, CO: Lynne Rienner.

Iheduru, Obiama M. 1999. *The Politics of Economic Restructuring and Democracy in Africa*. Westport, CT: Greenwood Press.

Ihonvbere, Julius O. 1996. "On the Threshold of Another False Start? A Critical Evaluation of Pro-democracy Movements in Africa." *Journal of African and Asian Studies* 31/1-2:125-142.

_____. 1998. "Where Is the Third Wave? A Critical Evaluation of Africa's Non-Transition to Democracy." In *Multiparty Democracy and Political Change*, eds. John M. Mbaku and Julius O. Ihonvbere. Brookfield, VT: Ashgate.

Imam, Ayesha. 1992. "Democratization Processes in Africa: Problems and Prospects." *Review of African Political Economy* 54: 102-105.

Imperato, Pascal J. 1996. *Historical Dictionary of Mali*, 3rd ed. Lanham, MD: Scarecrow Press.

Inglehart, Ronald. 1988. "The Renaissance of Political Culture." *American Political Science Review* 82/4: 1203-1230.

Inkeles, Alex, ed. 1991. *On measuring Democracy: Its Consequences and Concomitants*. New Brunswick, NJ: Transaction Publishers.

Isaac, Jeffrey. 1993. "Civil Society and the Spirit of Revolt." *Dissent* (Summer): 356-361.

Isichei, Elizabeth. 1977. *History of West Africa since 1800*. New York: Africana Publishing Company.

Issouf, Akandé. 1993. "Bénin: Deux Ans après la Démocratisation." *Information Économique Africaine* 236: 26-27.

Jackman, Robert. 1978. "The Predictability of African Coups d'État." *American Political Science Review* 72/4: 1262-1275.

_____. 1986. "Explaining African Coups d'État." *American Political Science Review* 80/1: 225-232.

Jackson, Robert H. and Carl G. Rosberg. 1982a. *Personal Rule in Black Africa: Prince, Autocrat, Prophet, Tyrant*. Berkeley: University of California Press.

_____. 1982b. "Why Africa's Weak States Persist." *World Politics* 35: 1-24.

_____. 1985. "Democracy in Tropical Africa: Democracy versus Autocracy in African Politics." *Journal of International Affairs* 38/2: 293-306.

Janowitz, Morris. 1964. *The Military in the Political Development of New Nations*. Chicago: University of Chicago Press.

Jeffries, Richard. 1993. "The State, Structural Adjustment and Good Governance in Africa." *Journal of Commonwealth and Comparative Politics* 31/1: 20-35.

Jenkins, J. Craig and Augustine J. Kposowa. 1992. "The Political Origins of African Military Coups: Ethnic Competition, Military Centrality, and the Struggle over the Postcolonial State." *International Studies Quarterly* 36/3: 271-291.

Johnson, John J., ed. 1962. *The Role of the Military in Underdeveloped Countries*. Princeton, NJ: Princeton University Press.

Johnson, Thomas H., R. O. Slater, and Patrick McGowan. 1984. "Explaining African Military Coups d'État, 1960-1982." *American Political Science Review* 78/3: 622-640.

Joseph, Richard, ed. 1989. *Beyond Autocracy in Africa*. Working Papers from Inaugural Seminar of the African Governance Program, February 17-18. Atlanta: Carter Center.

_____, ed. 1990. *African Governance in the 1990s*. Working Papers from the Second Annual Seminar of the African Governance Program, March 23-25. Atlanta, GA: The Carter Center.

_____. 1991. "Africa: The Rebirth of Political Freedom." *Journal of Democracy* 2/4: 11-24.

_____, ed. 1994. *The Democratic Challenge in Africa*. Atlanta, GA: The Carter Center.

Jouffrey, Roger. 1983. "Le Bénin Depuis 1981." *Afrique Contemporaine* 127: 34-43.

Kaba, Lansiné. 1986. "Power and Democracy in African Tradition: The Case of Songhay." In *Democracy and Pluralism in Africa*, ed. Dov Ronen. Boulder, CO: Lynne Rienner.

Kabaya-Katambwa, Jean-Jacques. 1986. "La Conception du Pouvoir et de la Démocratie en Afrique Noire après les Indépendances." *Le Mois en Afrique* 245-246 (Juin): 23-38.

Kamal, Ahmad. 1996. "Civil Society Finding its Place in the Twenty-First Century." *Journal of SID* 3: 68-69.

Kamrava, Mehran. 1993a. "Conceptualising Third World Politics: The State-Society See-Saw." *Third World Quarterly* 14/4: 703-716.

_____. 1993b. *Politics and Society in the Third World*. London: Routledge.

_____. 1995. "Political Culture and a New Definition of the Third World." *Third World Quarterly* 16/4: 691-701.

Kant, Immanuel. 1795. *Perpetual Peace*. New York: MacMillan.

Karl, Terry L. 1990. "Dilemmas of Democratization in Latin America." *Comparative Politics* 23/1 (October): 1-21.

_____ and Philippe C Schmitter. 1991. "Modes of Transition in Latin America, Southern and Eastern Europe." *International Social Science Journal* 128: 269-284.

Kasfir, Nelson. 1992. "Popular Sovereignty and Popular Participation: Mixed Constitutional Democracy in the Third World." *Third World Quarterly* 13/4: 587-605.

_____. 1998. "The Conventional Notion of Civil Society: A Critique." In *Civil Society and Democracy in Africa: Critical Perspectives*. London: Frank Cass.

_____, ed. 1998. *Civil Society and Democracy in Africa: Critical Perspectives*. London: Frank Cass.

Keller, Edmond J. 1993. "Towards a New African Order." *African Studies Review* 36/2: 1-10.

_____. 1995. "Liberalization, Democratization and Democracy in Africa: Comparative Perspectives." *Africa Insight* 25/4: 224-230.

_____ and Donald Rothchild, eds. 1987. *Afro-Marxist Regimes: Ideology and Public Policy*. Boulder, CO: Lynne Rienner.

Kemp, Kenneth W. and Charles Hudlin. 1992. "Civil Supremacy over the Military: Its Nature and Limits." *Armed Forces and Society* 19/1: 7-26.

Kérékou, Mathieu. 1995. *Préparer le Bénin du Futur: Réflexions d'un Citoyen sur le Devenir du Pays*. Porto-Novo: Centre Panafricain de Prospective Sociale.

Khagram, Sanjeev. 1993. "Democracy and Democratization in Africa: A Plea for Pragmatic Possibilism." *Africa Today* 40/4: 55-72.

Kholi, Atul. 1993. "Democratic Transitions in the Developing Countries." *Politica Internazionale* 21/2: 19-34.

Kim, Young C. 1964. "The Concept of Political Culture in Comparative Politics." *Journal of Politics* 26: 313-364.

Kimenyi, Mwangi S. 1989. "Interest Groups, Transfer Seeking, and Democratization: Competition for the Benefits of Governmental Power May Explain African Political Instability." *American Journal of Economics and Sociology* 48/3: 339-349.

_____. 1997. *Ethnic Diversity, Liberty and the State: The African Dilemma*. Cheltenham, UK: Edward Elgar.

Kohn, Richard H. 1997. "How Democracies Control the Military." *Journal of Democracy* 8/4: 140-153.

Koné, Samba S. 1990. *1990: Une Année Pas Comme les Autres*. Abidjan: Presses de la MICI.

Korn, David A. 1991. "Time for Change." *The Christian Science Monitor*. December 5.

Kothari, R. 1988. *State against Democracy*. New Dehli: Ajanta.

Kpundeh, Sahr John. 1992. ed. *Democratization in Africa: African Views, African Voices*. Summary of Three Workshops organized by the National Academy of Science. Washington, D.C.: National Academy Press.

_____ and Stephen P. Riley. 1992. "Political Choice and the New Democratic Politics in Africa." *The Round Table* 323: 263-271.

Kraus, Jon. 1991. "Building Democracy in Africa." *Current History* 90/553: 209-212.

Kumar, Krishan. 1993. "Civil Society: An Inquiry into the Usefulness of an Historical Term." *British Journal of Sociology* 44/3: 375-401.

Kunz, Franz A. 1991. "Liberalization in Africa: Some Preliminary Reflections." *African Affairs* 90/359: 223-235.

_____. 1995. "Civil Society in Africa." *Journal of Modern African Studies* 33/1: 181-187.

Laitin, David D. 1995. "The Civic Culture at 30." *American Political Science Review* 89/1: 168-173.

_____ and Aaron Wildavsky. 1988. "Political Culture and Political Preferences." *American Political Science Review* 82/2: 589-596.

Laloupo, Francis. 1992-1993. "La Conférence Nationale du Bénin: Un Concept Nouveau de Changement de Régime Politique." *Année Africaine*: 78-114.

Lancaster, Carol. 1991/1992. "Democracy in Africa." *Foreign Policy* 85: 148-165.

_____. 1993. "Democratisation in Sub-Saharan Africa." *Survival* 35/3: 38-50.

Landell-Mills, Pierre. 1992. "Governance, Cultural Change, and Empowerment." *Journal of Modern African Studies* 30/4: 543-567.

Lawson, Stephanie. 1993. "Conceptual Issues in the Comparative Study of Regime Change and Democratization." *Comparative Politics* 25/2: 183-205.

Lee, J. M. 1969. *African Armies and Civil Order*. New York: Praeger.

Leftwich, Adrian. 1994. "States of Underdevelopment: The Third World State in Theoretical Perspective." *Journal of Theoretical Politics* 6/1: 55-74.

Legum, Colin. 1986. "Democracy in Africa: Hopes and Trends." In *Democracy and Pluralism in Africa*, ed. Dov Ronen. Boulder, CO: Lynne Rienner.

_____. 1990. "The Coming of Africa's Second Independence." *Washington Quarterly* 13/1 (Winter): 129-140.

_____, ed. 1998. *Africa Contemporary Record*, Vol 23 (1990-1992). London: Europa Publications Ltd.

_____. 1999. *Africa since Independence*. Bloomington: Indiana University Press.

Lemarchand, René. 1968. "Dahomey: Coup within a Coup." *Africa Report* 13/6: 46-54.

_____. 1976. "African Armies in Historical and Contemporary Perspectives: The Search for Connections." *Journal of Political and Military Sociology* 4/2: 261-275.

_____. 1990. "Uncivil States and Civil Societies: How Illusion Became Reality." *Journal of Modern African Studies* 30/2: 177-91.

_____. 1992a. "African Transitions to Democracy: An Interim (and Mostly Pessimistic) Assessment." *Africa Insight* 22/3: 178-185.

_____. 1992b. "Africa's Troubled Transitions." *Journal of Democracy* 3/4: 98-109.

_____. 1994. "Managing Transition Anarchies." *Journal of Modern African Studies* 32/4: 581-604.

Lerner, Daniel. 1958. *The passing of Traditional Society: Modernizing the Middle East.* Glencoe, IL: Free Press.

Levallois, Michel. 1996. "Actualité de l'Afro-Pessimisme." *Afrique Contemporaine* 179/3: 3-15.

Levine, Daniel. 1988. "Paradigm Lost: Dependence to Democracy." *World Politics* 40/3: 377-394.

LeVine, Victor T. 1967. *Political Leadership in Africa.* Stanford: Stanford University Press.

_____. 1980. "African Patrimonial Regimes in Comparative Perspective." *Journal of Modern African Studies* 18/4: 657-673.

_____. 1987. "Military Rule in the People's Republic of Congo." In *The Military in African Politics,* ed. John W. Harbeson. Westport, CT: Praeger.

Lewis, Arthur W. 1965. *Politics in West Africa.* Oxford: Oxford University Press.

Lewis, Peter. 1992. "Political Transition and the Dilemma of Civil Society in Africa." *Journal of International Affairs* 27/1 (Summer): 31-54.

_____. 1998. "Political Transition and the Dilemma of Civil Society in Africa." In *Africa: Dilemmas of Development and Change,* ed. Peter Lewis. Boulder, CO: Westview Press.

Leys, Colin. 1982. "Economic Development in Theory and Practice." *Daedalus* 111/2: 99-148.

Lijphart, Arendt. 1969. "Consociational Democracy." *World Politics* 21/2 (January): 207-225.

_____. 1977. *Democracy in Plural Societies.* New Haven: Yale University Press.

_____. 1984. *Democracies.* New Haven: Yale University Press.

Linton, Ralph. 1945. *The Cultural Background of Personality.* New York: Appleton-Century.

Linz, Juan J. 1978. *The Breakdown of Democratic Regimes: Crisis, Breakdown and Re-equilibration.* Baltimore: Johns Hopkins University Press.

_____. 1990. "Transitions to Democracy." *Washington Quarterly* 13/3 (Summer): 143-164.

Lipset, Seymour M. 1959. "Some Social Requisites of Democracy." *American Political Science Review* 53/1: 69-105.

_____. 1960. *Political Man: The Social Basis of Politics.* New York: Doubleday.

_____. 1990. "The Centrality of Political Culture." *Journal of Democracy* 1/4: 80-83.

Lofchie, Michael F. 1968. "Political Theory and African Politics." *Journal of Modern African Studies* 6/1: 3-15.

Lombard, Jacques. 1958. *Dahomey: Sa Géographie, Son Histoire, Son Ethnographie.* Dakar, Sénégal: IFAN.

_____. 1967. "The Kingdom of Dahomey." In *West African Kingdoms in the Nineteenth Century,* eds. P.M. Kaberry and Daryll C. Forde. London: Oxford University Press.

Londregan, John and Keith Poole. 1990. "Poverty, the Coup Trap and the Seizure of Executive Power." *World Politics* 42: 151-183.

Lonsdale, John. 1981. "States and Social Processes in Africa: An Historiographical Survey." *African Studies Review* 24/3: 139-225.

_____. 1986. "Political Accountability in African History." In *Political Domination in Africa: Reflections on the Limits of Power,* ed. Patrick Chabal. Cambridge: Cambridge University Press. 126-157.

Loong, Wong. 1991. "Authoritarianism and Transition to Democracy in a Third World State." *Critical Sociology* 18/2 (Summer): 77-102.

Luckham, Robin A. 1971. "A Comparative Typology of Civil-Military Relations." *Government and Opposition* 6/1: 5-35.

_____. 1975. *Politicians and Soldiers in Ghana, 1966-1972.* London: Frank Cass.

_____. 1982. "French Militarism in Africa." *Review of African Political Economy* 24: 55-84.

_____. 1994. "The Military, Militarization, and Democratization in Africa: A Survey of Literature and Issues." *African Studies Review* 37/2 (September): 13-76.

_____. 1995. "Dilemmas of Military Disengagement and Democratization in Africa." *IDS Bulletin* 26: 49-61.

220   **Determinants of Democratization in Africa**

_____. 1996. "Democracy and the Military: An Epitaph for Frankenstein's Monster? *Democratization* 3/2: 1-16.

_____ and Gordon White, eds. 1996. *Democratization in the South: The Jagged Wave*. Manchester: Manchester University Press.

Luttwak, Edward. 1968. *Coup d'État: A Practical Handbook*. London: Allen Lane.

Lutz, James. 1989. "The Diffusion of Political Phenomena in Sub-Saharan Africa." *Journal of Political and Military Sociology* 17/1: 99-104.

Magang, David. 1992. "A New Beginning: The Process of Democratization in Africa." *The Parliamentarian* 4: 235-239.

Mair, Lucy. 1977. *African Kingdoms*. Oxford: Oxford University Press.

Magnusson, Bruce. 1996. "Benin: Legitimating Democracy, New Institutions and The Historical Problem of Economic Crisis." *Afrique Politique*: 33-54.

_____. 1999. "Testing Democracy in Benin: Experiments in Institutional Reform." In *State, Conflict, and Democracy in Africa*, ed. Richard Joseph. Boulder, CO: Lynne Rienner.

Makumbe, John Mw. 1998. "Is there a Civil Society in Africa?" *International Affairs* 74/2: 305-317.

Malwal, Bona. 1986. "The African System of Pluralism." In *Democracy and Pluralism in Africa*, ed. Dov Ronen. Boulder, CO: Lynne Rienner.

Mamdani, Mahmood. 1986. "Peasants and Democracy in Africa." *New Left Review* 156 (March-April): 37-49.

_____. 1990. "The Social Basis of Constitutionalism in Africa." *Journal of Modern African Studies* 28/3: 359-374.

_____. 1992. "Democratic Theory and Democratic Struggles in Africa." *Dissent* 39/3 (Summer): 312-318.

_____. 1995. "A Critique of the State and Civil Society Paradigm in Africanist Studies." In *African Studies in Social Movements and Democracy*, eds. Mahmood Mamdani and Ernest Wamba-Dia-Wamba. Dakar, Senegal: CODESRIA.

_____. 1999. "Indirect Rule, Civil Society, and Ethnicity: The African Dilemma." In *Out of One, Many Africas: Reconstructing the Study and Meaning of Africa*, eds. William G. Martin and Michael O. West. Chicago: University of Illinois Press.

_____ and Ernest Wamba-dia-Wamba, eds. 1995. *African Studies in Social Movements and Democracy*. Dakar, Senegal: CODESRIA.

Manizurraman, Talukdar. 1987. *Military Withdrawal from Politics.* Cambridge, MA: Ballinger Publishing Company.

Manning, Patrick. 1988. *Francophone Sub-Saharan Africa, 1880-1985.* New York: Cambridge University Press.

Marchal, Roland. 1998. "France and Africa: The Emergence of Essential reforms?" *International Affairs* 74/2: 355-372.

Markakis, John and Michael Waller. 1986. *Military Marxist Regimes in Africa.* London: Frank Cass.

Marks, Gary and Larry Diamond, eds. 1992. *Reexamining Democracy: Essays in Honour of Seymour Martin Lipset.* London: Sage.

Martin, Guy. 1983. "Les Fondements Historiques Économiques et Politiques de la Politique Africaine de la France: Du Colonialisme au Néocolonialisme." *Genève-Afrique* 21/2: 4-7.

_____. 1985. "Bases of France's African Policy." *Journal of Modern African Studies* 23/2: 189-208.

_____. 1986. "The Franc Zone, Underdevelopment and Dependency in Francophone Africa." *Third World Quarterly* 8/1: 205-235.

_____. 1993. "Democratic Transition in Mali." *Africa Demos* 3/2: 5-8.

_____. 1995. "Continuity and Change in Franco-African Relations." *Journal of Modern African Studies* 33/1: 1-20.

Martin, Michel-Louis. 1984. "Note sur le Changement Politique et Constitutionnel en République Populaire du Bénin depuis l'Indépendance." *Année Africaine*: 91-127.

_____. 1986a. "La Spécificité des Forces Armées Africaines." In *Les Armées Africaines*, ed. Institut Africain d'Études Stratégiques. Paris: Economica.

_____. 1986b. "The Rise and 'Thermidorization' of Radical Praetorianism in Benin." In *Military Marxist Regimes in Africa*, eds. Markakis, John and Michael Waller. London: Frank Cass.

_____. 1990. *Le Soldat Africain et le Politique: Essai sur le Militarisme et l'État Prétorien au Sud du Sahara.* Toulouse: Presses de l'Institut d'Études Politiques.

_____. 1995. "Armies and Politics: The 'Lifecycle' of Military Rule in Sub-Saharan Francophone Africa." In *State and Society in Francophone Africa since Independence*, eds. Anthony Kirk-Greene and Daniel Bach. London: St. Martin's Press.

_____. 1997. "Operational Weakness and Political Activism: The Military in Sub-Saharan Africa." In *To Sheathe the Sword:*

Civil-Military Relations in the Quest for Democracy, eds. John P. Lovell and David E. Albright. Westport, CT: Greenwood Press.

Marx, Karl. 1843. "Towards a Critique of Hegel's Philosophy of Right. Introduction." In *Marx Selections*, ed. A. W. Wood (1988). London: Macmillan.

Mauck, Gerardo L. 1994. "Democratic Transitions in Comparative Perspective." *World Politics* (April): 355-375.

Maurois, André. 1956. *A History of France*. Trans. Henry L. Binsse. New York: Farrar, Strauss & Cudahy.

May, John D. 1978. "Defining Democracy: A Bid for Coherence and Consensus." *Political Studies* 26/1: 1-14.

Mayrargue, Cédric. 1996. "Le Caméléon Est Remonté en Haut de l'Arbre: Le Retour au Pouvoir de M. Kérékou au Bénin." *Politique Africaine* 62 (Juin): 124-131.

Mbachu, Ozoemenam 1994. "Democracy in Africa: A Theoretical Overview." *Coexistence* 31/2: 147-157.

Mbaku, John Mukum. 1992. "Political Democracy and the Prospects of Development in Post-Cold War Africa." *Journal of Social, Political and Economic Studies* 17/3-4: 345-371.

_____. 1993. "Political Democracy, Military Expenditures and Economic Growth in Africa." *Scandinavian Journal of Development Alternatives* 12/1: 49-64.

_____. 1994. "Military Coups as Rent-Seeking Behavior." *Journal of Political and Military Sociology* 22/2 (Winter): 241-284.

_____ and Julius O. Ihonvbere, eds. 1998. *Multiparty Democracy and Political Change: Constraints to Democratization in Africa*. Brookfield, Vermont: Ashgate.

Mbembe, Achille. 1985. *Les Jeunes et L'Ordre Politique en Afrique Noire*. Paris: L'Harmattan.

_____. 1988. *Afriques Indociles*. Paris: Karthala.

_____. 1990. "Democratization and Social Movements in Africa." *Africa Demos* 1/1 (November): 4-18.

Mbikutsita-Lewanika, Akashambatwa and Derrick Chitala, eds. 1990. *The Hour Has Come: Proceedings of the National Conference on the Multi-Party Option*. Lusaka: Zambia Research Foundation.

McCaskie, Thomas. 1995. *State and Society in Pre-Colonial West Africa*, 2nd Ed. Madison, WI: University of Wisconsin Press.

McFerson, Hazel M. 1992. "Democracy and Development in Africa." *Journal of Peace Research* 29/3: 241-248.

McGowan, Patrick. 1975. "Predicting Political Instability in Tropical Africa." In *Quantitative Techniques in Foreign Policy Analysis and Forecasting*. New York: Praeger.

_____ and Thomas H. Johnson. 1984. "African Military Coups d'État and Underdevelopment: A Quantitative Historical Analysis." *Journal of Modern African Studies* 22/4: 847-882.

_____. 1985. "Forecasting African Coups d'État." *South African Journal of Political Science* 12/2: 19-31.

_____. 1986. "Sixty Coups in Thirty Years: Further Evidence Regarding African Military Coups d'État." *Journal of Modern African Studies* 24/3: 352-371.

McKinlay, R.D. and R. White. 1978. "The French Aid Relationship: A Foreign Policy Model of Distribution of French Bilateral Aid, 1964-1970." *Development and Change* 9/3: 459-478.

McKinlay, R.D. and R. Little. 1979. "The U.S. Aid Relationship: A Test of the Recipient Need and the Donor Interest Models." *Political Studies* 27/2: 236-250.

McLean, Iain. 1994. "Democratization and Economic Liberalization: Which is the Chicken and Which is the Egg?" *Democratization* 1/1: 27-40.

McNamara, Francis T. 1989. *France in Black Africa*. Washington, DC: National Defense University.

Médard, Jean-François. 1991. "Autoritarismes et Démocraties en Afrique Noire." *Politique Africaine* 43 (Octobre): 92-104.

_____. 1994. *États d'Afrique Noire: Formation, Mécanismes et Crises*. Paris: Karthala.

Médeiros, Francisco de. 1981. "Armée et Instabilité: Les Partis Militaires au Bénin." In *La Politique de Mars: Les Processus Politiques dans les Partis Militaires Contemporains*, ed. Alain Rouquié. Paris: Le Sycamore.

Meillassoux, Claude, ed. 1971. *The Development of Indigenous Trade and Markets in West Africa*. Oxford: Oxford University Press.

Memmi, Albert. 1967. *The Colonizer and the Colonized*. Boston: Beacon Press.

Messone, Nelson N. and Jean-Germain Gros. 1998. "The Irony of Wealth: Democratization in Gabon." In *Democratization in Late Twentieth Century Africa: Coping with Uncertainty*, ed. Jean-Germain Gros. Westport, CT: Greenwood Press.

Mill, John Stuart. 1863. "Types of Theorizing: A System of Logic." In *Comparative Perspectives: Theories and Methods*, eds. Amitai Etzioni and F. Dubow. New York: Basic Books.

Monga, Célestin. 1994. *Anthropologie de la Colère: Société Civile et Démocratie en Afrique Noire*. Paris: L'Harmattan.

_____. 1995. "Civil Society and Democratisation in Francophone Africa." *Journal of Modern African Studies* 33/3: 359-79.

_____. 1996. *The Anthropology of Anger: Civil Society and Democracy in Africa*, trans. Linda L. Fleck and Célestin Monga. Boulder, CO: Lynne Rienner.

Moore, Barrington Jr. 1966. *The Social Origins of Dictatorship and Democracy: Lord and Peasant in the Making of the Modern World*. Boston: Beacon Press.

Moose, George E. 1985. "French Military Policy in Africa." In *Arms and the African: Military Influences on Africa's International Relations*, eds. Foltz, William J. and Henry S. Bienen. New Haven: Yale University Press.

Morel, Yves. 1992. "Démocratisation en Afrique Noire: Les 'Conférences Nationales'." *Études* 376/6: 733-743.

Morgenthau, Ruth S. 1961. "Single-Party Systems in West Africa." *American Political Science Review* 55/2: 978-993.

Moss, Todd J. 1995. "U.S. Policy and Democratization in Africa: The Limits of Liberal Universalism." *Journal of Modern African Studies* 33/2: 189-209.

Moukoko-Mbonjo, Pierre. 1993. "Régimes Militaires et Transition Démocratique en Afrique: À la Recherche d'un Cadre d'Analyse Théorique." *Afrique 2000* 13: 39-58.

Mowoe, Isaac J. 1980. *The Performance of Soldiers as Governors: African Politics and the African Military*. Washington, D.C.: University Press of America.

Muller, Edward N. 1988. "Democracy, Economic Development, and Income Inequality." *American Sociological Review* 53/1: 50-68.

_____ and Mitchell A. Seligson. 1994. "Civic Culture and democracy: The Question of Causal Relationships." *American Political Science Review* 88/3: 635-652.

Munck, Geraldo. 1994. "Democratic Transitions in Comparative Perspective." *Comparative Politics* 26/3 (April): 355-375.

Mundt, Robert J. 1997. "Côte d'Ivoire: Continuity and Change in A semi-Democracy." In *Political Reform in Francophone Africa*, eds. John F Clark and David E. Gardinier. Boulder, CO: Westview Press.

Munslow, Barry. 1983. "Why Has the Westminster Model Failed in Africa?" *Parliamentary Affairs* 36/2: 218-228.

_____. 1993. "Democratization in Africa." *Parliamentary Affairs* 46/4: 478-490.

Murdock, George P. 1959. *Africa: Its Peoples and their Cultural History.* New York: McGraw-Hill.

Nannan, Sukhwant Singh. 1992. "Africa: The Move towards Democracy." *Strategic Analysis* 14/10: 1221-1232.

Nash, Kate. 2000. *Contemporary Political Sociology: Globalization, Politics, and Power.* Oxford: Blackwell.

Ndue, Paul Ntungwe. 1994. "Africa's Turn towards Pluralism." *Journal of Democracy* 5/1: 45-54.

Nelkin, Dorothy. 1967. "The Economic and Social Setting of Military Takeovers in Africa." *Journal of Asian and African Studies* 2/3-4: 230-244.

Neocleous, Mark. 1996. *Administering Civil Society: Towards a Theory of State Power.* London: MacMillan Press.

Newbury, Catharine. 1994. "Introduction: Paradoxes of Democratization in Africa." *African Studies Review* 37/1: 1-8.

Nicol, Davidson. 1986. "African Pluralism and Democracy." In *Democracy and Pluralism in Africa,* ed. Dov Ronen. Boulder, CO: Lynne Rienner.

Niebuhr, Reinhold and Paul E. Sigmund. 1969. *The Democratic Experience.* New York: Praeger.

Ninalowo, Bayo. 1990. "On the Structures and Praxis of Domination, Democratic Culture and Social Change: With Inferences from Africa." *Scandinavian Journal of Development Studies* 9/4: 107-117.

Nkrumah, Kwame. 1961. *Politics Is not for Soldiers.* Accra: Government Printers.

Nolutshungu, Sam C. 1992. "Africa in a World of Democracies: Interpretation and Retrieval." *Journal of Commonwealth and Comparative Politics* 30/3: 316-334.

Nordlinger, Eric A. 1970. "Soldiers in Mufti: The Impact of Military Rule upon Economic and Social Change in Non-Western States." *American Political Science Review* 64/4: 1138-1148.

_____. 1972. *Soldiers in Politics: Military Coups and Governments.* Englewood Cliffs, NJ: Prentice-Hall.

Nordlund, Per. 1996. *Organising the Political Agora: Domination and Democratisation in Zambia and Zimbabwe*. Uppsala: Uppsala University Press.

Norton, Augustus, R., ed. 1995. *Civil Society in the Middle East*, Vol. 1. Leiden: E.J. Brill.

Nwajiaku, Kathryn. 1994. "The National Conferences in Benin and Togo Revisited." *Journal of Modern African Studies* 32/3: 429-447.

Nyang'oro, Julius E. 1994. "Reform Politics and the Democratization Process in Africa." *African Studies Review* 37/1: 133-150.

_____. 1996. "Critical Notes on Political Liberalization in Africa." *Journal of African and Asian Studies* 31/1-2: 112-124.

Nzouankeu, Jacques-Mariel. 1991. "The African Attitude to Democracy." *International Social Science Journal* 43/2: 373-385.

_____. 1993. "The Role of the National Conference in the Transition to Democracy: The Cases of Benin and Mali." *Issue: A Journal of Opinion* 21/1-2: 44-50.

_____. 1994. "Decentralization and Democracy in Africa." *International Review of Administrative Sciences* 60/2: 213-227.

Odhiambo, Atieno. 1994. "Democracy and the Emergent Present in Africa: Interrogating the Historical Assumptions." *Afrika Zamani*, new series 2: 27-41.

O'Donnell, Guillermo. 1993. "On the State, Democratization and some Conceptual Problems." *World Development* 21/8: 1355-1369.

_____, Philippe C. Schmitter and Lawrence Whitehead. 1986. *Transitions from Authoritarian Rule*. Baltimore: Johns Hopkins University Press.

_____ and Philippe C. Schmitter. 1986. *Transitions from Authoritarian Rule: Tentative Conclusions about Uncertain Democracies*. Baltimore: John Hopkins University Press.

Ogot, Bethwell A., ed. 1972. *War and Society in Africa: Ten Studies*. London: Frank Cass.

Ogunjimi, Bayo. 1990. "The Military and Literature in Africa." *Journal of Political and Military Sociology* 18/2 (Winter): 327-341.

O'Kane, Rosemary H. T. 1981. "A Probabilistic Approach to the Causes of Coups d'État." *British Journal of Political Science* 11/3: 287-308.

_____. 1987. *The Likelihood of Coups*. Brookfield, VT: Avebury.

_____. 1989. "Military Regimes: Power and Force." *European Journal of Political Research* 17: 333-350.

Oke, Mathias F. 1968. "Survivance Tribale ou Problématique Nationale en Afrique Noire? Un Cas Concret, Celui de la Réalité Dahoméenne." *Études Dahoméennes*, Nouvelle Série 12: 5-10.

_____. 1969. "Des Comités Electoraux aux Partis Politiques Dahoméens." *Revue Française d'Études Politiques Africaines* 45: 45-61.

Olodo, André. 1978. "Les Institutions de la République Populaire du Bénin." *Revue Juridique, Politique, Independance, Coopération* 32/2: 647-802.

Olsen, Gorm R. 1997. "Western Europe's Relations with Africa since the End of the Cold War." *Journal of Modern African Studies* 35/2: 299-319.

_____. 1998. "Europe and The Promotion of Democracy in Post-Cold War Africa: How Serious Is Europe and for What Reason?" *African Affairs* 97/388: 343-367.

Onwumechili, Chuka. 1998. *African Democratization and Military Coups*. Westport, CT: Praeger.

Orkand Corporation. 1983. *Analysis of the Cause of Coups d'État in Sub-Saharan Africa, 1960-1982*. Silver Spring, MD: Orkand Corporation.

Osaghae, Eghosa E. 1998. *Structural Adjustment, Civil Society, and National Cohesion in Africa*. Harare: African Association of Political Science.

Osterdahl, Inger. 1997. *La France dans l'Afrique de l'Après-Guerre Froide: Interventions et Justifications*. Uppsala: Nordiska Afrika Institutet.

Otayek, René. 1997. "Démocratie, Culture Politique, Sociétés Plurales: Une Approche Comparative à Partir de Situations Africaines." *Revue Française de Science Politique* 47/6: 798-822.

Ottaway, Marina. 1993. "Should Elections Be the Criterion of Democratization in Africa?" *CSIS Africa Notes* 145: 1-5.

_____. 1997. "African Democratisation and the Leninist Option." *Journal of Modern African Studies* 35/1: 1-15.

_____, ed. 1997. *Democracy in Africa: The Hard Road Ahead*. Boulder, CO: Lynne Rienner.

Ottaway, Marina and David. 1986. *Afrocommunism*, 2nd ed. New York: Africana Publishing.

Owusu, Maxwell. 1992. "Democracy and Africa—A View from the Village." *Journal of Modern African Studies* 30/3: 369-396.

_____. 1997. "Domesticating Democracy: Culture, Civil Society, and Constitutionalism in Africa." *Comparative Studies in Society and History* 39/1: 120-152.

Oyugi, Walter O., et al., eds. 1988. *Democratic Theory and Practice in Africa.* London: James Currey.

Palmer, Robert R. and Joel Colton. 1971. *A History of the Modern World,* 4th ed. New York: Alfred A. Knopf

Paraiso, Alexandre. 1980. "La Loi Fondamentale et les Nouvelles Institutions de la République Populaire du Bénin." *Recueil Penant* 769: 288-306.

Parry, Geraint and Michael Moran, eds. 1994. *Democracy and Democratization.* London: Routledge.

Pateman, Carole. 1971. "Political Culture, Political Structure, and Political Change." *British Journal of Political Science* 1/3: 291-305.

Pateman, Carole. 1980. *Participation and Democratic Theory.* London: Cambridge University Press.

_____. 1996. "Democracy and Democratization." *International Political Science Review* 17/1: 5-12.

Patterson, Amy S. 1998. "A Reappraisal of Democracy in Civil Society: Evidence from Rural Senegal." *Journal of Modern African Studies* 36/3: 423-441.

Pelczynski, Zbigniew A. 1988. "Solidarity and the 'Rebirth of Civil Society' in Poland, 1976-1981." In *Civil Society and the State,* ed. John Keane. London: Verso.

Pérennès, Jean-Jacques et Hugues Puel. 1991. "Démocratie et Développement au Sud." *Économie et Humanisme* 319 (Octobre-Novembre): 11-19.

Perlmutter, Amos. 1977. *The Military and Politics in Modern Times.* New Haven: Yale University Press.

Peterson, David L. 1994. "Debunking Ten Myths about Democracy in Africa." *Washington Quarterly* 17/3: 129-141.

Pfaff, William. 1995. "A New Colonialism? Europe Must Go back into Africa." *Foreign Affairs* 74/1: 2-6.

Pinkney, Robert. 1994. *Democracy in the Third World.* Boulder, CO: Lynne Rienner.

Plattner, Marc. 1991. "The Democratic Revolution." *Journal of Democracy* 2/4: 34-46.

Pollard, Robert. 1992. "La Démocratie Ambiguë." *Année Africaine 1992-1993*: 17-57.

Potholm, Christian P. 1979. *The Theory and Practice of African Politics*. Englewood Cliffs, NJ: Prentice-Hall.

Press, Robert M. 1999. *The New Africa: Dispatches from A Changing Continent*. Gainesville: University Press of Florida.

Price, Robert M. 1971. "Military Officers and Political Leadership: The Ghanaian Case." *Comparative Politics* 3/3: 361-379.

Prunier, Gérard. 1991. "Violence et Histoire en Afrique." *Politique Africaine* 42 (Juin): 9-14.

Przeworski, Adam and Fernando Limongi. 1993. "Political Regimes and Economic Growth." *Journal of Economic Perspectives* 7/3: 51-69.

Pye, Lucian W. 1962. "Armies in the Process of Political Modernization." In *The Role of the Military in Underdeveloped Countries*, ed. John J. Johnson. Princeton: Princeton University Press, 69.

Quantin, Patrick. 1982. "La Vision Gaullienne de l'Afrique Noire: Permanences et Adaptations." *Politique Africaine* 2/5: 8-18.

Quantin, Patrick, ed. 1994. *L'Afrique Politique, 1994: Vue sur la Démocratisation à Marée Basse*. Paris: Karthala.

Rasheed, Sadig. 1995. "The Democratization Process and Popular Participation in Africa: Emerging Realities and the Challenges Ahead." *Development and Change* 26/2: 333-354.

Raynal, Jean-Jacques. 1991. "Le Renouveau Démocratique Béninois: Modèle ou Mirage?" *Afrique Contemporaine* 160/4: 3-25.

Rijnierse, Elly. 1993. "Democratization in Sub-Saharan Africa: Literature Overview." *Third World Quarterly* 14/3: 147-64.

Riley, Stephen P. 1991. "The Democratic Transition in Africa." *African Demos* 1/3: 5-8.

_____. 1991. *The Democratic Transition in Africa: An End to the One-Party State?* London: Research Institute for the Study of Conflict and Terrorism.

_____. 1992. "Political Adjustment or Domestic Pressure: Democratic Politics and Political Choice in Africa." *Third World Quarterly* 13/3: 539-551.

_____. 1993. "Post-Independence Anti-Corruption Strategies and the Contemporary Effects of Democratization." *Corruption and Reform* 7/3: 249-261.

Robinson, Ian. 1995. "Globalization and Democracy." *Dissent* (Summer): 373-380.

Robinson, Mark. 1999. "Governance and Coherence in Development Co-operation. In *Policy Coherence in Development Co-operation*, eds. Jacques Forster and Olav Stokke. Portland, OR: Frank Cass.

Robinson, Pearl T. 1994a. "The National Conference Phenomenon in Francophone Africa." *Comparative Studies in Society and History* 36/3: 575-610.

_____. 1994b. "Democratization: Understanding the Relationship between Regime Change and the Culture of Politics." *African Studies Review* 37/1: 39-68.

Ronen, Dov. 1974. "The Colonial Elite in Dahomey." *African Studies Review* 8/1: 55-74.

_____. 1975. *Dahomey: Between Tradition and Modernity.* Ithaca: Cornell University Press.

_____. 1980. "Benin: The Role of the Uniformed Leaders." In *The Performance of Soldiers as Governors: African Politics and the African Military,* ed. Isaac J. Mowoe. Washington, D.C.: University Press of America

_____, ed. 1986. *Democracy and Pluralism in Africa.* Boulder, CO: Lynne Rienner.

_____. 1987. "People's Republic of Benin: The Military, Marxist Ideology, and the Politics of Ethnicity." In *The Military in African Politics,* ed. John Harbeson. New York: Praeger Publishers.

Roniger, Luis. 1994. "Civil Society, Patronage, and Democracy." *International Journal of Comparative Sociology* 35/3-4: 207-220.

Rosanvallon, Pierre. 1995. "The History of the Word 'Democracy' in France." *Journal of Democracy* 6/4: 140-154.

Ross, Andrew L. 1987. "Dimensions of Militarization in the Third World." *Armed Forces and Society* 13/4: 561-578.

Roth, Brad R. 1995. "Evaluating Democratic Progress: A Normative Theoretical Perspective." *Ethics and International Affairs* 9: 55-77.

Roth, Guenther. 1968. "Personal Rulership, Patrimonialism, and Empire-Building in the New States." *World Politics* 20/2: 194-206.

Rothchild, Donald and Naomi Chazan, eds. 1988. *The Precarious Balance: State and Society in Africa.* Boulder, CO: Westview Press.

Rothchild, Donald and V.A. Olorunsola, eds. 1982. *State Versus Ethnic Claims: African Policy Dilemmas.* Boulder, CO: Westview Press.

Rouquié, Alain, ed. 1987. *La Politique de Mars: Les Processus Politiques dans les Partis Militaires Contemporains.* Paris: le Sycamore.

Rousseau, Jean-Jacques. 1762. *The Social Contract.* Harmondsworth: Penguin.

Rowley, Charles K., ed. 1997. *Classical Liberalism and Civil Society.* Cheltenham, UK: Edward Elgar.

Rubin, Barnett R. 1987. "Civil Liberties Movement in India: New Approaches to the State." *Asian Survey* 27/3: 371-392.

Rudebeck, Lars, ed. 1992. *When Democracy Makes Sense: Studies in the Democratic Potential of Third World Popular Movements*. Uppsala: Working Group for the Study of Development Strategies.

Rummel Rudolph J. 1985. "Libertarian Propositions on Violence within and between nations." *Journal of Conflict Resolution* 29/3: 419-455.

_____. 1995. "Democracies Are Less Warlike than Other Regimes." *European Journal of International Relations* 1/4: 457-479.

Rustow, Dankwart A. 1970. "Transitions to Democracy: Towards a Dynamic Model." *Comparative Politics* 2/3: 337-364.

Sachikonye, Lloyd M. 1995. *Democracy, Civil Society and the State*. Harare, Zimbabwe: SAPES Books.

Saga, Hugo. 1991. "Chaillot n'est pas la Baule." *Jeune Afrique* 1613 (November 27-December 3): 4-9.

Sahlins, Marshall D. 1976. *Culture and Practical Reason*. Chicago: University of Chicago Press

Sakamoto, Yoshikazu. 1991. "The Global Context of Democratization." *Alternatives* 16/2: 119-128.

Sandbrook, Richard. 1987. "Personnalisation du Pouvoir et Stagnation Capitaliste: L'État Africain en Crise." *Politique Africaine* 26 (Juin): 15-37.

_____. 1988. "Liberal Democracy in Africa: A Socialist-Revisionist Perspective." *Canadian Journal of African Studies* 22/2: 337-364.

_____. 1990. "Taming the African Leviathan." *World Policy Journal* 7/4: 673-701.

Sarkesian, Sam C. 1981. "Military Professionalism and Civil-Military Relations in West Africa." *International Political Science Review* 2/3: 283-297.

Sarraut, Albert. 1923. *La Mise en Valeur des Colonies Françaises*. Paris: Payot.

Sartori, Giovanni. 1987. *The Theory of Democracy Revisited*. Chatham, N.J.: Chatham House.

_____. 1991. "Rethinking Democracy: bad Polity and bad Politics." *International Social Science Review* 129 (August): 437-450.

Scarritt, James R. 1986. "The Explanation of African Politics and Society: Towards a Synthesis of Approaches." *Journal of African Studies* 13/3: 85-93.

Schatzberg, Michael G. 1993. "Power, Legitimacy and 'Democratisation' in Africa." *Africa* 63/4: 445-461.

Schmitter, Philippe. 1994. "Dangers and Dilemmas of Democracy." *Journal of Democracy* 5/2: 57-74.

_____ and Terry L. Karl. 1991. "What Democracy Is...and Is Not?" *Journal of Democracy* 2/3 (Summer): 75-88.

Schmitz, Gerald and Eboe Hutchful. 1992. *Democratization and Popular Participation in Africa*. Ottawa: North-South Institute.

Schraeder, Peter J. 1994. "Élites as Facilitators or Impediments to Political Development? Some Lessons from the 'Third Wave' of Democratization in Africa." *Journal of Developing Areas* 29/1: 69-90.

_____. 1997. "France and the Great Game in Africa." *Current History* 96/610: 206-211.

_____. 2000. *African Politics and Society: A Mosaic in Transformation*. New York: Bedford/St. Martin's Press.

Schumpeter, Joseph A. 1942. *Capitalism, Socialism, and Democracy*. London: Allen and Unwin (Reprint in 1976).

Seibert, Gerhard. 1999. "Sao Tomé and Príncipe: Recent History." In *Africa: South of the Sahara 1999*, 28th ed. London: Europa Publications Ltd.

Seitz, Steven. 1991. "The Military in Black African Politics." *Journal of Asian and African Studies* 26/1-2: 61-75.

Seligman, Adam. 1992. *The Idea of Civil Society*. New York: Free Press.

Serpa, Eduardo. 1991. "Madagascar: Change and Continuity." *Africa Insight* 21/4: 233-245.

Shah, Ghanshyam 1988. "Grass Roots Mobilization in Indian Politics." In *India's Democracy*, ed. Atul Kohli. Princeton: Princeton University Press.

Share, Donald. 1987. "Transitions to Democracy and Transition through Transaction." *Comparative Political Studies* 19/4: 525-548.

Shils, Edward. 1962. "The Military in the Political Development of the New States." In *The Role of the Military in Underdeveloped Countries*, ed. John J. Johnson. Princeton: Princeton University Press.

_____. 1991. "The Virtue of Civil Society." *Government and Opposition* 26/1: 3-20.

Shin, Doh Chull. 1994. "On the Third Wave of Democratization: A Synthesis and Evaluation of Recent Theory and Research." *World Politics* 47/1: 135-170.

Shivji, Issa G., ed. 1991. *State and Constitutionalism: An African Debate on Democracy*. Harare, Zimbabwe: SAPES Trust.

Siddiqui, Rukhsana A., ed. 1997. *SubSaharan Africa in the 1990s: Challenges to Democracy and Development*. Westport, CT: Praeger.

Sigelman, Lee. 1974. "Military Intervention: A Methodological Note." *Journal of Political and Military Sociology* 2/1: 275-281.

Sklar, Judith N. 1987. *Montesquieu*. Oxford: Oxford University Press.

Sklar, Richard L. 1983. "Democracy in Africa." *African Studies Review* 26/3-4: 11-24.

_____. 1986. "Democracy in Africa." In *Political Domination in Africa*, ed. Patrick Chabal. Cambridge: Cambridge University Press.

_____. 1987. "Developmental Democracy." *Comparative Studies in Society and History*. 29/4: 686-714.

_____. 1993. "The African Frontier for Political Science." In *Africa and the Disciplines*, eds. Bates, Robert H., Valentin Y. Mudimbe and Jean O'Barr. Chicago: University of Chicago Press.

_____ and Mark Strege. 1992. "Finding Peace through Democracy in Sahelian Africa." *Current History* 91/565: 224-229.

Skurnik, William A.E. 1970. "The Military and Politics: Dahomey and Upper Volta." In *Soldier and State in Africa: A Comparative Analysis of Military Intervention and Political Change*, ed. Claude E. Welch, Jr. Evanston: Northwestern University Press.

Smith, Robert S. 1976. *Warfare and Diplomacy in Pre-Colonial West Africa*. London: Methuen.

Smith, Tony F. 1993. "Making the World Safe for Democracy." *The Washington Quarterly* 16/4: 197-214.

Snyder, Richard. 1992. "Explaining Transitions from Neopatrimonial Dictatorships." *Comparative Politics* 24/2: 379-400.

Somerville, Keith. 1991. "Africa Moves Towards Party Pluralism." *The World Today* 47/8-9: 152-155.

Soresen, George. 1993. *Democracy and Democratization: Processes and Prospects in a Changing World*. Boulder, CO: Westview Press.

Spalding, Nancy J. 1996. "State-Society Relations in Africa: An Exploration of the Tanzanian Experience." *Polity* 29/1: 65-96.

Staniland, Martin. 1973. "The Three-Party System in Dahomey 1946-1956." *Journal of African History* 14/3: 291-312.

_____. 1973. "The Three-Party System in Dahomey 1956-1957." *Journal of African History* 14/4: 491-504.

_____. 1987. "Francophone Africa: The Enduring Connection." *Annals of the American Academy* 489 (January): 51-62.

Starr, Harvey. 1991. "Democratic Dominoes: Diffusion Approaches to the Spread of Democratic in the International System." *Journal of Conflict Resolution* 35/2: 356-381.

Stepan, Alfred. 1985. "State Power and the Strength of Civil Society in the Southern Cone of Latin America." In *Bringing the State back in*, ed. Evans, et al. Cambridge: Cambridge University Press, 317-343.

_____. 1988. *Rethinking Military Politics: Brazil and the Southern Cone*. Princeton: Princeton University Press.

Stepanek, Joseph F. 1999. *Wringing Success from Failure in Late-Developing Countries: Lessons from the Field*. Westport, CT: Praeger.

Stromberg, Roland N. 1996. *Democracy: A Short, Analytical History*. Armonk, NY: M.E. Sharpe.

Sullivan, William M. 1999. "Making Civil Society Work: Democracy as a Problem of Civic Cooperation." In *Civil Society, Democracy, and Civic Renewal*, ed. Robert K. Fullinwider. Lanham, MD: Rowman and Littlefield Publishers, Inc.

Sundhaussen, Ulf. 1998. "The Military: A Threat to Democracy?" *Australian Journal of Politics and History* 44/3: 329-349.

Suret-Canale, Jean. 1964. "Un Pionnier Méconnu du Mouvement Démocratique et National en Afrique: Louis Hunkanrin (25 Novembre 1887 – 28 Mai 1964)." *Études Dahoméennes*, Nouvelle Série 3: 5-30.

Sylla, Lanciné. 1982. "La Gestion Démocratique du Pluralisme Socio-Politique en Afrique: Démocratie Concurrentielle et Démocratie Consociationnelle." *Civilisations* 33/1: 23-63.

Tamás, G. M. 1994. "A Disquisition on Civil Society." *Social Research* 61/2: 205-222.

Tandon, Yash. 1991. "Political Economy of Struggles for Democracy and Human Rights in Africa." *Economic and Political Weekly* (June 22): 1554-1561.

Tangri, Roger. 1998. "Politics, Capital and the State in Sub-Saharan Africa." In *Civil Society and Democracy in Africa: Critical Perspectives*, ed. Nelson Kasfir. London: Frank Cass.

Tedga, Paul John Marc. 1991. *Ouverture Démocratique en Afrique Noire?* Paris: L'Harmattan.

Terray, Emmanuel. 1964. "Les Révolutions Congolaise et Dahoméenne de 1963: Essai d'Interpretation." *Revue Française de Science Politique* 14/5: 917-943.

_____, ed. 1987. *L'État Contemporain en Afrique.* Paris: L'Harmattan.

Thebold, Robin. 1982. "Patrimonialism." *World Politics* 34/4: 548-559.

Thompson, Virginia and Richard Adloff. 1958. *French West Africa.* London: Greenwood Press.

Tixier, Gilbert. 1966. "Les Coups d'État Militaires en Afrique de l'Ouest." *Revue de Droit Public et de la Science Politique* (Novembre-Decembre): 323-346.

Tordoff, William, 1997. *Government and Politics in Africa,* 3rd Edition. Bloomington: Indiana University Press.

Toulabor, Comi M. 1986. *Le Togo sous Éyadéma.* Paris: Karthala.

_____. 1991. "Transition Démocratique en Afrique." *Afrique 2000* 4 (January-March): 55-70.

_____. 1995. "'Paristroika' and the One-Party System." In *State and Society in Francophone Africa since Independence,* eds. Anthony Kirk-Greene and Daniel Bach. London: Macmillan.

Turrittin, Jane. 1991. "Mali: People Topple Traore." *Review of African Political Economy* 52 (November): 97-103.

Udogu, Ike E. 1996. "Incomplete Metamorphic Democracy as a Conceptual Framework in the Analysis of African Politics: An Explanatory Investigation." *Journal of African and Asian Studies* 31/1-2: 5-20.

United States Agency for International Development (USAID). 1990. *The Democracy Initiative.* Washington, D.C.: USAID.

Uzoigwe, G. N. 1975. "Pre-Colonial Military Studies in Africa." *Journal of Modern African Studies* 13/3: 469-481.

Valenzuela, Arturo. 1985. "The Military and Social Science Theory." *Third World Quarterly* 7/1: 132-143.

van de Walle, Nicolas. 1994. "Political Liberalization and Economic Reform in Africa." *World Development* 22/3: 483-500.

van Hoek, F. and J. Bossuyt. 1993. "Democracy in Sub-Saharan Africa: The Search for a New Institutional Set-Up." *African Development Review* 5/1: 81-93.

Vanhanen, Tatu. 1990. *The Process of Democratization.* New York: Crane Russak.

Vengroff, Richard. 1993. "Governance and the Transition to Democracy: Political Parties and the Party System in Mali." *Journal of Modern African Studies* 31/2: 277-299.

_____. 1994. "The Impact of the Electoral System on the Transition to Democracy in Africa: The Case of Mali." *Electoral Studies* 13/1: 29-37.

_____ and Moctar Koné. 1995. "Mali: Democracy and Political Change." In *Democracy and Political Change in Sub-Saharan Africa*, ed. John A. Wiseman. New York: Routledge.

Verba, Sydney and Lucien Pye. 1965. eds. *Political Culture and Political Development*. Princeton: Princeton University Press.

Viotti, Paul R. and Mark V. Kauppi. 1990. *International Relations Theory: Realism, Pluralism, Globalism*. New York: MacMillan.

Vittin, Théophile. 1991. "Bénin: Du 'Système Kérékou' au Renouveau Démocratique." In *États d'Afrique Noire: Formation, Mecanismes, et Crises*, ed. Jean-François Médard. Paris: Karthala.

Vivekananda, Franklin and Ibrahim James. 1990. "Militarism and the Crisis of Democracy in Africa, 1980-1985." *Scandinavian Journal of Development Alternatives* 9/4: 79-93.

Volman, Daniel. 1993. "Africa and the New World Order." *Journal of Modern African Studies* 31/1: 1-30.

Waltz, Kenneth N. 1979. *Theory of International Politics*. New York: Mcgraw-Hill, Inc.

Walzer, Michael. 1984. "Liberalism and the Art of Separation." *Political Theory* 12/3: 315-330.

Walzer, Michael. 1991. "The Idea of Civil Society." *Dissent* 38/2 (Spring): 293-304.

Wamala, A. S. 1992. "The Role of Workers in the Struggle towards Multi-Party Democracy: Africa's Colonial and Post-Colonial Experience." *Eastern Africa Social Science Research Review* 8/1 (January): 46-61.

Wauthier, Claude. 1981. "France in Africa: President Giscard d'Estaing's Ambitious Diplomacy." *Africa Contemporary Record*, 12, 1979-1980. New York: Africana, A120-127

Weede, Erich. 1984. "Democracy and War Involvement." *Journal of Conflict Resolution* 28/4: 849-664.

Welch, Claude E. Jr. 1967. "Soldier and State in Africa." *Journal of Modern African Studies* 5/3: 305-322.

_____, ed. 1970. *Soldier and State in Africa: A Comparative Analysis of Military Intervention and Political Change*. Evanston: Northwestern University Press.

_____. 1975. "Continuity and Discontinuity in African Military Organization." *Journal of Modern African Studies* 13/2: 229-48.

_____. 1983. "Military Disengagement from Politics: Lessons from West Africa." *Armed Forces and Society* 9/4: 541-54.

_____. 1985. "Civil-Military Relations: Perspectives from the Third World." *Armed Forces and Society* 11/2:

_____. 1986. "From 'Armies of Africans' to 'African Armies': The Evolution of Military Forces in Africa." In *African Armies: Evolution and Capabilities*, eds. Arlinghaus, Bruce E. and Pauline H. Baker. Boulder, CO: Westview Press.

_____. 1987. *No Farewell to Arms? Military Disengagement from Politics in Africa and Latin America*. Boulder, CO: Westview Press.

_____. 1988. "Obstacles to Disengagement and Democratization: Military Regimes in Benin and Burkina Faso." In *The Decline of Military Regimes: The Civilian Influence*, ed. C. Danopoulos. Boulder, CO: Westview Press.

_____. 1991. "The Single Party Phenomenon in Africa." *TransAfrica Forum* (Fall): 85-94.

_____. 1993. "Changing Civil-Military Relations." In *Global Transformations and the Third World*, eds. Robert O. Slater, Barry M. Schutz and Steven R. Dorr. Boulder, CO: Lynne Rienner.

Welch, Stephen. 1993. *The Concept of Political Culture*. New York: St Martin's Press.

Wells, Alan. 1974. "The Coup d'État in Theory and Practice: Independent Black Africa in the 1960s." *American Journal of Sociology* 79/4: 871-887.

_____ and Richard Pollnac. 1988. "The Coup d'État in Sub-Saharan Africa: Changing Patterns from 1956-1984. *Journal of Political and Military Sociology* 16/1 (Spring): 43-56.

West Africa, 1998. "Africa: What Future for Democracy." January 19-25.

Westebbe, Richard. 1994. "Structural Adjustment, Rent-Seeking, Liberalization in Benin." In *Economic Change and Political Liberalization in Sub-Saharan Africa*, ed. Jennifer A. Widner. Baltimore: Johns Hopkins University Press.

White, Gordon. 1994. "Civil Society, Democratization and Development: Clearing the Analytical Ground." *Democratization* 1/3: 375-390.

White, Dorothy S. 1979. *Black Africa and de Gaulle: From the French Empire to Independence.* University Park: Pennsylvania State University Press.

Whitehead, Laurence. 1996. "Concerning International Support for Democracy in the South." In *Democratization in the South: The Jagged Wave*, eds. Robin Luckham and Gordon White. Manchester, UK: Manchester University Press.

Widner, Jennifer A., ed. 1994. *Economic Change and Political Liberalization in Sub-Saharan Africa.* Baltimore: Johns Hopkins University Press.

_____. 1994. "Two Leadership Styles and Patterns of Political Liberalization." *African Studies Review* 37/1: 151-174.

Wignaraja, Ponna, ed. 1993. *New Social Movements in the South: Empowering the People.* London: Zed Books Ltd.

Wiking, C. 1983. *Military Coups in Sub-Saharan Africa: How to Justify Illegal Assumptions of Power.* Uppsala, Sweden: Scandinavian Institute of African Studies.

Wildavsky, Aaron. 1994. "Cultural Pluralism Can both Strengthen and Weaken Democracy." In *Research on Democracy and Society*, Vol. 2: Political Culture and Political Structure – Theoretical and Empirical Studies, ed. Frederick D. Weil. Greenwich, CT: JAI Press.

Wiseman, John A. 1986. "Urban Riots in West Africa, 1977-1985." *Journal of Modern African Studies* 24/3: 509-518.

_____. 1990. *Democracy in Black Africa: Survival and Revival.* New York: Paragon House.

_____. 1992. "Early Post-Redemocratisation Elections in Africa." *Electoral Studies* 11: 27-38.

_____. 1993a. "Democracy and the New Pluralism in Africa: Causes, Consequences and Significance." *Third World Quarterly* 14/3: 439-49.

_____. 1993b. "Leadership and Personal Danger in African Politics." *Journal of Modern African Studies* 31/4: 657-660.

_____, ed. 1995a. *Democracy and Political Change in Sub-Saharan Africa.* New York: Routledge.

_____. 1995b. "Introduction." In *Democracy and Political Change in Sub-Saharan Africa.* New York: Routledge.

_____. 1996. *The New Struggle for Democracy in Africa.* Brookfield, VT: Avebury.

Woodward, Peter. 1994. "Democracy and Economy in Africa: The Optimists and the Pessimists." *Democratization* 1/1: 116-132.

Woods, Dwayne. 1992. "Civil Society in Europe and Africa: Limiting State Power Through a Public Sphere." *African Studies Review* 35/2: 77-100.

World Bank. 1989. *Sub-Saharan Africa: From Crisis to Sustainable Growth*. Washington, DC: World Bank.

World Bank. 1992. *Governance and Development*. Washington, DC: World Bank.

Wunsch, James S. and Dele Olowu, eds. 1990. *The Failure of the Centralized State*. Boulder, CO: Westview Press.

Yagla, Wen'saa Ogma. 1978. *L'Édification de la Nation Togolaise: Naissance d'une Conscience Nationale dans un Pays Africain*. Paris: L'Harmattan.

Yannopoulos, Tatiana and Denis Martin. 1972. "Régimes Militaires et Classes Sociales en Afrique Noire." *Revue Française de Science Politique* 22/4: 847-882.

Yoder, John C. 1974. "Fly and Elephant Parties: Political Polarization in Dahomey, 1840-1870." *Journal of African History* 15/3: 417-432.

_____. 1998. "Good Government, Democratisation and Traditional African Political Philosophy: The Example of the Kanyok of the Congo." *Journal of Modern African Studies* 36/3: 483-507.

Young, Crawford. 1982. *Ideology and Development in Africa*. New haven: Yale University Press.

_____. 1994a. *The African Colonial State in Comparative Perspective*. New Haven: Yale University Press.

_____. 1994b. "Democratization in Africa: The Contradictions of a Political Imperative." In *Economic Change and Political Liberalization in Sub-Saharan Africa*, ed. Jennifer A. Widner. Baltimore, MD: Johns Hopkins University Press.

Young, Tom. 1993. "Elections and Electoral Politics in Africa." *Africa* 63/3: 299-312.

Zeleza, Paul T. 1994. "Reflections on the Traditions of Authoritarianism and Democracy in African History." *Afrika Zamani*, new series 2: 223-240.

Zimmerman, Ekkart. 1979. "Toward a Causal Model of Military Coups d'État." *Armed Forces and Society* 5/3 (Spring): 384-413.

Zolberg, Aristide R. 1966. *Creating Political Order: The Party States of West Africa*. Chicago: Rand McNally & Co.

_____. 1992. "The Specter of Anarchy: African States Verging on Dissolution." *Dissent* 39/3: 303-311.

Zunes, Stephen. 1994. "Unarmed Insurrections against Authoritarian Governments in the Third World: A New Kind of Revolution." *Third World Quarterly* 15/3: 403-426.

OFFICIAL DOCUMENTS

British Government. *Report on the British Mandated Sphere of Togoland.* Presented to Parliament by Command of His Majesty. London: His Majesty's Stationary Office, 1922-1958.

Gouvernement Français. 1950. *Annuaire Statistique de l'Union Française d'Outre-Mer 1939-1949.* Paris.

_____. Colonies de Dahomey et ses Dépendances. Cabinet du Gouverneur. Affaires Politiques. *Rapports Politiques, Économiques, et Divers de la Colonie du Dahomey 1896-1958* (Microfilm) Séries 2G. 200 MI. Archives Nationales, Paris.

_____. Affaires Politiques et Administratives. *Troubles de 1933: Rapports Divers sur les Événements, Correspondances, Extraits d'Articles de Presse, etc. 1933. Deux Cartons.* Archives Nationales, Lomé, Togo.

League of Nations. *Rapport Annuel du Gouvernement Français sur l'Administration sous Mandat des Territoires du Togo.* Paris: Imprimerie Générale Lahure, 1922-1939.

Nations Unies. 1957. *Avenir du Togo sous Administration Française.* Rapport No. A/3677. Deuxième Session, 25 Septembre 1957. New York: Nations Unies.

Nations Unies/United Nations. 1958. *Rapport Annuel du Gouvernement Français aux Nations Unies sur l'Administration du Togo Placé sous la Tutelle de la France.* New York: United Nations 1946-1958.

United Nations. 1950. *Official Records of the Seventh Session of the Trusteeship Council* (1 June – 21 July 1950). Reports of the United Nations Visiting Mission to Trust Territories in West Africa and Related Documents. Supplement No. 2 (T/798), "Special Report on the Ewe Problem." New York: United Nations.

République du Bénin. Conférence Nationale des Forces Vives. 1990. *Correspondances Reçues par le Comité.* 7 Vols. Cotonou.

République du Togo. 1991. *Rapports, Actes, et Divers de la Conférence Nationale Souveraine.* Lomé, Togo.

_____. 1991. *Séminaire National d'Information et de Sensibilisation Organisé les 22 et 23 Février 1988 à Lomé.* Lomé, Togo.

JOURNALS AND NEWSPAPERS

Africa Confidential (London)
Africa Contemporary Record
Africa Report (New York)
Bénin-Info (Cotonou, Benin)
Bulletin de l'Afrique Noire (Dakar, Senegal)
L'Enjeu (Cotonou, Benin)
Ehuzu (Cotonou, Benin)
Financial Times (London)
Forum de la Semaine (Cotonou, Benin)
Forum-Hebdo (Lomé, Togo)
Gazette du Golfe (Cotonou, Benin)
Le Héraut (Cotonou, Benin)
Jeune Afrique (Paris)
Journal Officiel du Dahomey
Journal Officiel de la République du Bénin
Journal Officiel de la République Populaire du Bénin
Journal Officiel de la République du Togo
Juris-Info (Cotonou, Benin)
Le Forum de la Semaine (Cotonou, Benin)
Le Matin (Cotonou, Benin)
La Nation (Cotonou, Benin)
La Nouvelle Marche (Lomé, Togo)
La Récade (Cotonou, Benin)
La Tribune des Démocrates (Lomé, Togo)
La Quinzaine Coloniale (Paris)
Le Monde (Paris)
Le Monde Diplomatique (Paris)
Marchés Coloniaux, later *Marchés Tropicaux et Méditerranéens* (Paris)
New African (London)
Togo-Presse (Lomé, Togo)
Tam-Tam Express (Cotonou, Benin)

West Africa (London)

THESES AND DISSERTATIONS

Ahovi, Antoinette A. 1988. "Le Mouvement Syndical Estudiantin et Scolaire au Dahomey: 1956-1974." Mémoire de Maîtrise. Université Nationale du Bénin.

Anignikin, Sylvain Coovi. 1980. "Les Origines du Mouvement National au Dahomey, 1900-1939." Thèse de 3e Cycle. Université de Paris VII.

Barandas, Kufoma. 1984. "'Mise en Valeur' et Changement Social au Togo dans L'Entre-Deux-Guerres (1914-1940)." Thèse de Doctorat, Nouveau Régime. Université de Paris I.

Bunche, Ralph J. 1934. "French Administration in Togoland and Dahomey." Ph.D. Dissertation, Harvard University.

Dossou, Léopold. 1973. "Le Mouvement Syndical au Dahomey, 1946-1969." Mémoire de Maîtrise. Université de Paris VII.

Frazer, Jendayi E.J. 1994. "Sustaining Civilian Control: Armed Counterweights in Regime Stability in Africa." Ph.D. Dissertation, Stanford University.

Gbedemah, Seti Yawo G.G. 1984. "La Politique d'Association au Togo sous Mandat de la France." Thèse de Doctorat d'État. Université d'Aix-en-Provence.

Heilbrunn, John R. 1994. "Authority, Prosperity, and Politics in Benin and Togo." Ph.D. Dissertation, University of California, Los Angeles.

Houngnikpo, Mathurin C. 1989. "Africa in Search of Peace." Master's Thesis, The Fletcher School of Law and Diplomacy, Tufts University.

Knoll, Arthur J. 1964. "Togo under German Administration, 1884-1910." Ph.D. Dissertation, Yale University.

Magnusson, Bruce A. 1997. "The Politics of Democratic Regime Legitimation in Benin: Institutions, Social Policy, and Security." Ph.D. Dissertation, University of Wisconsin-Madison.

INDEX

A

Ablodé, 157

Abomey, 66-68, 121, 124, 129, 171.

Abrahamsen, R., 10

Accords de Coopération, 153

Adandozan, 182

Adja, 66, 68

Adjahouto, 66

Adja Tado, 66

Adjaho, R., 69, 77-80, 90, 91, 128, 130, 156, 176, 183

Adjatchê, 66

Adjou Moumouni, B., 124

Adjovi, S., 78, 91, 94, 96, 125, 127, 130, 137, 174, 176, 183, 184

African-Carribean-Pacific Countries, 152

African Development Bank, 109

African leaders, 4, 8, 10, 30, 31, 35, 36, 47, 55, 57, 97, 147, 149, 152, 158, 181, 186, 191

African military, 8, 51, 52, 56

Afrique Occidentale Française (A.O.F.), 67, 143

Afro-pessimist view, 190

Agasouvi, 66

Agbelenko, D., 97

Agblemangnon, F. N'S., 73, 133, 134

Agoli-Agbo, 67

agricultural schools, 81

Aguëro, F., 9

Agyeman-Duah, B., 53

Aho, Ph., 123

Ahomadégbé, J. T., 68, 121-124, 126, 127.

aid rhetoric, 178

Aïkpé, M., 128, 172, 174, 175

Ake, C., 26

Akinjogbin, I. A., 67, 168, 180

Alam, M. B., 180

Algeria, 67, 119, 131, 152, 158, 178, 180, 181

Al-Hadj Omar, 142

Allada, 66, 67

Alladaye, M., 128

Allen, C., 8

Alley, A., 68, 124

Alliance pour la Démocratie au Mali (ADEMA), 111

Allison, L., 178

Almond, G. and S. Verba, 2, 9, 24, 60, 61

Amazons, 67, 182

Amegah, A-K., 97

Amegi, Y. M., 97

amicales, 169

amnesty, 75, 92, 98

Amouzou, J., 162

Andereggen, A., 14, 120, 141-
    144, 147-149, 157, 181,
    189
Anglo-French forces, 13
Animal Farm, 140
année blanche, 110
Anyang' Nyong'o, P., 16, 18,
    48
Apparatchiki, 91, 130
Apithy, S. M., 68, 121-124, 126
Aplahoué, 66
Arato, A., 41, 42
Arête, 169
Argyle, W.F., 168, 182
Aristotle, 60
armed forces, 5, 6, 17, 56, 74,
    94, 109, 113, 117-119,
    127, 130-138, 142, 173,
    182-184, 187, 188
Asante, 168
*Assemblée Nationale
    Révolutionnaire (ANR)*, 95
assembly of notables, 88
associational life, 3, 16, 45
Assogba, J., 128
Atakora mountains, 66
austerity program, 80, 82, 121,
    158
Austin, D., 8, 118, 158
authenticité, 158
autocracy, 30, 105
authoritarian leaders, 4
    regimes, 11, 12, 17, 24, 91,
        151
    rule, 2, 7, 189
    rulers, 3, 5
Ayittey, G. B. N., 37, 186
Ayoade, J. A. A., 29, 36, 46
Azaïs, G., 156, 159
Azevedo, M., 105

B

Baba, K. I., 141, 168, 185
Badjogoumê, H., 128
Baker, G., 39
Balandier, G., 37, 45
Banégas, R., 90, 91, 129, 156
Bangura, A. K., 56
Baraza, 171
Bariba, 66
Barnes, J. F., 61, 102-105
Batéké, 103
Bates, R. H., 58
Baule, La, 147, 148, 151, 159,
    160, 161, 163, 165, 181
Bayart, J-F., 7, 8, 11, 37, 40, 47,
    49, 58, 148, 152, 159
Baynham, S., 54, 86, 119, 178
Bebler, A., 8, 119, 120, 126
Beckman, B., 8
Beetham, D., 23, 27
Behanzin, 67
Benin, Republic of, 6, 13, 64
    People's Republic of, 13,
        155
Berg-Schlosser, D., 185
Berlin Conference, 13, 42, 52
Berlin Wall, 41, 90, 179
Bermeo, N., 124
Berton, G., 25, 90, 186
Biarnes, P., 141
Bienen, H. S., 8, 53, 56
Bills of Rights, 185
Bitam Declaration, 103
black market, 79
Bland, D. L., 6, 188
Blaney, D. L., and M. K. Pasha,
    39, 41
Boahen, A., 168-171, 182
Bodjolle, E., 132, 133

Boggio, P., 141
Bohiki affair, 121
Bokassa, 148, 153
Bongo, O., 102-105, 158
Boulaga, F. E., 85, 86, 90, 91, 172
Bourdieu, P., 167
Bourgi, A. and C. Castern, 90
Bouteflika, A-A., 180
Bovy, L., 57
Bowles, P., 179
Bratton, M., 3, 4, 35-38, 48, 103
Brinton, C., 87, 89
Bryant, C. G. A., 41
Buijtenhuijs, R. and E. Rijnierse, 24
Buijtenhuijs, R. and C. Thiriot, 24
Burkina Faso, 65, 72, 97, 162
Busia, K. A., 28, 44, 57
Buzan, B, Ch. Jones, and R. Little, 153

C

cahiers de doléances, 89
Calhoun, C., 41
Callaghy, T. M., 25, 37
Calonne, 88
Cameroon, 144
caravan trade, 142
Carbett, E. M., 120, 142-144, 157, 171
carte blanche, 58
Carter, J., 162
Cartwright, J. R., 8
Carving of Africa, 13

Catt, H., 25
CEAO, 155
Central African Republic, 148, 153
Cercles, 143, 169
Chabal, P., 7, 8, 25, 35-37, 97
Chafer, T., 82, 148, 157
Chaigneau, P., 54, 120, 148
Chaillot, 160
Chaîne du Togo, 72
Chalker, L., 179
Chan, S., 2
Chandhoke, N., 39-41, 49
Charlton, R., 25
Chateaubriand, 76
Chazan, N., 4, 7, 9, 32, 47, 62, 63, 117, 145, 147, 148, 151, 187
checks and balances,28, 37, 44, 173
Cheiffou, A., 114
Chenu, G-M., 8, 159
China, 155
Chinese Cultural Revolution, 109
Chipman, J., 52, 120, 146, 158, 179
Chirac, J., 151, 152
Chole, E., and J. Ibrahim, 186
Church, 17, 87, 88, 133
Citoyens, 170
civil-military problématique, 6
civil-military relations, 5, 6, 15, 182, 188, 190
civil servants, 9, 71, 92, 110, 122, 143
civil society, 5, 6, 8-14, 16, 38-60, 69, 90, 156, 182, 186

civilian coup d'état, 95
civilization, 54, 62, 143
civilize, 29
Civitas, 48
Clapham, C., 30, 31, 45
Clark, J. C. and D. Gardinier, 100, 187
Clarke, W. S., 70, 71, 80, 85, 86, 93-96, 99, 103-105, 108, 172
Clergy, 48, 87-89
client-states, 3
cocoa, 79, 80-82, 144
coffee, 79, 80-82, 101, 144
Cohen, 53, 142, 144, 186
Cohen, J. and A. Arato, 41, 42
Coleman, J. S., 50, 81, 157
Collier, R. B., 58
Colmar, 161
Colonialism, 30, 34, 36, 45, 47, 52, 58, 63, 117, 118, 145, 168-170, 191
Colonies Françaises d'Afrique (**CFA**), 145
Comité de Réconciliation Nationale, 136
Comité de Transition pour le Salut du Peuple, 111
Comité de l'Unité Togolaise (CUT), 74, 171
Comité Militaire de Vigilance, 123, 124
Comité Militaire pour la Libération Nationale (CMNL), 109
Comité Militaire Révolutionnaire, 175
Comité National d'Initiative Démocratique (CNID), 111

Commission Nationale des Droits de l'Homme (CNDH), 75, 97
Communauté Financière Africaine, 145
Communauté Française, 67
communism, 3, 60, 154
Compagnie Normande, 141
Compagnie Togolaise des Mines du Bénin (CTMB), 81
Compaoré, B., 162
comptoir, 141, 142
Comrades, 72, 119
Conac, G., 9, 25, 59, 158, 180
confederacies, 51
Confédération Nationale des Travailleurs du Togo (CNTT), 99
confinement, 89
Congacou, T., 123
Congo Republic, 12, 105
Conseil de l'Entente, 156
Conseil du Gouvernement, 143
Conseil Présidentiel, 143
Conseil Supérieur de la République, 109
consensus, 15, 32, 34, 57, 59, 63, 86, 95, 115, 151, 186, 189
consultations, 92
constituent assembly, 104
constitutional revision, 101
Conté, L., 12
Conteh-Morgan, E., 3, 9, 12, 30, 77, 86, 136, 165, 167, 172, 178-181
co-optation, 8, 105

Coquery-Vidrovitch, C., 29, 32, 37, 143, 144, 169-171, 182, 184
Cornevin, R., 13, 14, 65, 65, 66, 68, 72-74, 77, 78, 81, 82, 96, 120-126, 129, 130-135, 137, 168, 170, 173-183
correlates of democracy, 26
corruption, 3, 11, 32, 69, 91, 105, 121, 126, 136, 150, 180
Cot, J-P., 149, 159
Côte d'Ivoire, 15, 19, 50, 143, 144, 149, 151, 158, 168, 190
Cotonou, 66, 67, 77, 78, 93, 94, 121, 133, 156, 159, 161
Couffo, 66
Courrier du Golfe du Bénin, 169
Cox, R. W., 49, 50, 57
Crocker, C. A., 54
Crowder, M., 4
Cuba, 155
Cummings, G., 140, 146, 158

D

Dabezies, P., 9, 93, 119, 147
Dadjo, K., 131, 133, 136
Dahl, R. A., 9, 24, 25-27, 35
Dahomey, Republic of, 13, 65
Dakar, 142, 143, 170
Daloz, J-P. et P. Quantin, 25
Danes 73

Danhomê, kingdom of, 13, 66, 168, 171, 182-184
Dapaong, 72
Dealy, G. C., 34
death camps, 99
Declaration of the Rights of Men and Citizen, 89
De Gaulle, Ch., 140, 145, 147, 153, 178
Delaye, B., 98, 159-161
De Lusignan, G., 145, 149
democratic theory, 24
    transition, 23, 28
democratization, 1-16, 27
    from above, 16
    from below, 16
Demos, 7, 37
Demirovic, A., 42
députés, 71
De Souza, P. E., 126
De Souza, I., 94
De Tocqueville, A., 40, 59, 60
devaluation, 71, 80, 82
developmental dictatorship, 32
Diagne, P., 38, 185, 186
Diamond, L., 8, 11, 16, 43, 48, 59, 167, 187, 188, 190
diehard supporters, 95
diktat, 52
dilatory methods, 92
diplomatic negotiations, 51, 94
Directoire Militaire, 126
Discours Programme, 128, 153
divide and rule, 142
Do-Gbagri, 66

domaine réservé, 155
Dossou, 77, 91, 92, 93, 95, 96, 97, 121, 127, 130, 155, 174, 183
Dossouvi, L., 97
Dowden, R., 10, 85
Doyle, M. W., 2
Durkheim, E., 59

E

Eades, J.S. and C. Allen, 66-68, 70, 71, 93, 175
East Germany, 155
Eastern Europe, 1, 10, 11, 42, 59, 85, 88, 139, 167
Écho des Cercles du Dahomey, 169
Écho du Dahomey, 170
Échos, les, 110
Eckert, P., 167
École Nouvelle, 129
economic degradation, 8
economic doldrums, 105
Ehuzu, 129
Ekeh, P., 8
Ekloh, Y. K., 97
Eleazu, U. O., 55, 120
Ellis, S., 141, 161
embezzlement, 69, 90, 136
enfant terrible, 156
Englebert, P., 70-76, 97, 98, 106-115, 137, 157, 162, 172
Ergas, Z., 11, 56
Estates-General, 86, 88, 89
États-Généraux, 86

Étoile du Dahomey, 169
European Economic Community, 78
Éveil Togo-Dahoméen, 169, 171
Evolués, 120, 171
Ewe, 73, 74, 132, 135, 137, 157, 173
Ewe Reunification, 73
Éyadéma, G., 74-77, 83, 96-99, 132-138, 157-163, 172-177, 189

F

factional strife, 101
Fage, J. D., 141-143, 168, 169, 182
Faidherbe, L., 142
Falk, R., 180
Fang, 103
Fatton, Jr., R., 7, 9, 18, 42, 43, 90, 93
faux pas, 134
Federal Advisory Council, 143
Feit, E., 51, 55
Finer, S. E., 36, 55-57, 120, 121, 132, 140, 185
First, R., 8
Fitzsimmons, M. P., 84, 87-89
Fon, 66, 121, 123, 124, 129, 168
Fondation Friedrich Naumann, 95, 184
Fonds d'Aide et de Coopération (FAC), 82
foreign domination, 128, 154
France, 6, 13, 15, 29, 53, 67, 86, 90, 109, 120, 139-153, 161, 189

France d'Outre-Mer, 143
Franco-African Family, 148
Franco-African Summit, 148, 151
Francophonie, 145
Frazer, J., 52, 53
French Community, 13
French Sudan, 109
French Union, 109
Freund, B., 141, 142, 144, 147, 168
Front des Associations pour le Renouveau (FAR), 98
Fukuyama, F., 10, 167, 179
Fundamentalists, 180, 181

G

Gabon, 50, 100, 102-105, 144, 158
Gaile, C. M., 55
Gallie, W. B., 21, 143
Gallieni, J., 143
Gardinier, D. E., 100, 103, 105, 146, 148, 151, 180, 187, 189
Gbado, B., 94, 184
Geertz, C., 62, 168
Gendarmerie, 126
Gendzel, G., 59-61
Genné, M., 124
geopolitical division, 1
Geremek, B., 43
Ghana, 15, 28, 38, 65, 72, 74, 97, 133, 174
Ghanaian Military Academy, 117

Ghosh, A., 42
Giscard d'Estaing, V., 147, 153
Glasnost, 167
Glèlè, M. A., 13, 68, 77, 121, 125, 168, 170, 182, 184
Glickman, H., 165
God's blessings, 95
Godin, F., 78, 80, 122-125, 127, 175
Goldsworthy, D., 53
Good, K., 26
Goodenough, W. H., 167
Gordon, D. L., 30-32, 117
Gorée, 141, 142
Goulbourne, H., 35
Goun, 66
Gouverneur-Général, 143
Governance, good, 140, 149-151, 177
Gramsci, A., 40, 45
Grand-Popo, 65
Grandeur de la France, 147
Grievances, 4, 89, 104, 113, 133, 153
Griffiths, I. Ll.,141, 142, 146
Grilli, E. and M. Riess, 179
Gros, J-G., 2, 12, 13, 102, 178
Grunitzky, N., 74, 132-135, 158
Guézo, King, 93, 182
Guha, R., 42
Gulf of Guinea, 100
Gutteridge, W.F., 8, 56, 119
Gyimah-Boadi, E., 8

H

Habermas, J., 41

Hadenius, A., 3
Hamani, D., 112
handmaiden, 40
Hanneman, R. A., 187
Haugerud, A., 171
Haut Conseil de la République
    (HCR), 95, 115
haven of peace, 96
Hegel, G.W.F., 40
Heilbrunn, J. R., 8, 10, 11, 12,
    14, 59, 68, 74, 76, 78-82,
    91-99, 124, 126-130, 138,
    152, 169, 174, 184, 189
Held, D., 1, 18, 21, 27, 33, 35,
    40, 42, 49, 68, 145, 175,
    183
Hicks, J.F., 162
Hodges, T. and M. Newitt, 110,
    101
Hodgkinson, E., 78-82, 136
Holm, J.D. and P.P. Molutsi, 86
Hotel PLM-Aledjo, 93
Houphouët-Boigny, F., 148,
    149, 152, 158
Houngbédji, A., 72
Houngnikpo, M.C., 38, 57, 77,
    90
housing allowances, 71
Hull, R.W., 37, 43, 44, 51, 52,
    55, 182, 184
human rights, 1, 11, 15, 17, 26,
    35, 44, 75, 102, 127, 149,
    152, 162, 178, 187
Hume, D., 59
Huntington, S.P., 2, 6, 9, 10, 15,
    23, 25, 34, 56, 57, 186,
    188, 191
Hurd. D., 151
Hutchful, E., 8, 19, 39, 48, 49,
    119, 187

Hyden, G., 2, 10, 149, 150, 177

I

ideological divide, 3
idéologues, 130
Ifé, A., 162
Iheduru, O.M., 10, 28
Ihonvbere, J.O., 12, 57, 58, 86,
    139, 167, 186
Imperato, P. J., 109-111
income distribution, 102
industrial revolution, 140
injunctions, 104
Inkeles, A., 60
International Civil Aviation
    Organization, 115
international donors, 3
investment code, 101
Isichei, E., 119, 184

J

Jackson, R.H. and C.G.
    Rosberg, 30, 36
Janowitz, M., 56, 57, 118
Jaubert, 142
Jenkins, J. C. and A. J.
    Kposowa, 57
Jeune Afrique, 104, 108, 115
Johnson, J.J., 118
Johnson, T.H., R.O. Slater, and
    P. McGowan, 57
Joseph, R., 15, 28, 59
Jouffrey, R., 175
junta, 127, 155

K

Kaba, L., 35
Kabaya-Katambwa, J-J., 35, 37, 44, 57
Kabiyè, 73, 74, 97, 100, 131, 132, 137, 173
Kamal, A., 42
Kamrava, M., 62, 62
Kant, I., 2
karité, 78, 79
Karl, T.L., 9, 15, 24
Katanga, 148
Kaunda, K., 33
Kéïta, M., 109
Keller, E. J., 7, 27
Kérékou, M., 14, 15, 68-72, 80, 90-97, 127-131, 154, 156, 172-176, 183, 190
Kétou, 66
khumalo, 52
Kimenyi, M.S., 190
Kinship, 13, 31, 45
Kodjo, E., 97
Koffi, P., 127
Koffigoh, J., 76, 97, 99, 127, 160, 161
Konaré, A.O., 111
Koné, S.S., 11, 59, 159
Kokpon, 67
Korn, D. A., 76
Kothari, R., 42
Kouandété, M., 68, 94, 124-127, 175
Kountché, S., 112
Kpodzro, F., 160
Kpundeh, S.J., 9

Kunz, F.A., 28
Kyambalesa, H., 77, 90

L

Laclé, K.T.D., 97
Lagos (Nigeria), 67
Laitin, D.D., 62
Laloupo, F., 86, 94-96, 127, 129, 131, 156, 183
Lancaster, C., 179
Landowners, 88
Latin America, 9, 17, 36, 42, 100, 109, 132, 139, 154, 188, 190
laxisme-béninisme, 69
Leaflets, 89, 97, 134, 172
League of Nations, 13, 54, 73, 131
Lee, J.M., 8
Legum, C., 11, 35, 59, 97, 101, 106-115, 160, 190
Lemarchand, R., 32, 49, 123
Lerner, D., 34
Levallois, M., 33
LeVine, V.T., 37, 105-107
Lewis, A. W., 45, 52, 54, 141-144, 147, 157, 168-172, 184, 186
liberal democracies, 6, 31, 34, 38
Liberia, 15
Liberalization, 4, 11, 18, 25, 2, 28, 41, 70, 91, 92
Ligue Togolaise des Droits de l'Homme (LTDH), 97

Lijphart, A., 33, 34
Linton, R., 167, 191
Linz, J.J., 11, 16
Lipset, S.M., 2, 9, 11, 16, 24, 25, 33
Lissouba, P., 109
living forces of the nation, 93
living standards, 102
Loi-Cadre, 145
Loi Fondamentale, 94
Lombard, J., 66, 67
Lomé, 73
Lonsdale, J., 18
Louis XVI, 88
Luckham, R.A., 3, 8, 55, 119, 146, 153, 177, 187

M

Maastricht Treaty, 152
Magang, D., 35
Mair, L., 28, 37, 38, 44
Magnusson, B., 92, 96
Makumbe, J. Mw., 10, 43, 45, 48
Maïnassara, I.B., 115
Mali, Empire, 109
    Federation, 109
    Republic of, 109
Malinke, 167
Malwal, B., 36
Mama, F., 134
Mamdani, M., 37-40, 45
Manning, P., 45
Marchal, R., 77, 146, 149, 156, 160-162, 178, 189
Martin, G., 19, 86
Martin, M-L., 45, 119, 121, 128, 142, 149, 174, 187

Marx, K., 40
Marxism-Leninism, 92, 93, 96, 101, 129
Massamba-Débat, A., 105
Mauritania, 143, 146
Maurois, A., 87-89
Mayrargue, C., 70, 71
M'ba, L., 102
Mbachu, O., 44
Mbaku, J.M., 12, 57, 167
Mbembe, A., 11
McFerson, H.M, 26.
McGowan, P., 57
McKinlay, R.D. and R. White, 179
McKinlay, R.D. and R. Little, 179
McNamara, F.T., 143
Meatchi, A., 133-135
Médard, J-F., 44, 46, 47
Menelik II, 52
Messone, N.N. and J-G. Gros, 102-105, 140, 178
Mill, J.S., 14
Milongo, A., 109
Mina, 73
Ministère de la Coopération et du Développement, 147
mission civilisatrice, 143
Mitterand, F., 97, 147-149, 151, 159, 160, 162
Mlapa III, 73
Mobutu, S. S., 12, 97, 158, 187
modernization theory, 17, 24-26
Monga, C., 25, 47-49, 85
Mono River, 66, 100
monopoly trading rights, 101
monopoly of violence, 8
Montesquieu, P., 59, 60
Moore, B. Jr., 9, 15, 24, 26, 33

mouvement, 92
*Mouvement National pour une
    Société de Développement*
    (MNSD), 113
Mowoe, I.J., 56
Muller, E.N., 26
Mundt, R.J., 149
Munslow, B., 36
Murdock, G.P., 44
Museveni, Y., 33
Musterkolonie, 80
Mve, B., 104
Mzilikazi, 52

N

Nachtigal, G., 73
Natchaba, O., 161
national conference, 6, 7, 14, 69,
    76, 86, 90, 96, 137, 161,
    172, 183
national gathering, 76, 99, 100,
    109, 138, 176, 183
national reconciliation, 72, 101,
    133, 136
National University of Benin,
    130
Natitingou, 174
Ndue, P.N., 18, 19
Neocleous, M., 39-41
Ngouabi, M., 105, 106, 108
Nguni, 52
Niebhur, R. and P. E. Sigmund,
    34
Niger, 9, 12, 15, 40, 41, 50, 65-
    67, 78, 110, 112-116, 126,
    170, 187

Niger River, 65-66
Nigeria, 15, 19, 65, 67, 78, 79,
    126
N'kombo, E., 108
Nkrumah, K., 117, 118, 157
nobility, 48, 87-89
Nordlund, P., 48
North Korea, 155
Nwajiaku, K., 98, 130, 134-138,
    168, 172, 184
Nyang'oro, J.E., 80, 86
Nyerere, J.K., 33
Nzouankeu, J-M., 94, 95, 110,
    111

O

OCAM, 155
October Revolution, 122, 127,
    175
O'Donnell, G., 9, 15, 17, 24, 27,
    28, 191
Office Togolais des Phosphates
    (OTP), 81
Ogot, B.A., 51
Olsen, G.R., 151, 152, 159, 178,
    179
Olympio, S., 74, 75, 132, 133,
    135, 136
Olympio, G., 181
Onigbolo, 79
Onwumechili, C., 5, 6, 9, 12-14,
    19, 28, 37, 38, 50, 59, 68,
    123, 132, 185
Orwell, G., 140
Osaghae, E.E, 18, 49.
Oti, 72

Ouagadougou, 162
Ouatchi, 72
Ouémé, 66
Ousmane, M., 115
outside influence, 191
    pressure, 6
Owando, 108
Owusu, M., 29
Oyo Empire, 66
Oyugi, W., 18

P

pacification, 51, 52, 67, 142
palaver, 86
Palmer, R.R. and J. Colton, 87,
    89
Pamphlets, 89, 172
Parakou, 174
Paristroïka, 159
Parti Communiste du Dahomey
    (PCD), 174
Parti Congolais du Travail
    (PCT), 106-108
*Parti de la Révolution
    Populaire du Bénin*
    (PRPB), 92
Parti Démocratique Gabonais
    (PDG), 102
Parti Togolais pour le Progrès,
    74, 171
party-state
Pateman, C., 9, 33
Patterson, A.S., 39
Pelczynski, Z.A., 42
per capita incomes, 34, 102
Pérennès, J-J, et H. Puel, 100
Perestroika à la Béninoise, 129
Perlmutter, A., 57

personal rule, 18, 36, 37
petits nordistes, 131
Pfaff, W., 29
Phare du Dahomey, 169
phosphate deposits, 81
Pinto da Costa, M., 101
Plato, 39, 59
Plattner, M., 188
police state, 90
political accountability, 18, 26
political change, 5, 9, 14
political class, 9
political culture, 6, 14, 28
political freedom, 10
political overture, 8
political participation, 17, 23,
    38, 40, 44
political reforms, 3, 5
Pollard, R., 92
Pompidou, G., 147
popular struggle, 16, 18
Porto-Novo, 66, 67, 121, 167,
    170
Potholm, C.P., 37, 44, 182
power, absolute, 58, 102
pré-carré, 155, 181
Press, R. M., 3, 5, 12, 30
Presse Porto-Novienne, 169
pressures, endogenous, 4, 138
    exogenous, 4, 138
provincial estates, 87, 88
Prunier, G., 52
public morality, 112
public welfare, 43
puppets, 189
Pye, L.W., 55, 61, 63, 118

Q

Quantin, P., 25, 142

R

Radio Dahomey, 125
Radio Trottoir, 95
*Rassemblement du Peuple
    Togolais* (RPT), 74, 75-
    77, 97-99, 160, 161
*Rassemblement pour la
    Démocratie et le Progrès*
    (RDP), 111
Raynal, J-J., 140
Referendum, 68, 74, 75, 96,
    110, 113, 134
Renaissance du Bénin (RB), 70
Rijnierse, E., 24, 163
Riley, S.P., 8, 10, 180, 187
Robinson, 7, 90, 93, 95, 137,
    139, 150, 152, 167, 168,
    178
Roman Catholic Mission
    Schools, 98
Ronen, D., 35, 119, 121, 124,
    127, 153, 154, 156, 183
Roniger, L., 40, 41
Rousseau, J-J., 32, 59
Roussin, M., 162
Rowley, C.K., 39
Rubin, B., 42
Rufisque, 142
rule, direct, 37
    indirect, 37, 46
Rummel R. J., 2
Rustow, D.A., 10, 24, 35, 189

ruthlessness, 10

S

Sachikonye, Ll.M., 39
Saga, H., 99, 160
Sahlins, M.D., 63
Saïbou, A., 112-114
Saint-Louis, 141-143
Sakamoto, Y., 16
Salifou, A., 115
Sandbrook, R., 31, 35, 36, 185
Sao Tomé and Príncipe, 100-
    102
Sara Kawa, 158
Sarraut, A., 37
Sassou-Nguesso, D., 106-109
Savé, 79
Savi, 66
Schmitter, P., 9, 15, 17, 27, 28
Schmitz, G. and Sell, 24
Schraeder, P.J., 1, 58, 117, 118,
    140, 152, 165, 177, 180,
    181, 189
Schumpeter, J.A., 25, 26
Scientific Socialism, 69, 105
Scramble for Africa, 55
second liberation, 8, 140, 187
secteur parallèle, 78
Ségou, 142
Segbana, 174
Seibert, G., 101
self-fulfilling prophecy, 56
self-help associations, 40
Senegal, Republic of, 141, 190
    River, 141
Shah, G., 42

Shils, E., 55, 118
Shin, D.C., 27
Siècle des Lumières, 141
Sierra Leone, 12, 15, 19, 187
Sinzogan, B., 126
Sklar, 11, 30, 32, 33, 38
Smith, 51, 52, 182, 184
Socialism, 105, 154
Socialist path of development,
    106, 129
Société Nationale pour le
    Développement Rural
    (SONADER), 78
Soglo, Ch., 68, 122-124, 175
    N., 70, 71, 79, 80, 95
Solidarnozc, 42
Somba, 125, 127
Somerville, K., 140
Soudan, 109, 143, 144
sous l'arbre à palabre, 86
Southern Europe, 9, 17
Soviet Union, 1, 90, 146, 155
Spalding, N. J., 42
Spranger, C-D., 161
Stalemate, 89, 162
Statism, 180
Stepan, A., 9, 42
Stepanek, J.F., 15
Strasbourg, 165
strategic elites, 11
street protests, 108
Stromberg, R.N., 27, 33, 34,
    180
Sudanese Republic, 109
Sullivan, W.M., 42, 48
Superpowers, 1
Switzerland of Africa, 83
Sylla, L., 8, 30

Syndicat National de
    l'Enseignement Supérieur
    (SNES), 91

T

Tangri, R., 3
Taxpayers, 45
Tê-Agbanlin, 66
Technocrats, 123, 136
Terray, E., 120
terrorist attacks, 75
tête-à-tête, 98
Tevi-Benissan, T., 97
Third World, 1, 3, 5, 10, 25, 55,
    56, 62, 150, 165, 188
Thompson, V. and R. Adloff,
    106-108, 144
Tiers-Mondiste, 149
Tirailleurs Sénégalais, 142
Togoland, 13, 37, 74
Togo, Republic of, 6, 13, 65
Togolese Republic, 13, 74
Tordoff, W., 13, 33, 143, 144,
    147-149, 155, 161, 175,
    179, 185-189
Toulabor, C.M., 136, 137, 172,
    173, 177
Touré, A.T., 11
Traoré, M., 109-111
Triumvirate, 68, 127, 128
Trovoada, M., 102

U

Udogu, I.E., 9, 26, 30, 48, 49
Uhuru, 146
Ultimatum, 92

Union Démocratique des
  Peuples Togolais (UDPT),
  74
Union Démocratique du Peuple
  Malien (UDPM), 110, 111
Union Démocratique et
  Socialiste de la Résistance
  (UDSR), 149
Union des Forces du
  Changement, 181
Union des Syndicats des
  Travailleurs du Niger
  (USTN), 114
Union Générale des
  Travailleurs du Dahomey
  (UGTD), 122
Union Nationale des
  Travailleurs du Mali
  (UNTM), 111
United Kingdom, 13
Université Omar Bongo, 103
Uzoigwe, G.N., 51

V

vassal states, 169
Vengroff, R., 109
Versailles, 89
Vietnam, 155
Viotti, P. R. and M. V. Kauppi,
  153
Voix de la Révolution, 129
Volte-face, 46

W

Wage-earners, 87, 124

Waltz, K.N., 153
Walzer, M., 49
Wanké, D.M., 115
Weede, E., 2
Welch, C.E. Jr., 9, 56, 60, 61,
  118, 125
Westebbe, R., 69, 70, 90-92,
  128, 149
White, 3, 41, 42, 141, 142, 177,
  179, 185
Whitehead, L., 9, 17, 178
Whydah (Ouidah), 66, 141
Wildavsky, A., 61, 62
Wiseman, J.A., 5, 8, 10, 11, 17,
  25, 27, 99, 189, 191
Woods, D., 18, 39, 45, 49
World Bank, 70, 71, 82, 91, 110
World War I, 13, 52, 73, 145
World War II, 1, 54, 81, 119,
  149, 157

Y

Yhombi-Opango, J., 106
Yoder, J.C., 167
Yoruba, 66
Yorubaland, 51, 52
Youlou, F., 105
Young, C., 35
young turks, 127

Z

Zagnanado, 66
Zaire, 12, 97, 146, 148, 187
Zinsou, E.D., 68, 124-126

About the Author

Mathurin C. Houngnikpo is currently a Visiting Assistant Professor in the Department of International Studies at Miami University (Oxford, OH). He holds a *Maîtrise* in International Relations from the National University of Benin (Republic of Benin, West Africa), a Master of Arts in Law and Diplomacy from the Fletcher School of Law and Diplomacy at Tufts University (Medford, MA), a Doctoral degree in Political Science from the University of Paris VIII (France), and a Ph.D. in International Studies from the Graduate School of International Studies at the University of Denver (Denver, CO). Dr. Houngnikpo has published in such journals as *Peace Research, Africa Insight*, the *Journal of Political and Military Sociology, African Studies Review* and *Millennium*. He co-authored (with H. Kyambalesa) *Contemporary Problems Facing Africa and Viable Strategies for Redress*. His research interests include civil-military relations, conflict resolution, democratic transition, political and economic development, and leadership issues in the Third World in general, and in Africa in particular.